Family
Unfriendly

Also by Timothy P. Carney

*Alienated America: Why Some Places Thrive
While Others Collapse*

*Obamanomics: How Barack Obama Is
Bankrupting You and Enriching His Wall Street
Friends, Corporate Lobbyists, and Union Bosses*

*The Big Ripoff: How Big Business and Big
Government Steal Your Money*

Family Unfriendly

*How Our Culture Made Raising Kids
Much Harder Than It Needs to Be*

Timothy P. Carney

HARPER

An Imprint of HarperCollins*Publishers*

HarperCollins books may be purchased for educational, business, or sales promotional use. For information, please email the Special Markets Department at SPsales@harpercollins.com.

FIRST EDITION

Designed by Michele Cameron

Library of Congress Cataloging-in-Publication Data

Names: Carney, Timothy, author.
Title: Family unfriendly: how our culture made raising kids much
  harder than it needs to be / Timothy P. Carney.
Description: First edition. | New York, NY: HarperCollins, [2024] |
  Includes index.
Identifiers: LCCN 2023040697 (print) | LCCN 2023040698 (ebook) |
  ISBN 9780063236462 (hardcover) | ISBN 9780063236479 (ebook)
Subjects: LCSH: Parenting. | Child rearing.
Classification: LCC HQ755.8 .C3857 2024 (print) | LCC HQ755.8 (ebook)
  | DDC 649.1—dc23/eng/20230907
LC record available at https://lccn.loc.gov/2023040697
LC ebook record available at https://lccn.loc.gov/2023040698

24 25 26 27 28 LBC 5 4 3 2 1

To Katie, the greatest partner I could ask for in life's grandest endeavor

Birth rates and a welcoming attitude reveal how much happiness is present in society. A happy community naturally develops the desire to generate and welcome others, while an unhappy society is reduced to a group of individuals defending what they have at all costs.

—*Pope Francis*

Contents

Preface: Friday Night Lights

Baseball glove on one hand, metal bat in the other, little Charlie climbed into our Toyota Sienna, and we drove off for a night of tee-ball that would forever change our family life.

That was the day my oldest son would get hooked on baseball, which would trickle down to his younger brothers, but that wasn't the most important thing that happened on the back campus of St. Bernadette's that evening. I thought I was driving Charlie to a youth sporting event, but instead I was showing up at "Friday Night on the Field."

Monsignor Smith led the children in a baseball-themed prayer and then bellowed "Play ball!" And that's when we witnessed the miracle.

As Charlie and I ambled toward his dugout for the kindergarten tee-ball game, I noticed what the crowds of first and second graders were doing in the hour before *their* games began: *Whatever they wanted.* The same was true for the older kids—some started playing basketball on the blacktop, others bounced balls off the school building, and countless boys and girls swarmed the jungle gyms at either end of the large St. B's field.

And the parents? They were just as free. Old friends hugged warmly after a long winter. Neighbors chatted up neighbors or reached out to new parents like me. Some dads manned the grill at the snack shack, while others coached the tee-ballers.

The field—and the playgrounds, basketball courts, bleachers, and even some adjacent backyards—was positively alive that April night. It was a hundred families eating, drinking, and visiting. This sprawling scene was stereotypical Americana, but it was also in a way subversive. Mom wasn't hovering like a helicopter over little Oscar. The tee-ball coaches were just dads, and nobody saw this program as a path to dominance or a scholarship. There was no "enrichment" going on—just liberated kids, which in turn meant liberated adults.

"Friday Night on the Field" showed the way, I realized, to making suburban life more family friendly. For the rest of the spring, I would bring all the kids to the field on Friday nights. Sometimes my wife, Katie, and the baby would stay home for early bedtime and some peace and quiet while the older kids and I spent an evening amid the glow of an April sunset, the crack of the bat, and a few hundred kids set loose in an oasis of freedom in a culture where everyday parenting could be a harrowing slog.

At a fish fry a couple of years later at our home church, St. Andrew Apostle, the image of those Friday-night tee-ball games resurfaced as I spoke with our young priest, Father Bill. He asked what new things our parish could do for its people. He didn't want to compete with what the local mall, the county parks department, or the elite youth sports programs of the region offered. The church is supposed fill holes in our society, he said.

"What are the unmet needs of these people?" Father Bill asked me, gesturing to the dozens of families in the Multipurpose Room of St. Andrew's. The parish is dizzyingly diverse. In line for fried haddock that night were lobbyists and taxi drivers. Irish American dads who were baptized there in the 1970s sat with Eritrean parents who had arrived in Silver Spring last year.

"Middle-class and upper-middle-class suburban parents," he said. "What do they need that their world doesn't give them?"

My memory was flooded with the sounds of kids playing pickup basketball, the smell of burgers from the snack shack, the feeling of freedom both the adults and kids felt at St. Bernadette on those evenings. St. A should have its own Friday Night on the Field, I realized. Yes, there are other rec leagues. Yes there are plenty of places to get a burger. But I told Father Bill, "We need a place to bring our children—*and ignore them*—while we hang out with other adults."

Such an institution would meet a second need of suburban parents: a sports program for our children that wasn't intensive, didn't claim to be "elite" or "select," and didn't require *travel*.

So we refurbished the infield and the dugout, found a couple of grills, and launched our own tee-ball program.

Bring the whole family and a picnic blanket, we told the parents. We'll have burgers and dogs, and cover the costs with donations. "I do not consider this a first step to a Division I scholarship," I wrote to the parents in my recruiting email. One nervous dad of a first grader saw me the next morning and asked, "Do you mean we *already should have taken* the first step?"

I laughed. But when I reflected on this one dad's worry, I realized it was part of the larger problem we were trying to address: a plague of parental anxiety and exhaustion. Parents worry that they are failing if their kids are not prodigies by age eight, or aren't on the path to dominance in violin, tennis, or math. Most parents don't actually submit their child to the regimen of a Tiger Woods or a Serena Williams, but way too many parents feel guilty that they're not doing more.

Parents also worry that if they don't hover over their children at all moments, something horrible will happen—or they'll be judged as neglectful parents. Somehow Mom and Dad have become full-time chauffeurs, Secret Service agents, and playmates—while both parents work full-time jobs.

St. A's tee-ball was a smashing success, and it continued to run even after Katie and I left the parish for Virginia. Families kept coming on Friday night even when they had no tee-ball-aged kids—they craved the opportunity for low-pressure family time. This was far, far bigger than tee-ball and burgers.

I thought about the least pleasant parts of parenting for Katie and me—hours in the car, taking overscheduled kids to ballet and sports, worrying about some parent calling the county government on us if our children go to the playground alone, and the pure exhaustion of having to run these little people's lives—and realized these were a part of a culture-wide plague. I began studying the literature on American parenting and childhood, and I found epidemics of burnout.

One data point made my jaw drop: While today's dads do much more parenting than our dads did, and today's moms are employed much more than their moms were, today's moms nevertheless spend more time taking care of children than *their* mothers did. Someone has convinced us that parenting should involve much more effort than any generation before us put in.

This is madness.

I wrote this book in order to shout as loud as I can: the tiger moms and helicopter parents are doing it wrong. And if you are the average parent and are nagged by feelings of inadequacy, then the main thing you're doing wrong is worrying too much.

It's not your fault. Modern parenting madness isn't a foible of individual moms and dads. It is a cultural pathology that has massive consequences.

America has a family-unfriendly culture that makes parenting harder than it should be. It's not one part of our culture that is the problem. The problem lies with our parenting culture, our school culture, our dating and mating culture, work culture, the shape of our communities, and the individualistic and materialistic characters of our culture.

A culture that makes raising kids too hard will bring about a society that has fewer children. Sure enough, America is having fewer kids than ever before: the birthrate has been falling steadily since 2008, and there are now fewer children in America than there were a decade ago. The U.S. birthrate hit record lows even before the pandemic and has since returned to its steady downward trend. We're in the midst of a decades-long Baby Bust.

Yet sociologists tell us this is all good, that we are choosing "quality over quantity." Yes, they really use that expression. But their wording isn't merely indelicate; it's flat wrong. Today's maximum-effort, high-anxiety, low-trust parenting isn't high-quality parenting. It isn't producing better results for children or for parents. The American Academy of Pediatrics and other organizations have declared a "national emergency" in child and adolescent mental health.[1]

It's easy to attribute the Baby Bust and the stresses of modern parenting entirely to finances or affordability. Economics are part of the story here, but they are hardly the whole story—or even the most important part. We often fall into a purely economic explanations for cultural phenomena because as our culture becomes more alienated— as happenings like Friday Night on the Field become rarer—we begin to think only of the marketplace and the government. We see the price of daycare or summer camp and ask why the government doesn't cover these costs. We forget that there is another way—a way that involves mothers-in-law, pot-lucks, sidewalks, neighborhoods, pickup basketball, and low-stakes tee-ball. As a wise woman once said, it takes a village to raise a child.

Rebuilding that village requires reinvigorating the sentiments of neighborliness and duty to others, and family over career. To be a sane and happy parent, you need to be countercultural in our family-unfriendly culture.

"When the Streetlights Turn On"

If you're around my age—Generation X—you remember a different culture and an easier model of family life. "Come home when the streetlights turn on" was the standard instruction to twelve-year-olds around America. We played soccer or peewee football at the field down the road, played basketball at the local rec department, and come spring, we played Little League. Mostly, though, we played pickup sports. And in the summer, we rode our bikes until the streetlights turned on, or later.

Other people's parents or grandparents were on their front porches to help us—or yell at us—if we needed it.

We were less anxious and more free than today's kids are. And our parents were happier and less frazzled than we are as parents. There's data to prove this. One 2023 paper in the *Journal of Pediatrics* concluded that "a primary cause of the rise in mental disorders is a decline over decades in opportunities for children and teens to play, roam, and engage in other activities independent of direct oversight and control by adults."[2]

Worry and fear have become central to twenty-first-century American parenting, not because of actual dangers so much as from the sickly spirit of the age. The media tries to convince us that there are lethal threats to our children lurking around each corner. Even if we know this isn't true, we feel societal pressure to be terrified, as if fear were a virtue: *You're a bad parent if you aren't constantly worried, distrustful, and anxious.*

Some level of worry and fear, of course, is inherent in parenthood. Mom and Dad fall totally in love with a vulnerable little creature who feels like a second self, but who nevertheless possesses free will and independence. It's almost as if one of your internal organs could go off on its own and make bad decisions or fall prey to malefactors.

Yes, vulnerability is part of love. But twenty-first-century parenting fear is something else. If you read Facebook comments or follow mommy bloggers and Instagram momfluencers, you'll see there's a competition among parents: Who can be most creative or most all-encompassing in her fear or worry?

Our culture—and sometimes the government—nearly *mandates* helicopter parenting in middle-class and upper-middle-class circles. It takes an act of defiance to escape helicopter and overachievement culture. It's countercultural to let our children run free, out from under our eye, wasting time as they please. It violates the teachings of "quality over quantity" parenting, but it makes everyone happier and less anxious.

At St. Andrew's we built our Friday-night tee-ball program in part as a front in the war against these norms.

The first year we ran tee-ball, I started to notice a change. Some parents visibly transformed from helicopters, who always needed to be right behind little Connor, into fairly laissez-faire moms or dads. *Somebody's big sister is over at the playground, there's a parent there most of the time, and it's a playground for kids on a bed of mulch. The worst that can happen isn't that bad.*

When a mom walked away from the playground and grabbed a can of Miller Lite, I was as proud as if one of my players had run the bases in the proper order. I had helped build a place where parents could bring their children—and ignore them.

We also tried to build a place where youth sports were for the sake of fun and exercise. Millions of parents feel they have no choice but to enter the rat race of elite youth sports. I suppose some parents *want* to spend their weekend at a field hockey tournament in Delaware, but most of the moms and dads are there because they never felt they had a choice. And again, those who do manage to resist sometimes feel guilt—*Is Lila going to fall behind her peers?*

But we need to remember that intensive parenting is merely the most visible symptom of a deeper rot.

If we've come to think there might be a trained kidnapper around every corner and that we really cannot trust our neighbors, we have unwittingly adopted an uncharitable view of our fellow man. If we believe we will have failed as a parent if our kid misses the honor roll or gets cut from varsity, then we have an impoverished view of our own children. And if we hold a zero-sum view of thriving in life—that one man's gain is another's loss—then it becomes harder to love our neighbor and welcome others. These dark views are rooted in bad *anthropology*—a misunderstanding of humanity.

Bad anthropology fosters an overly individualistic, materialistic, and pessimistic culture, which is family unfriendly. We now see individual autonomy as the highest good and self-actualization as the purpose of life, and we see other people as competitors over a finite pie. This worldview obviously fits poorly with parenthood and the self-sacrifice it inevitably requires, but it does something else we might not always notice: it erodes the social bonds that make parenthood possible for others.

Have kids if you want, American culture seems to say, *but don't ever allow this lifestyle choice of yours to impose any burden on us.*

In our modern world, where parenthood is now a calculated, super-planned decision, parenting seems to demand constant super-planning. The burden falls almost entirely on Mom and Dad alone, since having kids was *their* decision, after all.

And in this atmosphere, of course, many folks are *choosing* child-lessness and fewer folks are *choosing* larger families. But some choices are made under duress, and it looks like that's the case in our Baby Bust. Surveys show that Americans still think the ideal is 2.7 children, but in the end we average below 1.7.

To borrow the language of ecology for a moment, American culture is a suboptimal habitat for the human family.

Economics is part of this explanation, for sure. Our governments and our employers need to make changes, in part to fix the finances of family life. But study the contours of our Baby Bust and our anxiety closely and you'll find that dollars and cents cannot fully explain the difficulty of raising kids and the aversion to having kids. The wealthy in America are just as likely as the middle class to find parenting too hard. The Baby Bust is not correlated with poverty, but actually with wealth.

It's not an individual problem, then, and it's not simply an economic problem, which is why we keep coming back to the culture. If we make our culture more family friendly, parents and kids will be happier, and we'll probably have more kids.

Anti-Family Forces

Beyond the Travel Team Trap and the helicopter culture, we have plenty of anti-family forces in our culture.

The very shape of our neighborhoods keeps kids from walking or riding their bikes around and thus forces parents to spend a decade or more in Car Hell—shuttling, dropping off, picking up, hanging around, buckling, unbuckling. . . .

It takes a village to raise a child, but our culture is less communal and more individualistic. Thus parents are stuck turning to the market or to the government to provide the support that ought to be provided by neighbors, community institutions, and extended family.

On the money front, we have plenty of public policies that increase the cost of starting a family (for instance, by creating a housing short-age). Plus, there are a handful of reforms by which local and national policies could make parenting more affordable. The big picture is this: Governments, employers, and other institutions need to abandon the idea of neutrality and instead take a side—the pro-family side.

Social media and smartphones are a culprit here, too. So are our attitudes toward work. In fact, we've largely replaced traditional (pro-family) religions in America with a new religion of *workism*. We look to work to find meaning and self-worth, which crowds out family and also fails to deliver on self-worth.

Now, some readers may roll their eyes at the notion of a mere dad spouting off about parenting and birthrates. I assure you that in these pages, plenty of women—moms and not-moms—will do the talking. But more important, the very attitude that dads don't have much of a say in childbearing and child-rearing is at the heart of our cultural problems. Humans aren't made to raise kids alone. Marriage is part of this story. If we view pregnancy and kid-raising as a "woman's issues," we've already lost and let men off the hook.

Others will wonder if I am just peddling my own values here. That's a fair question, and the reader deserves to know where I am coming from.

My wife and I have six children. Yes, we're Catholics (as the tales from St. B and St. A might have given away). Our kids, as of this writing, have forty first cousins. Our big family is tied up with our view on parenting culture.

A big family means you have to do things differently, but it's not just necessity. Our big family is also a reflection of *why* we do things differently. We don't subscribe to the sociologists' theory of "quality over quantity"—though our kids are all top-shelf, I assure you. We don't follow the cultural norms of family planning. We try very hard not to let our worldly ambitions for our children control our lives. And we have dozens of friends who live the same way, providing us with a network—a family-friendly subculture—that is valuable beyond words.

Throughout the stories and observations in this book, you'll see my faith reflected (probably in ways I don't even notice), but I spend more time on other faiths, such as Orthodox Judaism and the Church of Jesus Christ of Latter-day Saints. You'll hear from dozens of secular voices, too, and my arguments don't require you to accept anything as dogma or revealed truth. Check the endnotes right now if you like: social science and economics do the heavy lifting here.

And the social science—specifically the demographics—tells us a dark story. Parenting madness and our Baby Bust are part of a deeper sadness.

"Happier men and women prefer to become parents sooner," researchers have found.[3] Adults who report greater general happiness or life satisfaction are more likely to become parents. Studies have found this using all sorts of methods. So a sadder culture today means fewer births tomorrow.

The future looks dim to most Americans. By a two-to-one margin, Americans believe that our standard of living will be worse a generation from now.[4] Millennials and Generation Z are even more pessimistic.

One reason: fear and sadness are the bread and butter of the Western media. In any corner of daily life, the press can find a reason for terror or despair. In the days before Thanksgiving 2021, under the headline "To Breed or Not to Breed" and an illustration of a burning, lonely, and dim planet, the *New York Times* ran the litany of twenty-first-century evil: "A rise in political extremism, at home and abroad. A pandemic that has killed more than five million. Thousand-year floods that wiped out Western European towns. West Coast wildfires that grow more unimaginable in scale each summer. Faced with such alarming news, some prospective parents wonder: How harmful might it be to bring a child into this (literal and figurative) environment?"[5]

But the fear and sadness are not just about the climate or a pandemic. We have to come back to anthropology: we simply do not see people as good.

"Would Human Extinction Be a Tragedy?" was the *New York Times* headline in 2018. It was part of a growing genre. "Would Extinction Be So Bad?" asked a headline in the *New Statesman* in August 2021. "Given the amount of suffering on Earth, the value of the continued existence of the planet is an open question."

This despair is not confined to newspaper headlines. It shows up in men dropping out of the labor force and women giving up on marriage. It shows up in therapists' offices, with record numbers of teenagers reporting depression and anxiety. It shows up in darker places, with increased suicide attempts, especially among teenage girls.

And the deep sadness, fear, and despair show up in our collapsing birthrate. If life is bad, why make more of it?

This sadness is coming to characterize and consume our culture. It's not a personal thing anymore. It's a civilizational sadness.

The sadness is real, and it's harmful. But the sadness is grounded in error. The dark story making us sad is a lie.

More importantly, there is a way out of this valley of anxiety, stress, fear, despair, and sadness. There is a way of life that makes family easier, makes parents less anxious, and makes kids happier. You don't need a time machine to access this life. It actually exists in America today.

A Better Way to Parent

I began our story on those tee-ball fields because I believe what we created there were villages that served as an antidote to our culture's anti-family pathologies and an antidote to sadness. I wrote this book because I believe we can fix our culture and make a more family-friendly America.

These chapters will take you to family-friendly oases as well as the all-too-typical places that are hostile to raising kids. We will visit travel-baseball winter workouts in a wealthy suburb, and the shuttered elementary schools now hosting senior yoga.

We will also visit a Mormon college with a bridal shop and a baby boutique right off campus. We will visit the neighborhoods where kids still roam free like their parents did.

We will meet parents who have fallen into the Travel Team Trap and have escaped. We will spend days among families who rest easy knowing that some neighbor, somewhere, will help their children if need be. And we will meet parents who realize that the good life for everyone involves losing track of their kids.

You'll see what the happiest parents, with the happiest kids (and often with the *most* kids), are doing—and what they're *not doing*.

Spending every minute supervising, planning, driving, and fretting—and spending every dime on training, enriching, and keeping kids busy—isn't high-quality parenting. It's just following the dumb rules of a family-unfriendly culture.

So, Dear Reader, please send the kids outside, grab a drink, and don't stop reading until someone comes back starving or bleeding.

Family
Unfriendly

CHAPTER 1

Have Lower Ambitions for
Your Kids

B aseball isn't fun," Coach told the boys gathered inside for their first workout of the year. "*Winning* baseball is fun."

The scene in the Baseball Zone Training Center that winter night was as different as could be from the idyllic Friday Nights on the Field where Charlie first swung a bat six years earlier.

Spring was two months away, and I was already doubting my decision to sign Charlie up for a twelve-and-under "select" baseball team. After years of successfully avoiding the rat race of elite youth sports in the Washington, D.C., suburbs, I had my first real encounter with this hypercompetitive beast. I use *competitive* in a narrow sense here: after the team's sixth loss in seven games, the head coach would quit. "I'm washing my hands of this mess," he would tell the parents.

Yes, the team's infield defense was often a mess. The relief pitching was always a mess. That's because twelve-year-old boys are a mess. But by the logic of today's middle-class and upper-middle-class parenting culture, our team's 1-and-6 start wasn't simply unfortunate; it was *shameful*.

This attitude—equating youth sports success with moral rectitude and seeing failure on the field as a failure of character—shone through before our players got their first at bats.

Our boys jogged off dejected after the top of the first inning of their season opener. Errors and infield hits led to a 6–0 deficit. I wasn't surprised; this was the first inning of baseball many of these kids had played in two years thanks to the pandemic lockdowns. But when the boys got near the dugout, the head coach yelled, *"No!"*

He yanked them away and made them take a knee on the grass near third base. Then he berated them. Pointing at the pitcher, Coach yelled, "I'm not angry at Colton* for the batters he walked or the runs he gave up. I'm angry at you for making him get six outs!"

Angry. At eleven- and twelve-year-olds. For booting ground balls.

The attitude was contagious. A few weeks later, my son bobbled a grounder, igniting a rally that would lead to an epic last-inning come-back for the other team. That night I found myself telling my wife, "I really need to hit Charlie grounders every day, so that he doesn't make those errors."

A week later it was still light out after Sunday dinner, and Charlie asked me to hit him fly balls in the "Wayback"—the grass field with a baseball backstop behind our house. Thinking of those errors and losses, I suggested we drive to a nearby high school with a good dirt infield so I could hit him grounders instead. We argued for a minute, until finally he said, "Dad, I just think fly balls are more fun."

I had almost turned a backyard father-son outing into a training session. My boy wanted to play ball with Dad, and I was fretting about his fielding percentage. I was falling into a trap. And it's a trap that ensnares millions of American moms and dads, making their roles as parents less fun and more stressful.

---

* Throughout this book I changed the names of other people's children for the sake of privacy. I also changed some place-names for the same reason.

We had already paid the exorbitant team fee (about four times as much as we have paid before or since for any team), and it was too late to put Charlie on any other team. We felt stuck with this select team for the spring. But we concluded pretty early on that we would escape for the saner confines of local rec ball as soon as possible.

Throughout the spring I saw how many had already been snared. At one game, the other team had a twelve-foot-by-six-foot color banner with all the players' photos printed on it. Some teams provided top-of-the-line, four-hundred-dollar "Cat 9" bats to the players (the cost of which was folded into team fees, thus upping the ante for simply giving your kid some baseball).

I chuckled one day as I walked down to the field and saw a sign posted by the field administrator that read:

Please Remember:
These are kids
This is a game
Coaches are volunteers
Umpires are human
Your child does not play in MLB

After the game, I wasn't chuckling. The sign, it turned out, was necessary, but ignored. The parents saw much more at stake in the games' outcomes—and in their sons' stats—than they should have.

Charlie's select team continued to lose, and the boys continued to have one or two practices a week alongside two or three games. For most kids, this was in addition to their school or rec teams. A few Saturdays, I got texts from my friend, the dad of Charlie's lifelong friend: "Hey Bobby wants to play some baseball with Charlie in the Wayback." Every week I declined because Charlie had a game or practice.

One Friday night, the coach belatedly announced a Saturday practice. We hadn't told Charlie about it by the time my friend texted on Saturday morning, Is Charlie free to hang out with Bobby today? Yes, I replied. Send Bobby over.

A couple of twelve-year-olds got to spend a day acting like twelve-year-olds. After half an hour of throwing and hitting balls to one another, I think they ran to the creek to catch rat snakes. I have no doubt that I made the right decision that morning in having Charlie skip practice, but at the time it was a hard choice to make.

The Travel Team Trap is easy for any parent to fall into. One need not be an achievement-obsessed parent or a dad living vicariously through his son in order to get caught up in overcompetitive youth sports. What's so pernicious about this system is how it drags in the unwilling and unsuspecting, which then creates more momentum for the system. Like every factor in our national parenting headache, it's self-perpetuating. It robs the kids and parents who buy into the travel system, and it robs those who don't.

Our own experience with select baseball was only *bad*, not *awful*. But I've spoken to a hundred parents whose lives have been totally captured by the Travel Team Trap or its equally pernicious cousins in Irish dance, violin, or theater.

Our culture teaches parents that you need to hone your daughters and sons into high achievers at a young age, and that you have to give them every advantage possible: tutors, lessons, equipment, private training. It takes up all of your money and your time.

Overly ambitious parenting, often unchosen or unconsciously chosen, is one big reason that parenting seems so hard and so costly in modern America. If you think that raising kids requires you to hire personal trainers and drive every weekend to lacrosse tournaments three counties away, or that you need to pull every possible lever in order to get your daughter into Cornell—lest you risk failing as a parent—you will believe you cannot possibly have more than one or two kids.

And it's a vicious circle. "With fewer children, parents become more child-centric," as Kevin DeYoung, a father of nine, puts it. "And as parents become more child-centric, they do not see how they could possibly have more than one or two children."[1]

The first prescription for curing our national parenting headache and making a more family-friendly America, then, is convincing everyone to have lower ambitions for their children.

"Quality" Parenting

Where did overambitious parenting come from? Why does our culture just accept it, rather than see it as a pathology? The blame may lie in our modern tendency to see life in economic terms. Consider the phrase "Quality over quantity," which is a saying you may use for your work output, or perhaps for your wardrobe. It's not typically how you talk about your children. But it is how economists talk about your children, and it's how they explain low and falling birthrates in wealthy societies.

Melissa Kearney of the Brookings Institution explains that "smaller families among higher income people—either over time or across place—could reflect a 'quantity-quality' trade-off." She grants that this is an "unfortunate label that is common in economics jargon."

"The idea," Kearney writes, "is that as societies become richer, parents may opt to have fewer children and spend more per child, investing in greater 'quality,' say, through expenditures on education and enrichment." In other words, Americans are having babies less often because we're spending so much time and effort on each one.

But this definition of "quality" parenting is at odds with everyone's *quality* of life. If you define "quality" as spending tons of money and time giving your kid "advantages," aimed at measurable worldly success, you're shortchanging yourself, your kids, and the world.

When it comes to sports, music, dance, or even academics, extraordinary "investment" in each kid doesn't pay off as much as you might think—for your kid or for you. Often the extra effort backfires. (As far as the supposed trade-off with *quantity* of children, you might be surprised how much you can still provide each kid with what matters: unconditional love, a good example, and close relationships that will last a lifetime.)

Yes, organized activities for your kids are good. They give children a chance to belong to something bigger, to strive for excellence, to cope with failure, and maybe to find something they love to do. But the point of ballet lessons or youth sports shouldn't be to get Susie national recognition or get Chad a Division I scholarship. Even in academics, you probably should skip the tutor you're hiring in order to get Eleanor into Yale.

The inputs and outcomes by which the upper-middle class measures "quality" of parenting are all distorted. American parents overplan their children's lives and place too much of their own worth as parents in the material and worldly successes of their kids.

Parents, especially college-educated and ambitious parents, would find parenting less daunting if they realized two things:

First: What really matters is not that your child get into an Ivy, dominate as a varsity pitcher, or go to nationals in Irish dance. Those are good things, yes, and should be celebrated when they happen. But they are icing on the cake. What matters far more is that you give your kids a happy childhood and build an environment for them that cultivates the virtues that will make them happy and good adults with meaningful lives. And there are often trade-offs between the pursuit of achievement and the pursuit of happiness.

Second: You have less of an impact on your children's outcomes than you think. To a large extent, each child is his or her own person. Nature, chance, environment, and social circle will determine the adult he or she becomes more than parental nurture will. That may sound a bit depressing at first, but upon reflection it becomes liberating. Parenting doesn't have to be as intensive as your yoga classmates make it out to be, and parents don't need to have everything as put-together as your typical Instagram momfluencer.

Instead of planning every hour of the week to maximize your child's chances of success, try having fun. That might mean a walk in the woods, or hitting fly balls, or watching a movie. It will certainly mean a lot more letting your kids run free while you drink coffee with your spouse.

Giving yourself permission to do those things means internalizing a piece of counterintuitive good news: your kid probably isn't a prodigy, and so you should relax.

Your Daughter Is Not Serena Williams

One summer night I found myself at a backyard cookout talking to Dan, the athletic director at a D.C.-area high school. I lamented how other people's kids were specializing in sports at age twelve, how their parents were hiring pitching coaches, and how my kids would be competing for playing time against only-children whose parents have the money and time to make travel baseball or basketball their life. Dan shrugged.

"At the end of the day, it's about raw ability." This wasn't any consolation for me. My sons and daughters, having inherited their parents' genes, might be out of luck by this accounting. (To give you an idea, both Katie and I were described by our respective high school basketball coaches as "scrappy.") But it was definitely bad news for those super-intensive parents who had fallen into the Travel Team Trap.

Dan has seen kids give up their social lives and their second and third sports for lacrosse and then lose the starting job to some naturally athletic basketball player who decided a spring sport would be fun. Matt Turner, the starting goalie for the U.S. national team in the 2022 World Cup, didn't play soccer at all until he got to high school. Jacob deGrom, the most skilled baseball pitcher of a generation, became a pitcher his junior year of college. Ultimately, whether your child becomes a star athlete is out of your hands, and all of your investment can only make small differences around the edges. The price you pay in money and time to put your child in Next Level Lacrosse has zero guarantee of taking him to the next level.

"Parents barely affect their children's prospects," explained Bryan Caplan in his 2011 book, *Selfish Reasons to Have More Kids*. "If parents gave themselves a big break—or redoubled their efforts—kids would turn out about the same."[2]

The entire upper-middle-class culture preaches the opposite and convinces parents to turn child-rearing into something so costly and time intensive that more than one or two kids is unimaginable. "Modern parenting has turned kids into a heavy burden," Caplan writes. "But it's not our kids that changed; it's us! We frequently meet demands that our elders would have rejected out of hand."

Lora is a mom of four in Florida. Her kids were all in college and high school by 2021 when she came across an old photo: Lora's oldest daughter was in a basketball uniform, her second daughter in different basketball uniform, one son was dressed for baseball, and the youngest for soccer. Four kids, dressed for four teams in three different sports, all hanging around the gym for Big Sister's game.

This sounds cute, but for Lora it wasn't a happy memory. "I look back on those early years," Lora told me, "and remember the stress and tears of being overcommitted. I hated that sports and activities controlled our family vacation schedules and our own kids' birthday dinners. Literally everything was dictated by the game and practice schedule. . . . And I was working a bunch of jobs to pay for it all."

This meant lots of driving, dropping off, and picking up. "The stress level of planning each day was absolute insanity, and no one had fun when Mommy was in 'organizing mode.'"

This takes a toll. The No. 2 reason parents gave the *New York Times*' pollsters for having fewer kids than they ideally would is "I want more time for the children I have."[3] For a single mom, or a working-class couple who has to work sixty hours each, this answer means one thing. For college-educated suburban and urban married parents, though, this answer often means, "I need to pour tons of time and energy and money into guaranteeing each of my children succeeds."

The time commitment of sports and activities deters adults from starting families. Kelley, thirty-one, told my focus group she wasn't ready for kids yet. Her life is a bit disorderly, and "the last thing I want to do is be the absent parent that doesn't show up at recitals."[4]

"Absent parent," though, isn't the only alternative to giving your kid "every advantage." What's more, being "present" as a parent often means trading out some of the "recitals" for taking a family walk or having a family game night. But this isn't the message preached by the prophets of progress.

"With fewer children to support," explained Brookings Institution scholar Isabel Sawhill, "parents and society can both invest more in each child, helping them to climb the ladder and become productive citizens in their adult years."[5]

This is the "quality-over-quantity" message, and to many ears it simply sounds like the *right* thing to do. Who wouldn't "invest more in each child"?

Well, parents' and kids' stress levels—and the plummeting birthrate—suggest we may be overinvesting.

And there's a deeper problem here. If we invest in something, we expect it to return some value to us. If our investments are all aimed at tournament trophies, good grades, blue ribbons, or college scholarships, then we are sending the message that the *value* we see in our children is in their worldly accomplishments. Every parent is rightly thrilled when Jack or Lila aces the SATs, but if we convey through our time, money, rewards, praise, and criticism that these accomplishments are what matter most, we send our children the message that they are valuable *because* of their successes. It's hard to imagine a message that more sells our kids short.

Hear the Music

Amylia is the sort of public school teacher they make movies about. She's taught music in inner-city New York and D.C. She works weekends and mentors kids who often have no other adult they can lean on. Her band students perform concerts that make the community proud.

If you ask her about what makes *her* proud, she might bring up Victor. "A really bright student," she says. Victor was Amylia's piano student at New York City's High School for Environmental Sciences. "He was eccentric."

Victor did not become a professional pianist. When he regales Amylia with his exploits, it's more likely to be about ballroom dancing or mountain climbing or geology. Music is still big for him, though. "It's definitely something that enriches his life," she tells me. "He's a very expansive person."

That word *expansive* caught my ear. Amylia is proud of Victor, but for things that are far beyond the reaches of band curriculum. The goal of Amylia's music class was never to churn out professional pianists, or get anyone first chair in the Vienna Philharmonic. It was to give kids the experience of being on a stage, of rehearsing and seeing themselves improve, of being part of a team.

These are skills with utility far beyond music, but the music itself is also key. Learning a love of music will enrich a kid's life.

When caught in the trap of a travel team or an elite youth orchestra, it's difficult to remember the *purpose* of these activities. Part of the confusion comes from a fact of human nature that can sound backward: we often need to aim at a lower target to hit a higher one.

Starting your daily run thinking, "I need to get into shape," is less likely to elicit maximum effort than starting with the thought, "I need to do 5K today in under twenty-two minutes." Your ultimate reason for running might be leg strength, expanding lung capacity, living longer, endorphins, or training for another sport. But a prudent person sets goals that are less abstract, more concrete, shorter term, and more measurable. Achieving these smaller goals (a twenty-two-minute 5K) may not be necessary for achieving the *real* goal (fitness), but *working hard* at such lower goals is necessary for hitting the higher one.

So we trick ourselves. Even more so, we trick kids. The true purposes of youth sports—developing body control, learning teamwork, experiencing adversity, learning the value of hard work, dealing with failure, being gracious in success—are probably impossible to attain unless the kids are aiming at more visible goals, such as earning first chair, winning a game, scoring a basket, or clocking a personal best for the 400 meters.

Success and accomplishments in youth sports and music and ballet are the means to an end. Our max-effort, achievement-obsessed culture wrongly sees these *means* as the *ends* themselves. Coaches and parents turn a good experience into an ordeal.

Amylia has seen intense parents ruin their kids' love of music by turning it into a job, as if the goal of music instruction is getting an oboe scholarship to Swarthmore. If your son is throwing a good fast-ball in Little League, and you're thinking, "He'll need to develop a curveball in order to make the JV squad," then you're missing out on the beauty of his throwing a good fastball. Parents can ruin sports or music for themselves and for their twelve-year-old by treating it as simply a means to sports and music at the next level.

"I wonder how much those kids even enjoy it," she tells me sadly. How appalling to take such lovely things as music and youth and turn them into toil.

Specialization

What's worse is when our kids' pursuits, rather than *expanding* their world as music did for Victor, narrow it.

Specialization is tempting, but costly. Unfortunately, specialization at a young age is now the overwhelming norm.

If you followed the Milwaukee Brewers in September 2003, you got to see a twenty-seven-year-old rookie named Pete Zoccolillo. A former all-American from Rutgers, "Petey Zocc" was also my teammate on the 1995 Pelham (N.Y.) Pelicans varsity baseball team. In four years on varsity, Zocc collected headline after headline in Pelham for his pitching and his hitting. Pete also led our varsity basketball team to a league title his senior year.

But the Zocc headline that sticks in my head the most was the one in our county paper just before his senior year, reporting that Zoccolillo—already starring in baseball and basketball—would not be playing varsity soccer. The soccer players all grumbled that the preseason feature article about our squad focused on the one player who was *not* playing.

What's remarkable *today* is that it was remarkable *back then* that one of the county's best baseball players—a future Major Leaguer—was giving up his third-best sport at age seventeen in order to play fall baseball for the Bayside Yankees, which would give him a chance to get recruited by colleges.

These days it would be a big story if a baseball player of that caliber played high school soccer at all, *and* lettered in basketball for four years. Pete had already been recruited by Rutgers Baseball when he led Pelham basketball to the league title. "It was a different time," Pete recalls. "We all played two or three sports."

Pete now has three of his own children and professionally runs a youth baseball program and training facility, making him very familiar with today's youth sports environment. "There's not many three-sport athletes left. Everyone's starting to focus on one sport . . . trying to specialize."

This specialization in youth sports is pernicious, Pete argues. It's also spreading like a virus. "The demand is there for year-round training," Pete finds. Parents and coaches want their kid to be doing baseball twelve months a year, which precludes other activities, such as basketball, music, or simply hanging out.

As a trainer, Pete sees the physical harms of specializing and the physical benefits of playing different sports. Yes, skipping fall baseball for soccer or cross country means giving up some hours in the batting cages and innings on the mound. It may lead to your son "falling behind" the other boys who are all-baseball-all-the-time. But it makes your son healthier and stronger: "You use different muscles, and get different strengths from playing different sports in different seasons."

The same argument applies against specializing in one position in a given sport. However, if you see your twelve-year-old as competing against every other twelve-year-old third baseman in the county, you will think the point of a baseball season is developing your son into an expert third baseman. In that case, you're going to get irritated if the coach rotates him to first base or puts him in the outfield— *he's missing a chance to get reps at his position.* But that attitude— that your son's development as a baseball player is the main thing *at stake* in a baseball game—is the wrong attitude. It leads parents to narrow their kids' childhood instead of expanding it. It turns a game into a job.

Burnout

If the reason for year-round baseball was that kids love baseball so much more today, it might not be that bad. But most youth baseball players quit by age thirteen. The quit rate is 70 percent across all youth sports,[6] and burnout is a plague among young athletes. The consequences of this burnout are real.

"What we're seeing is a rash of injuries among young players," NBA commissioner Adam Silver said before the 2017 NBA Finals. He called out the "broken" AAU system—the nationwide youth basketball organization that promises to turn child ballers into pros, or at least get them full rides to college.[7]

"What our orthopedics are telling us," Silver said, "is they're seeing wear-and-tear issues in young players that they didn't used to see until players were much older."

The result: "Kids are broken by the time they get to *college*," says Dr. Neeru Jayanthi, director of sports medicine research at Emory University. Kids specialize, overwork their bodies, and then they break. And when the body doesn't break, often the spirit does.

You might be tempted to write off "burnout" as a symptom of snowflake kids or their coddling parents. But avoiding burnout isn't about avoiding adversity in life.

This is about the human body and mind needing rest and variety. This is about how childhood is naturally a time of experience and experimentation, trial and error. Childhood ought to be, to use the term of Amylia the music teacher, *expansive*.

This old wisdom has been shunted aside by overambitious upper-middle-class suburban parents. We have lost belief in the inherent value of human beings—a value independent of their accomplishments and instead rooted in their very nature. Rather, elites have embraced a harshly meritocratic worldview in which academic or extracurricular success is an outward sign of inward grace. The result is a rat race in which parents push their kids into specialization, which seems modern and savvy.

As so often happens, though, the old wisdom is bolstered by the new science. Starting in the 2010s, college athletic departments, youth psychiatrists, and pediatricians have studied burnout's causes and treatment. The lack of an offseason is a central factor. Sports medicine has increasingly discovered the value of cross-training for strengthening and loosening muscles and connective tissue. Playing other sports or doing nonsports activities is a great natural way to cross-train.

Young athletes who specialized were twice as likely to suffer a hip or knee injury as other young athletes. Specializers also develop more negative attitudes about sports—and their lives in general—than those young athletes who vary their physical activity more. You could see the physical harm as an outward sign of the inward damage.

University of Kansas medical researchers in 2020 systematically combed through all the research on youth sports specialization and athlete burnout. Along every dimension, they found specializers worse off than other kids. "Athletes who specialized reported higher levels of burnout than athletes who did not specialize. Specializers reported greater exhaustion and sport devaluation than athletes who were samplers."[8]

One crucial and maybe surprising finding: the main effect of specialization was diminishing kids' sense of accomplishment. That proves how self-defeating it all is. The kid who gives up hiking, fishing, and soccer to dedicate nine months a year to tennis is likely not going to come away with the perception that hard work and dedication pay off.

Unless your daughter is Venus or Serena Williams, there will always be plenty of girls better than her at her sport. The further you go down the road of travel sports and national tournaments, the clearer it becomes that hundreds of kids are better and *always will be better* than your kid.

If your son spends all his time and effort trying to become the best jump shooter in the state, there is a 99.9 percent chance that he will fail. Failure isn't bad in itself. It's good for kids to fail. But it's bad for them to fail at something by which they've defined their own value.

It is very easy for a young athlete to see her pursuit of athletic excellence as her purpose in life. There is a high chance she attaches her identity and her worth to her success at this sport—especially if she notices that her mom and dad spend all their free time and significant money on her training.

Not every specializer comes to resent the sport or feel burnt out. Many kids simply love a single sport and never want to do anything else. But kids often want things that are bad for them, and that's where parents need to come in to say, "Hey, kid, *take a break*."

Sam, a suburban dad my age in the D.C. area, wished he had said this to his son Rickey. Rickey loved baseball. He wanted to play all the time. Then Rickey hit a growth spurt early and became the most feared slugger in McLean Little League. "By sixth grade, college recruiters were talking to me."

Soon Little League wasn't enough, and it was travel ball. "I fell into the Travel Team Trap—*hard*," Sam told me at the bar one day, shaking his head at his own mistakes. "In ninth grade, he played ninety games. . . . Every weekend, we were headed out to a tournament in Rocky Mount, North Carolina, or something."

But pretty rapidly in his teens, Rickey's love of the game waned. He was soon doing the bare-minimum work, and eventually he dreaded baseball. He was done with the game before turning fifteen. Is it any wonder? A game had become a job.

But here's the worst part, and if you are a parent of a teenage athlete, you may have been thinking this thought during this whole section: when so many other parents choose this specialization and professionalization, it almost *forces* unwilling parents to follow the same destructive route. That's why I call it the Travel Team Trap.

The Travel Team Trap

"Something has happened in youth sports since I was a kid," Meg told me in 2021. Meg is a mom in suburban Virginia. She and her husband, Paul, both come from big families and they have a big family—about eight kids, as best as I can count.

"I loved playing year-round, low-key CYO sports as a kid," Meg says, referring to the Catholic Youth Organization. "You don't have that opportunity anymore."

This is the "culture shift" Pete Zoccolillo has seen in the customers for his baseball programs, and in the coaches he competes against or who come through his facility. The fact that Pete and I were ever teammates shows how different it was back then. I was a middling athlete who never could hit the best fastballs. I could chase down fly balls, run the bases, lay down bunts, and I hustled my butt off. (My nickname one summer was "Dirt.") I never played fall ball, my parents never paid for special training, and nearly every coach I ever had was either a gym teacher or a dad who was volunteering.

Yet my senior year I was the starting center fielder for the varsity team, which had always been the pinnacle of my realistic aspirations. Luck, athletic ability, and a hundred factors beyond a kid's control will determine outcomes, but a kid who loves a game, has moderate talent, and tries hard should at least have a chance to start in the outfield for his high school team.

That's not realistic in much of America today. "It's a pretty tough climb to get playing time" on a high school team if you're not playing year-round, Zoccolillo explains.

Will and Kate are a couple who experienced the overprogramming nightmare in Chicago—theater, martial arts, and a team sport for each kid all at the same time. They moved to the D.C. area during the pandemic and used the disruption in their life as an opportunity to intentionally dial everything down—one activity at a time. Now their kids are happier, but some would say they are paying a price.

Their Mary is playing softball in the spring and wants to take piano lessons in the offseason. But there is no offseason in the Travel Team Trap. "All of her teammates are doing not just fall ball, they're doing winter training, they're doing summer travel ball."

Will says they don't regret opting out of the insanity, but "the one downside is it does feel like your kids can be left behind in the sports world at a superyoung age given the amount of specialization that is introduced so young among their peers. . . . They play all year round and on multiple teams and clubs—it's hard or impossible to catch up if you don't commit to the same pace."

Melina is a mom of four from Finland who has raised her children both in the U.S. and overseas. Her experience in the U.S.: parents who want sports for their kids have no choice but to buy into the overserious, overscheduled rat race.

The first problem is that organized sports are often the only possibility for outdoor activity. "Communities and neighborhoods are not set up for children to safely roam around," she says, "and other children are not available for group games." When pickup games do sprout up to Melina's delight, neighborhood moms report on the local message boards that a bunch of unsupervised kids are on the field "up to no good."

One of my favorite memories from my own youth was weekly pickup football games in the fall and winter. There was a group of about fifteen boys we would call on, and most weeks we got a quorum. (You needed four-on-four for a good tackle football game.) We also played pickup basketball year-round. We'd grab a court outdoors during good weather. In rain or 90-degree heat, my friend John Dolan would ask the pastor at Our Lady of Perpetual Help for the key to the gym.

Our parents' contribution to this was typically letting us use the phone to plan and making us take off our muddy clothes before walking through the house. There was no sign-up, no entry fee, no practices, and no equipment to buy. We lived in a walkable and bikeable town. We also had one another. If your sons are the only boys looking to play pickup football, it's not going to happen.

Also, Melina points out, coaches and organizers are often the ones making it so hard for parents: "Year-round sports, extra clinics, and summer training camps become the expectation at a very young age to participate in a way that feels adequate. Also, if you want to do two different activities such as youth orchestra and soccer, time commitments would clash and the child was blatantly punished for it."

The coaches see the youth programs as feeders for travel programs. If you're not "all in," many coaches don't want to use up a roster spot for you. That attitude makes sense if you're running a baseball farm system, where the purpose is to feed the major-league squad. It's perverse for youth sports.

This is the worst part about it. Not that your kids will get left behind athletically, but that they will be considered shirkers if they do what kids naturally do—try to have a childhood where their games are fun and their experiences are varied.

These elite and superintensive programs also harm the regular old volunteer-run recreational leagues. Little Leagues and rec basketball leagues around the country are finding it hard to field enough teams to even have a season.

The problem of falling numbers is especially acute in baseball, where the game becomes a joyless slog if pitchers can't find the strike zone and every inning features walk after walk with only the rare ball put in play. "The rise of privatized sports," writes John W. Miller, who had coached one of these elite teams, "has drawn the best pitchers away from volunteer-based leagues, raising the likelihood that a local recreational team lacks the skills needed for a decent game, driving average players to find other sports or to quit. Or, if they can afford it, to seek out private clubs."[9]

Exacerbating the harm, the kids left behind in the withering rec league are more likely to be working-class or poor, which means they are less likely to have a parent available to coach, thanks to more single moms and more rigid or unpredictable work schedules.

Another key thing lost in this overplanned childhood is age mixing. If your kids' "free time" is entirely organized, adult-led stuff, it's likely all age-segregated. It's great for your kids to play with their peers, but there are real benefits to them playing with and hanging out with kids significantly older or younger.

"[A]ge-mixed play is qualitatively different from play among children who are all similar in age," says play psychologist Peter Gray. "It is more nurturing, less competitive, often more creative, and it offers unique opportunities for learning."[10] An obvious example: Two four-year-olds cannot play catch. But a four-year-old can have a catch with a twelve-year-old who can accurately lob the ball underhanded to the little guy.

My own kids, with a ten-year age span from number one to number six, regularly prove this rule. Brendan outgrew playing make-believe on his own by eleven. But at age thirteen, he would still create complex worlds and quests for his younger siblings running around the backyard. They got a more advanced game than they would have had, and Brendan got to use mental muscles that could be atrophying.

My daughter Meg at age eleven was sharing a room with Eve, aged six, and walking her to and from school every day. The two had very few planned activities after school and so a lot of time together. Meg visibly grew in maturity from the responsibility and improved her reading so as to read Eve bedtime stories. For her part, Eve got an up-close, personal, and accessible role model of what a Big Girl looked like.

Who has time for niceties, though, when you're in the parental rat race?

High-Stakes High School

Some parents enter the rat race because they don't have or can't see alternatives, but many enter because they are desperate for a way to finance college—and that sprint starts earlier and earlier.

"I didn't get recruited until the fall of my senior year," said Zoccolillo, my friend who became a college all-American and a major leaguer. "Nowadays we have kids who commit [to a college] as freshmen in high school."

This is part of a bigger problem: high-stakes high school. It's the idea that children direly need to succeed in their teens in order to pave the path to life success.

In 1999, researchers at Columbia University Teachers College and Yale School of Medicine discovered something brand-new: teens in wealthy suburban school districts were more likely to abuse drugs than were teens in low-income school districts. This reversal wasn't merely about rich kids being able to afford more drugs. The upper-middle-class suburban high schoolers were far more likely to show signs of depression, anxiety, and worry—and suburban drug use was linked to these maladies.[11]

When you consider that poorer school districts have more violence and crime, and that children there are more likely to lack a father at home, and in general lack the conveniences and joys that money and class bring, this is amazing. Why is being an upper-middle-class tenth grader more stressful than being a poor tenth grader?

It's the message of high stakes at a young age—or "high-quality parenting," as some scholars would put it.

"Excessive pressures to achieve and isolation from parents" were two factors identified by Columbia researcher Suniya Luthar.[12]

A huge part of that pressure is simply *getting into a good college.* In fact, the pressure that harms so many affluent kids may not come primarily from the parents, but from the schools they send their kids to. If your daughter's high school—public or private—sold itself to you as her best path to the Ivy League, it might also be her most likely path to anxiety and depression.

"[S]chools that prioritize getting into top universities," psychologist Leonard Sax explained, "schools that place a premium on superior academic and extracurricular performance—so-called 'high-achieving schools'—are now associated with increased risk of anxiety, depression, and substance abuse."[13]

Luthar has spent decades studying the stress of the college-bound upper-middle-class kid, sometimes called "affluenza," and found that the problem is getting worse. "There is little reason to believe that the problems of affluent youth end upon completion of high school. . . . [C]ollege counseling centers are dealing with unprecedented numbers of students with serious problems including not just substance abuse but also unipolar or bipolar depression, anxiety and eating disorders, and nonsuicidal self-injury."

Just as the pressure doesn't end in high school, it doesn't begin there either. "New York's 4-Year-Olds Are Mastering Zoom to Get into Elite Kindergartens"[14] ran the Bloomberg News headline in fall 2020. The article explained the pandemic-era process of getting one's kid into Dalton or any other elite New York City private school.

"Test-prep and tutoring companies have kicked into gear," Bloomberg reported, "offering products marketed around the brand-new test.

Bright Kids, a Manhattan-based tutoring and publications company, sells a $375 workbook that says it covers all the concepts" kids will see in the Zoom interview.

Where does all this insane pressure come from? Sometimes it's parents who simply don't see any way to afford college without a merit scholarship, so they place the family's financial solvency on young Oliver's pitching arm or Tiara's GPA. Other times, it's parents who measure their own value as parents by their kids' success. Many parents just want to put their kids in the "best" middle school or high school, but they unconsciously allow others to define *best* for them— and that becomes "most likely to get your kid into the Ivies." That school, in turn, applies immense pressure on kids.

The net result is a generation of kids who carry anxiety and depression into their adulthood. Another result is parents who are less happy, who find parenthood more stressful than it has to be.

It's a trap. But there is a way out.

How to Escape the Travel Team Trap

"When everyone goes *right*," Nicki Bush-Sawyer says, describing other parents who fill their days with "scheduled activities every day, packed weekends," and focusing obsessively on test scores, "it's difficult to go *left*."

Nicki is a scientist, married, raising a kid in the suburbs. She admits to feeling "pressure to go with the majority." It's not competitive pressure or blindly following the crowd. She wants her son to journey through childhood with his classmates. "He'll be working with them and competing with them for years. We know what is right for our son (usually), but have to consciously and consistently step away from the swirl of cultural norms and expectations" in order to give him what he needs.

It takes a deliberate and constant effort to extract yourself from the Travel Team Trap. But any parent can do it. The whole process starts with lowering your ambitions for your kids when it comes to sports,

music, dance, or whatever, and understanding that these good things
are means to more important ends: the building of life skills, good
habits, and virtues.

Where you go from there will vary depending on many factors
in your life, but mostly on what will make you and your children
happy. For Eve, a mom in Chicago, "boredom is a muse." Leave your
kids alone for long periods, and they will make their own fun. A lack
of parent-free, unstructured play is a root cause of the current child
mental-health crisis, experts argue.

When Lora escaped the Travel Team Trap, it wasn't for lazier weekends, but for family activities, such as kayaking and hiking. Her kids
won't go pro in backpacking with mom, and nobody will hand them a
trophy or scholarship for it. Regular weekend outings make it impossible to commit to an elite basketball or soccer team. But Lora's family
became a much happier one when they gave up striving for individual
success and started climbing mountains together.

I once heard a varsity baseball dad lament that his younger son
had switched to lacrosse: "Nine years of baseball down the drain."
No! Nine years of baseball is great because *baseball* is great. Now he
gets to expand his sports experience! If you have an athlete, there's
a good chance he or she would be happiest trying a new sport every
year. Baseball this spring, lacrosse next year, then tennis the following year. Your kid may never "get ahead," but *getting ahead is not the
point of childhood.*

Maybe he would be happiest playing one sport, and in the offseason doing the school play—or nothing. Most years, my wife and I try
to use sports-free or sports-light fall seasons to help our kids find their
footing academically. (And we need to block off October evenings for
that Mets World Series run that will come one of these days.)

Just because your kid enjoys basketball or violin doesn't mean you
have to get her on a team or an orchestra. And if you do decide to sign
her up for some formal program, it doesn't have to be the most elite
program around.

The best team for your kid is often the one that practices across
the street, or the one that runs as an after-school program. Instead of

"Next Level Lacrosse," maybe look up next-door lacrosse. Sports and activities should work for your family, not the other way around.

One of the most powerful antidotes to the Travel Team Trap is siblings. Having many kids not only makes travel sports much harder, it also makes it feel less necessary. John is a dad I know through school and baseball. I've coached his younger son, Sammy, a good baseball player. John attributes that to one thing: Sammy has an older brother, Ozzie. "You know that ten-thousand-hours thing?" John says, referring to the theory that ten thousand hours of practice make one an expert. "Sammy got those ten thousand hours in our front yard with Ozzie."

Playing Is Supposed to Be Fun

After Charlie's select team head coach quit seven games into the season, a few parents spoke up: our boys weren't having fun. The pressure made them lose more. Early in the season, the boys held a few late leads, but they never felt good about it. They were too nervous they would mess it up—especially since they knew what sort of scolding they would get if they blew the game.

After the parental intervention and the coaching change, everyone relaxed, and by the end of the season, they were having fun. They tied a good team late in the regular season, and then pulled off an upset win in the playoffs. We took the summer off from organized baseball, and in the fall, Charlie asked to switch back to his old rec team. The competition, the umpiring, and the field quality were all less impressive than with his select team, but I have never seen a group of boys have more fun playing baseball than the "Green Goblins" of 2021.

What's more, Katie and I often skipped Charlie's games that fall. Don't get me wrong, I loved watching that team, but some game days, I opted to take the younger kids to the park, or simply to get some rest. The Goblins' coach was happy to pick up Charlie on his way to the field. Counter to the travel-team narrative, the whole family didn't have to be present for Charlie to play baseball and benefit from it.

In one very close Goblins game, Charlie was playing second base in the last inning with a one-run lead. He made a mental error, making a futile throw to home plate, allowing the opposing batter to reach safely. That kid then scored the winning run in a one-run game.*

When Charlie came to the car after the game, he looked a little dejected, but he said, "I know I should have thrown to first base instead of home on that play. I had thought through what I would do before the pitch, but I didn't adjust after the ball hit the pitcher's glove."

As a former ballplayer and a coach, I was impressed Charlie had realized his mistake. As a dad, I was thrilled that my teenage son was admitting a mistake and coming up with a way to do better in the future.

I realized during the drive home that it was *good* that Charlie had made that mental error and cost his team the game. That's because ambitions for my kids aren't low, after all. I'm not trying to make them premier athletes or musicians. I'm trying to help them become men and women of virtue. That's something my wife and I cannot do for them. We can only give them the opportunities to make their own mistakes and learn their own lessons.

Ambitions

We've mentioned several solutions for the Travel Team Trap: Stop seeing accomplishments as the goal and start seeing activities as good in themselves. Turn away from the intensive and toward the expansive. But there's a final one that is far bigger in scope: lower your ambitions for your kids' success . . . but also raise your expectations for them way higher than you ever dreamed.

---

* Charlie at this point has requested that I mention some of his defensive highlights of his 2021 baseball season so as not leave the impression that he only makes game-losing errors. I will mention that he was the winning pitcher on the select team's only regular-season victory, and for the Goblins, he pitched scoreless final innings to save one-run leads in two consecutive games.

Let me explain what I mean. "Have lower ambitions for your kids" is a motto I came up with many years ago for reminding parents that D-I scholarships, MVP trophies, and first-chair clarinet may be good things, but for many parents and kids, striving for them will not maximize happiness.

The motto is also a joke.

Our ambitions for our kids ought to be astronomical, if we're talking about the things that truly matter. As a Catholic, my ambition for my children is the highest: that they share in the glory of God for eternity in heaven. In more secular terms, my ambition for them is to develop the virtues that lead to a life of meaning, lasting satisfaction, and true happiness. It doesn't get much higher than that.

And *of course* I care about the worldly accomplishments and joys. I get competitive, and I relish in my kids' victories and achievements. Seeing Charlie sprint to the outfield as the starting center fielder for his middle school teams warmed my heart. Seeing Brendan bring home a straight-A report card put me in a good mood for a weekend. Following Meg's successes in overcoming a learning disability brings tears to my eyes. But watching them make up absurd games on the front lawn, laughing and enjoying one another, is just as good. Joy, regardless of outcome or performance, is more important.

"I don't see the need to compete with others in what activities my children participate in," my wife's cousin Cassie explains. She has a very different perspective, thanks to her oldest daughter, Isabel. "With all the extra tutoring and therapies my daughter with Down syndrome endures every day of her life, I have allowed her to find her own joy. And she did . . . dancing is her life."

Isabel has tried multiple dance styles, including hip-hop. "She's amazing," Cassie says, as a typical proud mom. "She knows the entire dance routine. She may be off a beat or two, but she steals the show each and every time. Only because she exhibits pure happiness and joy for what she's doing." If you are blessed with an Isabel in your life, it's easier to keep things in perspective.

When my nephew John Paul was born, his shoulder got stuck, his arm was fractured in delivery, he was covered in bruises, and he wasn't breathing well at all. At times he wasn't responsive to stimuli. It was scary and harrowing, and also physically grueling for his mom, Elena. When John Paul's dad, Pat, finally stepped out of the hospital for an hour or two, he met up with me and his childhood friend, Father Drew Royals, at the Corner Pub in Silver Spring. Pat needed support and prayers, but he also needed a pint and some brotherly jocularity. We joked about how tough JP would be as a teenager, beating up his big brothers with a laugh: "They had to break my arm when I was born just to give the rest of you a fighting chance."

Pat and Elena soon learned the cause of those birth issues: John Paul had spinal muscular atrophy (SMA), a debilitating congenital disease for which there is no cure. Elena, in one of her regular dispatches on the Internet, wrote of how this diagnosis tested her faith. "Something both Pat and I have struggled with in recent days has been how to find the balance between striving for the faith that won miraculous cures for Jesus' followers, and embracing God's will as Christ himself did."[15]

How much should she ground her hope for her son in what he might accomplish and grow into if a cure is developed? She wrote to John Paul, "While we will always pray for your health, our happiness is not rooted in it."

Around nine months, doctors detected cognitive decline, and it came as a painful shock to Elena. "It's not that I was really hoping you were going to go to Harvard, and it certainly does not change how incredibly beautiful your life is," she wrote. Then she corrected herself: "In my humble and unbiased opinion, you just got a little more beautiful."

"Any little thing that we might attribute to human merit, we do," Elena confessed in a letter to John Paul. We talk about how survivors are so strong and kids are so smart. "You make it clearer that the true value of human life is not in the outer displays of human ability, but rather in the God-given power of the immortal soul to love and inspire love."[16]

Even for those without Elena's faith, this truth holds. A child with a severe disability allows us to see that human life, in and of itself, is a blessing. Achievements, success, brilliance, speed, strength, nimbleness, and beauty are all good things, wonderful to behold and worthy of celebration. But in our modern age, we confuse these good things with the Good. We wrongly believe that the good things about other people are the things that make them good.

Having children, in the modern secular view, is or ought to be entirely an individual choice. *Some people elect to have kids, and that's fine, just like some people elect to own a boat. In contemporary America and Western Europe, we are enlightened and liberated from tradition, biological clocks, and God's commandments.* Parenthood is no longer thought of as the natural consummation of marriage or natural part of adulthood. *We smart people have kids only if we have decided after plenty of deliberation and calculation that having a kid is the utility-maximizing choice for us right now.*

This creates problems, one of which is too-high worldly ambitions for our own kids. "Once having children is defined as an individual choice," writes Paula Fass in *The End of American Childhood*, "American parents often imagine that when they do not succeed or are less than completely successful . . . it is somehow their fault. Having made the choice, they are somehow obligated to do it right."[17]

The cultural elites of Western Europe and the United States pride themselves on their secularism. Our culture believes we have overcome past superstitions and are more humane and equal as a result. But as our culture and our elite belief system is stripped of the idea of the divine, it loses the idea of fundamental human dignity.

Pat and Elena, in contrast, never lost their grip on that idea. Their John Paul never grew up to take down his big brothers. At most, he could wiggle his toes, grip Elena's finger, and smile. Soon he lost even that ability. At fourteen months old, John Paul passed away.

Father Drew delivered the funeral homily, and part of it he addressed directly to Pat and Elena. "You saw so clearly that John Paul's life possessed a dignity that was radically equal to that of everybody else."

Once we realize that we all have innate value—that we are good no matter what we accomplish—we might worry less about our children's accomplishments. Hypercompetitive childhood, achievement obsession, and the Travel Team Trap are as massive as they are because our meritocratic secular society has forgotten that we have innate value.

We need to invert and expand the motto of Charlie's former coach: *Successful* kids aren't good. *Kids* are good.

CHAPTER 2

"Hey, Parents, Leave Your
Kids Alone"

H ow do you do it?"
You get that question a lot when you have six kids. I relish the question because it gives me an opportunity to explain my "systems" for doing things the big-family way—what my kids would call "life hacks." For instance, I developed a *system* for trips to the zoo.

I pack snacks, get there early on a Saturday (most animals are out before the official opening time), park for free on Connecticut Avenue, and let each kid choose one must-see animal.

The National Zoo in Washington, D.C., is on a long, steep hill, and Connecticut Avenue is at the top. That means we visit the animals on a leisurely stroll downhill, then hoof it about a mile uphill back to the minivan. I realized during my first visit that this last part had to be an athletic event. No more looking at animals at this point—just mountain climbing. With the nine-month-old strapped onto my chest, I loaded the two-year-old into the front of the double stroller and the four-year-old into the back. There was a skateboard-type thing on the back of the stroller for the five-year-old. They all got juice boxes. The seven-year-old walked on my right, and the eight-year-old walked on my left. Then we marched up the mountain, stopping once for a water break.

Many fellow zoo-goers gawked, some cheered, most smiled. Once, I saw a kid tug his father's hand and point at our little marching platoon of six kids and a father—"Look over there, Dad!"

The Carney family went to the zoo and became an exhibit.

This isn't rare. When people learn how many kids we have, I once told a *New York Times* writer for an article on big families, some react as if they "found out we went around in a horse and buggy and drew all our water from the well."[1]

The author of the article, Laura Vanderkam, who has five kids herself, interviewed a handful of big families for the story and included an insight that is certainly more valuable and relevant than any of my "systems."

The most important observation was this: Big families "often learn a liberating secret: Many 'requirements' of modern parenting aren't requirements at all."

A leading cause of America's parenting headache is the belief that we need to do so much. There's a norm of maximum-effort parenting, and in some cases, helicopter parenting—with constant hovering and surveillance of our children—is considered mandatory.

But looking at big families is revealing, and Vanderkam in the *Times* had some eye-opening research: "while mothers of three children experienced more stress than mothers of one or two, mothers of four or more experienced less; a Norwegian study found that living in a large family was associated with lower levels of stress and anxiety in children, too."

Put another way, if you ask a mom or dad of six, seven, or eight kids, "How do you do it?" the truthful answer is, "To be honest, I often just don't."

The "secret" here is simple: *You don't have to do all the parenting things you think you need to.* Yet our culture increasingly demands intensive parenting, which makes the whole family thing a bigger headache.

If American culture is to become more family friendly, we need to abandon maximum-effort helicopter parenting. What the sociologists call "high-quality" parenting often manifests itself as a steady state of anxiety—which is not, in fact, good for children or their parents.

We know that anxiety and fear are bad for us, but somehow our culture has convinced us that, for parents, anxiety and fear are a requirement. This is a lie. It is a fruit of our culture, and particularly of our changes over the past two generations.

The "Demands" of Modern Parenthood

The mid-1960s housewife is, in American elite culture, the model of a benighted and oppressed woman, enslaved to the duties of the home while their husbands worked nine to five and then rested. Hard data lends credence to this stereotype. In 1965, in a given week, American mothers had about ten hours when their primary activity was taking care of children. This doesn't count the many hours where Mom was doing something else and simultaneously helping or tending to her children—washing the dishes while reminding Davey to brush his teeth and get in his pj's. Meanwhile, dads were averaging fewer than three hours a week.

Since then, dads have stepped up. Studying time diaries—detailed accounts of a day's activities—and survey data, Suzanne Bianchi and other scholars found that, from 2.6 hours of primary parenting a week in 1965, dads increased to 5.0 hours in 1995, and then 6.5 hours in 2000.[2] That's 2.5 times as much father-kid time as their parents. And it's held steady for about twenty years.[3]

And the moms? Surely they're replacing time at the playground with time at the office, or finally getting some Me Time, right?

Hardly.

Mom's weekly primary-parenting load *increased* from 8.8 hours in 1975 to 12.9 hours in 2000. That is, while Modern Dad put in an added 3.8 hours a week of parenting compared to what his own father did, Modern Mom added 4.1 extra hours.[4]

And again, this doesn't count multitasking or family activities that involve the children. Parenting was a married mom's primary or secondary activity for 18.9 hours a week in 2000, a 5-hour increase over 1975, while married dads put in 8.6 hours all told—up nearly 4 hours from a generation earlier. In the twenty years since 2000, those numbers haven't really changed[5] (as long as we bracket those months in 2020 when millions of parents suddenly became homeschool proctors and sole playmates for their kids).

The bottom line: in this century compared to last, Dad is spending more time with the kids, and Mom is working more hours outside the home, yet Mom is *still* spending more much time taking care of kids—all while family size shrinks. Something has gone wrong here.

"Stay-at-home moms used to just tell their kids to go out and play," as parenting author Bryan Caplan puts it. "Now, moms *and* dads tag along with their kids as supervisors, or servants."[6] Some of this is moms and dads doing what they enjoy—like me at the zoo. A lot of extra parenting time, though, is moms and dads doing what they feel is expected—or demanded—of them. This is where a large family can actually be liberating.

"When you eventually get past two or more kids, you have to accept that not everything is going to be perfect," explained Kristin Reilly, a mom of seven. Some people will judge you for being a bit of a mess, but most won't. In fact, many people will find joy in it.

A front lawn scattered with bicycles and scooters and wagons is a beautiful sight. If a neighbor comes over for coffee and your house isn't perfect, more likely than judging you, she's apt to be relieved and encouraged that you, too, are not totally put together. Hand-me-downs are the norm for our kids. Even our oldest ones get their jeans and hoodies from older cousins.

My wife mostly gave up baking birthday cakes or cupcakes when our oldest was five because she found a local bakery that sells unfrosted cupcakes for cheap. Soon enough, that same oldest started doing the baking for most birthdays.

This isn't laziness. It's sanity. Doing less means the less you do is better—the sort of quality-over-quantity trade-off I can get behind—and it makes everyone happier.

I find the most common trigger for my being a bad parent, getting irrationally angry or yelling at my kids needlessly, is too-high expectations for myself. Maybe from reading *Cheaper by the Dozen* or from listening to certain moms and dads of ten, I have become subconsciously convinced that I should be able to run my own household like a well-trained military unit—you know, because of my *systems*. My ego wants to answer "How do you do it?" with "We run a real tight ship."

So when getting our ship out of the dock looks less like less a squadron of Navy SEALs and more like a bunch of mackerel flapping on the deck, I am angered not by the prospect of my children getting a late slip, but because my own self-image—as a militaristic tough guy with optimal systems who can whip a rowdy bunch into shape—has been shattered.

Being happy in the morning requires chilling out. *Of course* I should try to teach the virtues of focus, punctuality, and obedience. But I shouldn't freak out if the nine-year-old doesn't exhibit those virtues all 180 school mornings.

That's my own foible. Other parents worry a lot about their kids *looking* right. Or they constantly compare their children's development against official milestones or neighbor kids. Many parents become helicopters because they are terrified of a broken skull from a fall off the bottom of the slide. A greater number helicopter because they have been led to believe they are *supposed* to constantly supervise little Tanner, and that doing anything less makes one a bad mom.

But these "demands of modern parenthood" are not demanded by your children or by human nature. They trickle out into the culture, through an irresponsible media that peddles sensationalism and from bullheaded government authorities who think they know better than parents how to raise kids.

"Risk management used to be a business practice," author Malcolm Harris wrote in his book about Millennials, and "now it's our dominant child-rearing strategy."[7] *Toddlers may never be left in a room alone. Young children must always have constant close supervision. Older grade schoolers still cannot walk anywhere by themselves. Mom and Dad should be at every practice and every game. God forbid you ever leave a child "unattended" in public.*

Society paints a daunting picture of "good parenting." Whether it's constant hovering or spectacularly twee arts and crafts or intensely enriching "vacations," our culture portrays parenting as a much bigger lift than it should be. Most American parents could benefit (themselves and their kids) from ignoring their children a bit more and trying a bit less hard.

Most of all, parents and kids would benefit from a lot less fear.

Fear can be a gift, and sometimes fearlessness is imprudent. But modern American parenting culture is overwhelmed by excessive fear. Parents are told to fear stranger abductions, cracked skulls, missed milestones, sex trafficking, processed foods, homegrown foods, unmasked schoolrooms, unbleached surfaces, melting ice shelves, and everything else. We come to fear these things—and we fear being judged if we don't take extreme precautions against them. This fear trickles down to our children, who grow into adults who see family formation as the most terrifying thing imaginable.

Is it any wonder that the Millennials, the safest, most protected generation, are terrified by the idea of having kids?

The Illusion of Control

Wedded to the mandate of fear is the illusion of control. Someone or something has convinced twenty-first-century adults that with enough effort we can eliminate risk and uncertainty from our lives. "The biggest lie," says Lenore Skenazy, founder of the "free-range parenting" movement, "is not just that every second is fraught with danger, but that you can control it." We need to stop trying to control what we can't.

I learned a long time ago to avoid commenting on the fraught battlegrounds of nursing, sleep training, and co-sleeping, but let me mention it for a moment. The newborn stage is a unique one, and intensive parenting at that point seems to be good for mom often as much as for baby. There's one school of thought, called "attachment parenting," that involves keeping your newborn in or right next to your bed, carrying her in a sling, and nursing her indefinitely. This wasn't our style, but for many parents it works and makes their families happier.

My proposal here involves parenting *after* those precious moments. However you parent for the first three or twelve or eighteen months, at some point many moms, dads, and kids would benefit from what could be called *detachment parenting*.

Yes, raising children is the most important job that parents have. But no, that doesn't mean that the best way to do it is through constant attention and constant presence. Parents' sanity matters, and our sanity is served by time away from our kids. Children's ability to develop into independent adults requires parents to leave them alone a bit. Raising kids is a bit like smoking pork shoulder: it's not going to be quick, and you do need to check the thermometer from time to time, but you'll get the best outcome if you avoid constantly lifting the lid and prodding the meat.

Having lower expectations for your kids is important. It's also important to have lower expectations for yourself. My wife and I have at least dozen friends with as many kids as us or more. Most of us have realized that we will skip the Travel Team Trap, never have the time to helicopter, eventually lean on the older kids to entertain and take care of the younger kids, and rely on free childcare from in-laws, grandmas, aunts, and neighbors.

Parenting will always be exhausting, but if you choose a model of parenthood that rejects the elite trends of the day, you can make it less exhausting per child. Then, hopefully, you can have more children. If our culture shifts in this direction, the parenting headache will be relieved, and more young adults will find family appealing.

"Once you adjust the kind of parent you plan to be," in the words of Bryan Caplan, "you should also reconsider the number of kids you want to have."[8]

This is not counseling neglect. Kids need parents to take care of

them, feed them, clothe them, show them unconditional love, hug
them, teach them to ride a bike, bake brownies with them, put them to
bed, clip their toenails, bathe them when they're little, and teach them
right from wrong. Hundreds of thousands of American kids experience
serious neglect in the U.S.[9] This is a huge problem. But it's not a problem we can solve with this book.

It's a safe bet that the reader of this book is far, far less prone to
neglect, and more prone to its opposite—overparenting. Helicoptering is not just for elites anymore, either; like most social changes, it's
trickling down to the working class.[10] Overparenting is booming. And
it's harming kids.

Childhood anxiety, for one, is rising in part as a result of helicopter
parenting. The *Journal of Pediatrics* in 2023 pinned the rise in teen
anxiety to a lack of childhood independence. "[C]hildren who have
more opportunities for independent activities are not only happier in
the short run, because the activities engender happiness and a sense
of competence," write the authors, "but also happier in the long run,
because independent activities promote the growth of capacities for
coping with life's inevitable stressors."[11]

A huge predictor of childhood anxiety is what researchers call
"maternal over-control." A 2012 paper in the journal *Child Psychology
and Human Development*, for example, gave children two widely used
questionnaires: one to test for anxiety and one to test for maternal
control.[12]

The study asked kids how often they experienced certain interactions with their parents or certain feelings toward them. The most
relevant statements included the following:

- "I wish my parents would worry less about what I am doing."
- "When I come home, I have to account for what I had been doing
  to my parents."
- "My parents forbid me to do things other adolescents are allowed
  to do because they are afraid that something might happen to me."
- "My parents get overly anxious that something might happen to me."

Parents who demanded an account for a kid's every minute, who
were constantly anxious that "something may happen," and who gave

their kids less freedom ended up with kids who themselves were more anxious. The data suggested a very precise cause and effect: maternal overcontrol causes children to perceive themselves as less competent, and children who feel less competent feel more anxious. They approach the world with more fear, maybe because they were ushered through their childhood in fear.

"Students who reported having overcontrolling parents reported significantly higher levels of depression and less satisfaction with life," reported a separate 2014 study published in the *Journal of Child and Family Studies*.[13] This corroborated a similar study of 317 college students published in 2011, which concluded that "helicopter parenting is negatively related to psychological well-being and positively related to prescription medication use for anxiety/depression and the recreational consumption of pain pills."[14]

"Rafts of research," writes early childhood expert Elliot Haspel, "prove that intensive parenting mainly serves to burn out parents while harming children's competence and mental health."[15]

Parents spend lots of time and energy trying to build up their children's self-confidence and self-esteem. The best way to accomplish these goals is often to leave your kids alone a bit more. This requires swimming against the cultural tide, and rejecting the lie that a *good* parent has to be constantly afraid. That pernicious lesson, that fear is good parenting, hits parents' ears long before they ever get to hold their baby in their arms.

Expecting in Anxiety

"Drinking any amount of alcohol at any time during pregnancy can harm your baby's developing brain and other organs," the website of the March of Dimes states. "There's no safe time to drink alcohol during pregnancy."[16]

The Thou Shalt Nots during pregnancy are endless. No coffee, no turkey sandwiches, no salami, no sushi, and so on. Nine months of this weird fast is daunting enough to deter plenty of women from ever considering motherhood. Those who follow all the rules are probably less likely to tolerate a second or a third pregnancy.

Emily Oster, an economist, looked into the studies behind the dire warnings against alcohol during pregnancy. One study found that any amount of drinking while pregnant correlated with more aggressive children—a seemingly good reason to warn pregnant moms off booze. But correlation is not causation, so Oster went looking for something else in the study that may have caused aggression.

The something else turned out to be *cocaine*. In a study comparing drinking moms to nondrinking moms, the very small number of cocaine-using moms are included on the drinking-mom side of the ledger—and they seem to be statistically responsible for the correlation between drinking and childhood aggression. When you control for cocaine use, the aggression problem goes away, Oster explained in her 2014 book, *Expecting Better: Why Conventional Pregnancy Wisdom Is Wrong, and What You Really Need to Know.*

Oster wrote the book because when she got pregnant, all the information she received from doctors, nurses, books, articles, or the Internet lacked anything resembling risk-reward analysis. "[P]regnancy medical care seemed to be one long list of rules," she wrote. "In fact, being pregnant was a lot like being a child again. There was always someone telling you what to do."

The study above—reflecting the fact that there are a statistically significant number of moms using cocaine—makes it clear that many mothers really do need someone to tell them what not to do (and lots of help not doing it). And the reams of advice for pregnant moms definitely do some good. Babies are, for example, more pleasantly plump on average these days than two generations ago, thanks to improved knowledge about nutrition and the massive decrease in cigarette smoking by expecting moms. Also, excessive drinking by pregnant moms can significantly harm baby and mom.

But if you are an educated mom who reads books, articles, or websites about pregnancy, you are more likely to be overly worried, because you are told that everything you could possibly want to eat, drink, or do poses some dire threat to your baby. Too much exercise, too much sitting around, outdoor air, and too little sunshine are dangerous. Don't go to concerts.[17] Don't spend time near highways or busy roads.[18] Don't "touch dirt . . . where cats may have been."[19] The World Health Organization has called for a campaign to discourage all drinking by all women "of childbearing age."[20] And while you assiduously follow all of these rules, you'd better not get stressed out.

"I wondered," author Kim Brooks wrote while trying to follow pregnancy rules, "how it was possible that any healthy baby had ever succeeded in being born."[21]

The rules of pregnancy are always issued as absolute diktats, even though, as Oster found, the data backing some of them was questionable. Moreover, the idea that all benefits have costs never factors into the equation. It wasn't that Oster was willing to run a 10 percent risk of disabling her child in order to have a more pleasant pregnancy. It was that she expected to find some discussion of the probabilities, the costs, and the risks, yet she found none.

"The key to good decision making is taking the information, the data, and combining it with your own estimates of pluses and minuses," Oster wrote.[22] When it came to alcohol, she granted that the reward (enjoying a glass of wine) was negligible if the risk (threat of IQ loss or excessive aggression for her baby) was statistically significant. But given the low quality of the data behind many pregnancy recommendations, she found that often "the existing rule is wrong. In others, it isn't a question of right or wrong but what is right for you and your pregnancy."

Studies that relied on randomized controlled trials—the kind that can clear out confounding correlations, such as the cocaine-Merlot overlap—convinced Oster that the abstinence-only teachings on alcohol or caffeine were not well grounded. She looked at the data and concluded that a solitary glass of wine at night, and anything less than four cups of a coffee a day, were fine for her during pregnancy.[23] Smoking was a no-go.

Oster's goal was to help mothers make better decisions, but also to relax. This latter part was probably her most radical view in a culture that holds that parents (especially moms) show their virtue through constant anxiety. What we really need is a lot less worrying, even if that occasionally results in you losing your kids.

Lose Your Kids

QUANTICO, VIRGINIA, my phone read. I knew exactly what this call was.

"Sir," said the U.S. marine on the other end, "we have your son, Seán."

I was slightly relieved and embarrassed when I thanked the man. But only slightly. The thing is, I kind of knew Seán was "missing," which means he wasn't *really* missing. It was the second time that week I had "lost" him.

I was driving my six kids (ages fourteen through four) home from Williamsburg, Virginia, and had, on a whim, pulled over to visit the National Museum of the Marine Corps, just off Interstate 95. My wife was home during this three-day, late-summer jaunt so that she could sort through the hand-me-downs, count school uniforms, find fall clothes, and generally get us ready for the school year. Also, she needed a break after three months at home with all six kids.

Being a dad is lovely in these circumstances. Our culture, despite all the changes over the past two generations and all the talk of equality, still holds far too low standards for dads parenting in public. Obviously, this should change, and society should raise the bar. But while the bar is low, it's gratifying for me to hurdle it and earn the applause of strangers.

I'm not saying it's *easy* to wrangle six kids single-handedly, and I'm obviously no expert wrangler. One got away, as I've already mentioned, a couple of times.

The first incident that weekend was a bit scarier than the Quantico incident, because the first time, I hadn't intended to lose Seán.

I had planned the trip to Williamsburg's Great Wolf Lodge, an indoor water park, with my friend Pat, who has three kids, the same ages as my older three. We had chosen our suites in the lodge across from one another, and at night, the nine kids and two dads spread between the two suites. I thought Pat had Seán. Pat figured I had Seán. At some point, we realized nobody had Seán.

Panic in such a moment is unavoidable. But if you examine the contours of the panic, you see it's a complex set of emotions, thoughts, and fears.

Your mind races through all the possible explanations, from terrifying to fine. *Could he have fallen into a ditch? Did somebody kidnap him? Maybe he's hiding, and playing a game. Maybe he got confused about which floor we were on.*

As you do your panicked search and he's not in first places you check (sometimes to your relief, as you check the bottom of the swimming pool), you experience other emotions and thoughts. Bafflement is one. Anger at some other kid or adult you can somehow blame for this. *If Eve hadn't been so stubborn about putting on her pajamas, I would have checked on Seán ten minutes ago.*

I kept arresting my worst thoughts because I knew they were all implausible. It's not that no abductor has ever snatched a kid from a hotel hallway, but the odds of that happening, and of Seán not screaming bloody murder, are approximately zero. If you parent based on your worst imaginable fears, as opposed to parenting based on probabilities and risk assessments, you will go crazy.

So, after I deployed all the older kids to search for him, I kind of calmed down, even though I could come up with no explanation for Sean's absence. I didn't need an explanation, because fourteen years of parenting had pounded an intellectual humility into my head. My children had, hundreds of times, done things I never could have possibly thought up on my own.

Also, I knew my kid. Some kids are born runners or lack a healthy fear of the unknown. I was blessed with children who all value independence while being bound by a certain invisible tether that will allow them to wander a bit, but never too far. Seán was on the property, I was certain.

Then my phone rang. The caller ID told me the call was coming from inside the lodge. Seán was found; I knew before answering.

But in that next half second, as I answered, the most confusing emotions hit me. I never worried he was found dead or wounded. I worried that the voice on the other end would be the police. Mixed with relief at my lost sheep being found was terror that I would face judgment and ramifications for being an imperfect shepherd.

"Hello," I answered apprehensively.

"Hi, Dad, where *are you*?!" Seán asked, a bit impatiently, as if I were the one who had disappeared.

Fear of Judgment

Losing your kid makes you feel like a bad parent, and you assume everyone else judges you as such.

This fear of judgment makes parenthood scarier for Kara Schoenherr, a married woman in Arizona who spoke to the *New York Times* for an article titled "Why American Women Everywhere Are Delaying Motherhood." Schoenherr grew up in rural Illinois and spent her days riding her bike "and coming home when the streetlights came on."

Parenting in that way seemed manageable to her. Parenting by today's standards does not. "Back then you could let your kids do whatever and you wouldn't be judged," Kara, then twenty-seven, told the *Times*. "Now there's so much mom shaming. You are looked down on if you are not fully focused on your kid."[24]

Parents simply don't allow their kids to be alone anymore. On average, American parents won't let a nine-year-old play in the front lawn unsupervised, won't leave an eleven-year-old home alone for even an hour, and won't let a thirteen-year-old play at the local park without adult supervision. It is maddening and exhausting for parents.[25]

"Come home when the streetlights turn on" may be the most common phrase I heard from Gen X parents talking about their own childhoods. It was liberating for us kids and liberating for our parents. Parents set boundaries and rules, and then set their kids free. But most adults today, like Schoenherr, believe that for various reasons that's not okay anymore. Some believe the world is less safe today than it was thirty years ago (that's mostly false), and others just believe the world is more judgmental (that's mostly true).

Helicopter parents are often parents who are simply following the rules because it's expected of them. One mother told author Kim Brooks that she would never let her kids out of her sight in a store, even though "[s]he knew it was irrational."

"Are you afraid someone will hurt them?" Brooks asked.[26]

"No," the other mom answered. "I don't know, I guess it's other people. I worry that if I let them out of my sight, other people will see us and think I'm doing something wrong. . . . I don't know if I'm afraid for my kids, or if I'm afraid other people will be afraid and judge me for my lack of fear."[27]

The fear of other people's disapproval—including the authorities—is, sadly, based in experience. Free-range parenting guru Lenore Skenazy runs a website, LetGrow, which published a letter in 2022 from a dad who had pizza with his four-year-old daughter at a Costco. Dad got up a couple of times—once to fill the sodas, a second time to get napkins, never walking more than a few feet away from their table. After sitting down to eat, "someone sitting behind me tapped me on the shoulder. He said something like, 'You know that's a no-no, right?' Then he let me know he works for Child Protective Services."

Every parent, according to this ethos, must assume every stranger is a skilled and effective kidnapper who has the motive and means to snatch your child and speed off in a waiting getaway car. This is absurd. It teaches children to be constantly afraid, it stunts their independence and confidence, and it makes it a hundred times harder to bring children anywhere. If Millennials have let this Secret Service agent image of parenthood sink into their heads, it's no wonder they think raising children—or more than one at least—is basically impossible.

"If you live in a culture that decides that you can't leave a child without adult supervision," as Skenazy put it when she and I spoke, "then having kids is signing up for something different than my mom signed up for."

"The World's Worst Mom" is one title Skenazy proudly wears. It comes from the time she let her nine-year-old ride the New York City subway alone.[28] She had her reasons for doing it, and she was intentional in how she went about it (she rode with her son many times, coaching him before leaving him at Bloomingdale's for his solo ride home), but that didn't stop the flood of opprobrium when she shared the story. The experience didn't drive Skenazy into a shell, but instead made her realize the need for more free-range parenting.

"My kid wears a helmet," Skenazy writes, "got strapped into a car seats, always wears his seat belt. But I don't believe kids need a security detail every time they leave the house."[29]

In fact, kids need the opposite.

Set Them Free

Young human beings need to experience the sensation of risk, and they're likely to get it one way or another.

Early childhood expert Ellen Sandseter concludes that risky play has given humans an evolutionary advantage by helping us overcome fears. If parents try to suppress that God-given desire for risky play, most kids will find other ways to satisfy that appetite. If they don't, they'll never overcome the fears everyone must to become a functioning adult.

"The everyday efforts we make to prevent kids' distress—minimizing things that worry them or scare them, assisting with difficult tasks rather than letting them struggle," writes Kate Julian, senior editor at the *Atlantic*, after reviewing child psychiatry literature, "may not help them manage it in the long term. . . . If we want to prepare our kids for difficult times, we should let them fail at things now, and allow them to encounter obstacles."[30]

For their sake—and your own—let your kids encounter the forks and bumps in the road. Exploring the world—unchaperoned—is "the most important [type of play] for the children," Sandseter says. "When they are left alone and can take full responsibility for their actions, and the consequences of their decisions, it's a thrilling experience."[31]

Early in the spring of 2020, when nearly all parents in Montgomery

County, Maryland, were enforcing social distancing rules on their kids, a thread started on my local online "NextDoor" group, fretting about other people's kids playing basketball outside, young women walking close together, or even a dad pushing his child in a swing that may have been used by another dad and kid earlier in the morning.

In the midst of this competitive COVID-fear-peddling, one neighbor warned that—as teenagers had no school, no activities, and were barred from going over to friends' houses—"I have seen quite a few children, not accompanied by adults, entering parkland and streams." The weather was mercifully beautiful that week of lockdown, and the neighbor worried "that warm weather brings out ticks, snakes, etc., and accidents may happen in unsupervised areas."

Walking with one's siblings was literally the only thing kids were allowed to do in those days, and this worried neighbors enough that they took to the community message board. There was a contest, it seemed, to come up with something to fear that nobody else had mentioned yet.

If you're not ready to let your kids wander around the neighborhood for an entire day, or if they are too young for that, I recommend what I did in Quantico: take them to a good museum and set them free. Brendan was in the Cold War exhibit. My daughters took in the World War II section. I have no idea what Seán did, but I knew that he and his siblings would be safe. Within the bounds of all reasonable probabilities, the worst that would happen was Seán getting a bit confused and stressed, and me getting a call from security again. The alternative was making all six kids go at the same pace through the same exhibits in the same order. I've tried that, and it's neither fun nor edifying.

And that's the point: if you never lose your kids, you're probably not having enough fun. Kids who never lose sight of their parents will not learn how to take initiative to solve their own problems. Getting lost as a kid—which means something different at different ages—inoculates one from separation anxiety at age eighteen, Sandseter has found. Meanwhile, parents who always have eyeballs on their kids will be anxious and exhausted and less willing to go on fun adventures.

A large part of parenting is placing your children in settings where they will ultimately be safe from the worst outcomes when things inevitably go wrong. I would have much less tolerance for losing my child while sea kayaking or in a high-crime neighborhood at night. But a lodge built for and crowded with families is like a walled garden. The museum in Quantico has one exit, and it is literally patrolled by U.S. marines. Barring a one-in-a-million freak accident—the sort of thing that *could* happen anywhere but almost certainly *won't* happen—being lost will be a temporary thing with a happy ending.

Will there be anxiety and fear in the meantime? Sure. But keeping your kids from scary experiences should not be a goal.

Young brains are elastic. Childhood is supposed to be expansive. For a child, learning and growing is largely being exposed to many things and protected from a few really bad things. Why do you consider taking your kids to New York City or Yellowstone? Because you want to show them that the world is big, diverse, and contains endless wonder. For a twelve-year-old brain, though, a five-hour open-ended bike adventure with two buddies might do more to convey the expanse, wonder, and diversity of the world than being dragged for five days around Paris.

"When I was 9 or 10," one dad friend of mine wrote, "I would tell my mom that my friend and I were going to go ride our bikes 'somewhere,' and got as a response to be back by dark if I wanted dinner. This was entirely normal at the time and is unimaginable now, despite the fact that 1986 was just objectively a *much* more dangerous year than 2021."

Have you ever gone back and read parenting magazines from a generation or two ago? Markella Rutherford did that systematically, reviewing 565 advice columns and parenting articles for her book *Adult Supervision Required.* Here's one telling conclusion:

> Early twentieth-century parenting advice showed evidence of a strong emphasis on children's need to develop independence and competence apart from parents. . . . For example, children walked unaccompanied to school, roamed around and played in neighborhoods alone and in groups, rode their bikes all

over town, hitch-hiked around town, and ran errands for their parents, such as going to the corner store or post office. These descriptions of freedoms to roam have disappeared from contemporary advice. Instead, parents today are admonished to make sure that their children are adequately supervised by an adult at all times, whether at home or away from home.[32]

Society needs to stop this competitive fear, and realize that we're killing both childhood and parenthood with all our rules. The real fight isn't convincing parents to overcome their fears, but changing our culture and our laws so that parents have one less thing to fear.

Criminalized Parenthood

I have been lucky in the times I lost Seán. I'm not talking about finding him again—that was nearly guaranteed. I'm talking about how I've been treated.

The *very* first time I lost Seán, he was four. The police were waiting for me in the Nature Center parking lot. They were there to make sure Seán was safe, and when it was clear that I was really Seán's dad, and when I gave the believable and not-totally-irresponsible explanation of how the heck I had left a four-year-old in a parking lot unattended for twenty-five minutes, the police were satisfied and ready to move on.

I benefited, in all likelihood, by being a well-dressed, passably groomed white dad. My car was a very responsible Honda Odyssey. I hadn't abandoned him. I was visibly rattled and relieved. The police saw that Seán seemed healthy and was happy to see me, and he was not nearly as rattled as I was. The one detail that didn't check out was my appearance.

The cops had asked Seán to describe me. To him, my defining trait was that I was old.

"*How* old?"

"REALLLLY old."

"Like, older than Santa Claus?"

"Maybe. About the same age."

The Park Police had gotten a call about a solo four-year-old and had decided, thankfully, that their job was making sure the four-year-old got safely reunited with his parents. They hadn't decided that their job was to find a bad guy to prosecute. The front desk at Great Wolf Lodge apparently had the same approach. The marine at Quantico only wanted to talk to me about how charming Seán was.

Other parents (surely moms more than dads) have had less pleasant and more judgmental experiences. For some parents, losing their kids and then finding them can also result in something far worse. It may not simply be dirty looks or judgy comments. You may fall under the full force of the law.

Helicopter Mandates

Kim Brooks's life was ruined for a few years—and almost permanently—by a culture and legal system that tries to criminalize parental violations of some overstrict parenting code, regardless of safety.

Brooks caved to her four-year-old son's demand to bring him along to Target, where she was headed to make a single purchase before flying home from a visit to her mother's house in Virginia. When the two got to Target, the boy didn't really want to go into the store—he had just wanted to ride in Grandma's car and play with the iPad that resided there. Rather than trigger a meltdown, Brooks assessed the situation. It wasn't even slightly hot out, it was cloudy, this was a very safe parking lot, and she would be in the store only a few minutes. She locked the doors, cracked the windows, and made her single purchase as quickly as possible. Her boy barely knew she was gone.

But a fellow shopper noticed and was appalled. Rather than offer help in some way, she started filming. Then she sent the video, along with Grandma's license plate number, to the local police. A few hours later, while Brooks was flying home to Chicago, the police showed up at Grandma's door. *Help us find her, or we'll haul you off in the back of the cruiser right now.* Brooks hired a lawyer and worried about it for a year before she learned that there was a warrant for her arrest. Her crime: "contributing to the delinquency of a minor." That little Felix was never delinquent and was never harmed didn't matter. Brooks flew to Virginia, turned herself in, and agreed to parenting classes and community service in exchange for getting the charge dropped.

Criminalization of parenting decisions is common in twenty-first-century America, as are laws that basically require helicopter parenting. Child Protective Services and the Montgomery County Police detained the two children of Alexander and Danielle Meitiv for more than five hours in April 2015. The authorities finally returned the two children, and then launched a months-long investigation into the parents. The suspected crime? Letting their children, ages ten and six, walk to the local playground together without adult supervision.

Maybe you would never do that, but as free-range parents, the Meitivs had raised their kids to be street smart and independent. Their kids were, in fact, safe on their walk to and from the playground. That didn't matter to the person who called the cops, whose assumptions of danger and neglect were divorced from any realistic threat assessment. And it didn't matter to the police or CPS, who, by taking the kids away from their parents, became the harm they claimed to guard against.

You see these stories everywhere. When ten-year-old Braylin Harvey of Chicago was picked up from school seven minutes late, the school reported this as neglect to the Illinois Department of Child and Family Services. "The investigator asked [his mother] to provide contact information for people who might reassure the department that she's a good mother," Skenazy reported.[33]

Sadly, too often "being a good mother" means "being afraid," regardless of what the real risks are.

Bad Risk Assessment

"It's not that nothing bad will ever happen," Skenazy told me over Zoom, "but to act as if every second it's about to happen is *more* wrong."

No matter what you do, you cannot keep your children completely safe. This thought is unnerving but undeniable. All parents know this, even if only subconsciously.

Which brings us to the real problem behind helicopter mandates: *bad risk assessment*.

Of course you shouldn't leave your four-year-old in a car on a 90-degree day, or in a mall parking lot for two hours. But if you show up at your sister's house for a cookout in April, and your two-year-old is asleep in the back seat of a minivan parked behind the house, you can roll down the window and let the kid sleep. So "leaving a kid in a car" is not in itself intolerably risky. It's the circumstances that should dictate when it becomes too risky for you.

Cable news will try to terrify you into believing children are likely to be snatched up if you turn your head away for a moment. We've all heard the horrific stories, and we all know the names—Etan Patz, Polly Klaas, Adam Walsh, Elizabeth Smart. Every parent's heart breaks for what these boys and girls and their parents went through and are still going through. But they're familiar names for reason: these utterly unthinkable cases are extremely rare.

You have probably read that 800,000 children go missing every year. Almost all of them are runaways rather than abductions. The minority that are classified as abductions are bad situations, but they are not cases of strangers snatching an unattended kid walking home. These are almost all family abductions—an ex-husband not returning the kids on time, or a young mom skipping town with the kids while her boyfriend is at work.

The "stereotypical" abduction, in which a stranger grabs a kid or lures them and takes him away, happens about 100 times a year in America, according to Justice Department numbers.[34] About 10 kids per year were murdered as part of a stereotypical abduction, and about 50 were targeted for sexual abuse or rape. This is out of 75 million children in the U.S.

We would all do anything to prevent these things from happening. But when something is a one-in-a-million risk, that means it is much harder to prevent.

"The statistics show that this is an incredibly rare event, and you can't protect people from very rare events," explains noted statistician Trevor Butterworth. "It would be like trying to create a shield against being struck by lightning."

"Statistically speaking," Brooks writes, "it would likely take 750,000 years for a child left alone in a public space to be snatched by a stranger."

And those horrifying hot-car deaths? Fewer than forty occur per year, according to Brooks. It's not a made-up risk, but it's less of a risk than the drive to the store. Somehow, though, our culture has decided that the risk of leaving your child in a car is never acceptable under any circumstance.

But leaving a kid in a car isn't the only risk a parking lot poses—just ask my wife. One summer day, in broad daylight, while walking in the marked crosswalk of a parking lot, a car ran her down, putting her in the emergency room. Thankfully, our kids were not with her. But bringing your kids from the car to the store and back—when your hands may be on a grocery cart—presents its own danger. If it's cold and rainy and you'll spend more time crossing the parking lot than grabbing your takeout, you might be safer leaving your ten-year-old and eight-year-old in the car. At the very least, that judgment should be up to you. But CPS and the people who will call them don't engage in such risk assessment.

If you could easily reduce the odds of an abduction from one in a million to one in two million you would. But if doing so required you never letting your child outside the home, you wouldn't. Every time you buckle your kids into a car seat or bring them to a pool, you are accepting a very small risk in exchange for some other good. As a society, we accept that risk-reward calculation—as long as we don't say it out loud.

A Culture of Fear

Parents don't have a duty to fear. Of course, fear will always be part of parenting. Love makes us vulnerable and brings with it fear of loss or failure. But our culture has given us a distorted picture of the size and the nature of threats. Even worse, our media and authorities have given us something new to fear: being blamed unjustly for something happening to our kids.

Because the Meitivs lived in our part of Maryland, I ended up in a lot of discussions about their free-range parenting at the time. Most friends agreed that the police should not have detained the kids, but they also said they would never let their kids walk to the park alone. The most common phrase I heard from mothers was "I would never forgive myself if something happened." Lenore Skenazy has had moms tell her, "I do not want to be the one on TV explaining my daughter's disappearance."

Deep down, this fear is about *failing as a parent*. It's not so much that something will happen to our kids, but that something *preventable* will happen to them. This is sensible, because although we don't admit it out loud, we simply cannot keep our children completely safe. Yet our media and our culture have convinced us that we are morally obligated to pretend that we can.

This is the challenge for Skenazy. It's behind my wife's repeated comment when I've left the kids alone at the playground: "I'm not afraid of kidnappers; I'm afraid of CPS." We're afraid of judgment. We're afraid of being caught being insufficiently afraid. And so fear has become central to parenting.

Parents naturally have an instinct to protect their children from harm. Chris, a twenty-eight-year-old man, explained during a focus group that he was nowhere near ready to have children. "I'm not grown-up enough," he said. He offered many indirect reasons for not committing to marriage and family, including problems with the world ("climate change" and "pop culture" were huge negatives), but eventually he got personal: "I'd also be terrified that I'm like doing a bad job and messing up the kid."

When COVID hit in March 2020, the first thing America did was shield the children. Closing schools in the second week of March was the first serious response by most families, localities, and states. This was natural, and at the time it seemed reasonable. COVID seemed like a really bad flu, and we knew that flu was particularly dangerous for children. We knew that anywhere you put together dozens of kids, germs will thrive.

By the summer, we had discovered how miraculously safe young children were from coronavirus. Yet most big-city schools didn't open in fall 2020. The data was undeniable by spring 2021, yet for another year, lockdowns, restrictions, and mandates were justified on the basis that children, and later babies, could not yet be vaccinated. A year, and then eighteen months, and then two years—the same behavior and attitudes continued in some circles, especially among the ruling class and media class in large cities.

"Parents of children under five stuck in grueling COVID limbo," ran the *New York Times* headline in January 2022. "With Omicron, parents of kids under 5 are even more stressed," was CNN's banner. ABC News ran with "Parents with children under 5 feel like it's still 2020."

In most kids, COVID, including the Omicron variant, was equivalent to a minor cold. An unvaccinated four-year-old was far, far safer than his vaccinated parents, yet parents felt they had to mask their tiny ones, or even keep them hidden away. Fear became the default setting among millions of parents.

"Being constantly wired like this," wrote pediatrician Lucy Mc-Bride in the *Atlantic*, "carries a cost: Rational thought is hijacked. Our risk tolerance goes down. Our instinct to protect shifts into overdrive. We default to primitive thought patterns including black-and-white thinking (*School isn't safe until all kids are vaccinated*)."[35]

Constant fear is bad for us. "Marinating in a toxic brine of fear and uncertainty can make us sick—whether from fatigue and insomnia or irritability and burnout," McBride wrote. "And when our children hear us processing endless loops of *what if* thinking, they can become worried and depressed too."[36]

Sure enough, when the masks came off and cities, states, and even the Centers for Disease Control and Prevention (CDC) began to make it clear that we were going to live with the virus, fear in some quarters actually went up as fast as case rates went down. Schools found they had to deal with a whole new wave of anxiety.

My five-year-old didn't wear a mask anywhere but school: county rules declared that it was unsafe to be at school—even outdoors—unmasked. One morning, realizing she was unmasked at the school parking lot, Eve covered her mouth in a panic. I couldn't tell whether she thought school air was poison, her own breath was poison, or showing her face was somehow profane.

Little Eve couldn't explain. Her fear was inchoate, as is the fear of so many parents. Fear can become such a part of parenting that we don't know exactly what we're afraid of. The mantle of fear is now part of the mandatory dress code of parenting, our religious garb, from the first positive pregnancy test until at least the eighteenth birthday.

Like the Travel Team Trap, this is a cultural problem. In fact, most of the problems that make parenting harder—and that make young adults decide they aren't up to the task—are cultural problems, which require cultural solutions. But there are policy problems, which can be solved by governments and employers. Let's begin the tour of policy problems by taking a quick stroll—or rather, drive—through Car Hell.

CHAPTER 3

Want Fecundity in the Sheets? Give Us Walkability in the Streets

Kate and Will were a young couple in Chicago living the life they thought they wanted.

An educated stay-at-home mom and a high-achiever dad, they had the means and the desire to keep their four kids busy with tons of enriching activities. Pat, a middle schooler, played baseball and had tae kwon do five days a week. Mary, also in middle school, had softball practice or games three times a week, plus games on the weekend. She was also doing dance. During theater season, Mary rehearsed two nights a week.

"The kids would come home from school, have a snack, and jump in the car," Will explained. "Drop Kid One off at Activity A. Drop Kid Two off at Activity B. By the time you do that, it's time to pick up Kid One."

This meant lots of fast-food meals on the go. "Potbelly's in the car was the usual dinner," Will recalled. "You'd get home at eight or eight thirty. That was every night, and that was not unusual among our friends." Pat and Mary's younger siblings "kind of lived in the car with Kate. . . . It was miserable for our toddlers and newborn to get shuttled around all day."

They had fallen into the Travel Team Trap, which meant that their real home was not their split-level ranch in Oak Lawn, but their Chrysler Pacifica. It's a particular torment of twenty-first-century parents: Car Hell.

Car Hell deserves its own discussion not just because of how it makes parenting harder, but because it is a part of our culture that flows directly from policy choices. Our cities, counties, and suburbs were built in a certain way due to the decisions of planners, politicians, and bureaucrats. If you're currently living in Car Hell, you have to wonder whether any of the planners had ever heard of children—or had ever been children themselves.

This discussion that starts in the third row of a Pacifica will not only cover the shape of our streets and sidewalks but also the other deliberate choices by people in power that make parenting harder. Our streets are less kid friendly because of policy choices. Family homes are more expensive because of policy choices. And many jobs are less accommodating of parents because of policy choices.

This is a discussion about policy—government policy and corporate policy—but it's also a discussion of philosophy and anthropology. Do we shape our world around commerce and technology or for people and families?

The Lower Circles of Car Hell

Some of us grown-ups look back on our own childhoods and remember riding our bikes to a friend's house, or walking a mile to baseball practice. But as twenty-first-century parents, many of us have never known anything other than Car Hell. Thanks to the shape of modern suburbs and the demands of helicopter parenting and travel teams, we seem to spend every waking hour that is not at work in a car with our children, or in a car getting our children.

When the kids are little, you have to buckle them into the car seat. And because you absolutely, positively cannot leave kids in the car for half a second unaccompanied, you're buckling and unbuckling and re-buckling and re-unbuckling if you are going more than one place. Maybe they're potty trained, but that doesn't help much in the car. And (I would like a major medical school to study this) the instant you strap your kids into the car, at least one child will be overcome by an overwhelming, life-threatening thirst. It could be a kid who has never once asked for water and who never drank the water you gave him at home or used the water fountain at the park you were just at. But when you are driving the twenty minutes home from that park, he will die unless you get him water *now*.

When the kids are older, Car Hell takes on a different nature—maybe the kids aren't as miserable every minute they are in the car, but now they have so many more places to go. If your teenager's school, sports, activities, parties, and even hangouts with their buddies are a car ride away, the chances are you're driving them to all of the above. You have suddenly taken on a second job as an unpaid cabbie, and because you sometimes have to say no, your kids don't see their friends or play pickup basketball as much as they'd like. Into that void rushes social media.

Most suburban parents know Car Hell, and any suburban parent who doesn't live in Car Hell thanks God for this. In Falls Church, a suburb of D.C., there is one end of a block occupied by four large Catholic families, most of whom have been friends for two decades and who maneuvered to live almost right next to each other. A local sportswriter once visited this end of Pearl Place and learned of the pickup games that are regular fare. He wrote, "this little slice of baseball heaven has enough kids to field two complete baseball teams if everyone decides to play on any given day."[1]

Now, if you drove through Pearl Place, you might not call it a slice of any sort of heaven. The homes are small, the road is narrow, and one of the houses is often overgrown with vines. But the weekends or summer afternoons I've spent on Pearl Place reminded me of a summer camp—but a camp where the counselors mostly spent their time gardening, driving to Home Depot, or just chatting with one another. The kids are free and make up their own fun with each other—and the kids from surrounding blocks ride their bikes or run on foot to Pearl Place. Yes, the parents here need cars to get to the supermarket or church or high school. But for simply keeping the kids happy and occupied—and sometimes this is our highest need—nobody has to climb behind the wheel or buckle a buckle.

If you ask my kids their favorite summer vacation ever, they'll tell you about the week we spent on Monhegan Island in Maine. Some people go to Monhegan for the sea air. More go for the thriving art scene. We went because there are basically no cars, and we could just let our children run around without our ever having to take them anywhere. *That's* a vacation.

Walkability might sound at first like a niche concern, but every parent knows exactly how oppressive Car Hell can be and how liberating walkability or bikeability is for kids—and in turn for parents. It's a good place to begin a discussion of pro-family public policy because walkability is inherently a governmental matter. After all, it's the government paving the roads and building the sidewalks—or not building them.

And as a small but revealing example, the very way we fit our children into our cars (or don't fit them) is shaped by public policy.

Car Seats as Contraception

The buckling, unbuckling, and re-buckling are the part of Car Hell the Baby Boomers didn't go through. When I was a kid, on our annual long drive from Manhattan to the coast of Maine, I would lie in the back of the station wagon, between my brothers' duffel bags and my dad's golf bag, for the whole five-hour drive.

In the twenty-first century, obviously, that wouldn't fly. We now have car seat mandates. At first their infant carriers get buckled in. Then there is the second set of rear-facing car seats. Then forward-facing, five-point harnesses. Then the booster seat. The age and weight at which we are required to buckle our children in slowly creeps upward over the years. There are some safety benefits to these mandates, but there are plenty of headaches.

One is the physical act of buckling. You need to dig your hands under your kids' butts into some sort of slurry of goldfish, toddler saliva, and butt sweat, yank out the buckle, and then get the two other straps. If you own a minivan, you might be doing this while standing in the middle row. If you drive a Toyota Camry, though, you're contorting your back to reach into the back seat to pull off this feat of dexterity.

And if that Camry is your largest car, the regulations requiring car seats have settled any family-planning questions you might still have: you will have no more than two children, because you couldn't possibly fit three car seats, or even two car seats and a booster, into that back row.

"Car Seats as Contraception" was the title of the social science paper that proved this.[2] The researchers took advantage of the fact that car seat mandates rolled out at different times in different states. They found that married parents of two kids were much more likely to stop at two kids when car seat mandates went into effect. Corroborating the hypothesis that the car seats had this impact, the anti-natal effect was limited to married mothers of two, and didn't really apply to unmarried parents or moms going from one child to two, or three kids to four.

It's a small example, but it shows an important message: government policy and Car Hell can make parenting so much harder that it actually prevents huge numbers of kids from ever being born.

We shouldn't see Car Hell as an inevitable part of modern parenting. A different world existed not long ago—and in fact, exists still in some places. In many others, however, government planning has eliminated the possibility of walking.

My brother John lives less than half a mile from the park where his daughters play softball. His girls are confident, competent, and grew up walking to school in New York City until they moved to the outer suburbs during the pandemic. Yet either my brother or his wife has to drive the girls to softball games and practice. Why? The two roads that go from their street to the fields have no sidewalks, have narrow shoulders (often with cars parked on them), and because it's often a few miles between stop signs or traffic lights, drivers are typically hitting 50 miles an hour on the straightaways. A kid on foot or riding her bike would not be safe.

When they start high school, walking or biking the 1.4 miles won't be an option for the same reason, so instead they'll spend thirty minutes on the bus—longer than it would take them to ride a bike.

When we lived in Montgomery County, there was a great creek at the end of our road. It was perfect for fishing or catching rat snakes or walking dogs. But for most of the walk to the creek, there was no sidewalk along the road. To get to friends' houses or the 7-Eleven, my kids would have to cross Randolph Road and Georgia Avenue, massive roads with at least three lanes in each direction, and crosswalks spaced far apart. The built environment of these suburban or exurban places was antihuman, and thus condemned us to Car Hell.

Having a park, library, or Main Street you can walk to isn't simply "nice." It has serious positive effects on families, according to research by my colleagues Dan Cox and Ryan Streeter at the American Enterprise Institute.[3] "[P]eople who live in proximity to neighborhood amenities are happier, more socially connected, and more inclined to help others compared with people who live in low-amenity areas," Streeter concluded. "They're also more civically engaged and enjoy higher levels of trust at work and in their community."[4]

More concretely, kids need to walk. When I was thirteen, my friend Mike Boyle and I would spend entire summer days simply wandering. We would take walks of maybe eight hours, venturing beyond the boundaries of our very nice little town of Pelham, crossing into the Bronx, where there was—a bit surprisingly—a network of horse trails. The simple decisions of which fork to follow, when to turn back, or which route to take were real decisions with real (though not actually grave) consequences. It was a thrill.

Not only do fewer kids get lost on long walks these days, but fewer even walk to the corner store, the ballfields, or school. In 1969, more than 40 percent of American school kids walked or biked to school.[5] By 2016, that number was about 10 percent.[6] American teenagers in particular walk less and less every year. Researchers led by Boise State University kinesiologist Scott Conger compiled studies of every wearable distance-traveled measuring device, from pedometers to Fit-Bits. Since 1995, every device saw a downward trend in all sorts of physically activity, most notably walking.[7] Adolescents' daily steps fell by 1,500 each decade—and the researchers specifically cited a reduction in walking to school. Over three decades, that's a reduction of five miles every week. That's well over a thousand miles, just in high school.

Fairland is a neighborhood in Montgomery County where county government deliberately prevented walkability, density, and the placement of commerce too close to homes. They wanted to create a rural feel. The result was wide roads, few crosswalks, few sidewalks, and a handful of strip malls. Dan Reed, a writer, grew up in Fairland and wrote about it. "What this looked like for me, a teenager: one of my closest friends riding his Razor scooter down a literal highway to hang out with me; biking around a golf course because I couldn't get anywhere else safely; my dad driving across the street to a job interview; begging for rides to Olney or the Mall in Columbia."[8]

Reliance on cars makes life more of a hassle for parents and less enriching for kids.

My brother-in-law Pat moved closer to his boys' school for the sake of "family culture," as he puts it—the boys are free to run down to the field for pickup soccer, or hang around school without it involving the labor of Mom or Dad. What's more, Pat tells his kids, "You deserve fifteen minutes on your own, walking between places, to think." If you are shuttled everywhere by a live-in cabbie, you don't get that.

Unwalkable neighborhoods aren't just bad for kids, they're also bad for adults. While the need for an adult chauffeur increases parents' time with their kids in a way that robs the kids of independence, conversely they also make adults more isolated from other adults. The unwalkability of modern suburban life is one reason American adults, including parents, have fewer friends. "Why should it require explicit scheduling to see a friend who lives 'within striking distance'?" asked Dave Roberts in a Vox essay on land use and friendship. "Why shouldn't proximity do some of the work? The answer, for many Americans, is that anything beyond a few blocks away might as well be miles; it all requires a car. We do not encounter one another in cars. We grind along together anonymously, often in misery."[9]

Modern America has been built in an overly car-centric way, and we've mostly come to accept it because we don't know anything else. But wherever we grew up many of us remember a time when our friends really were all within walking or even shouting distance. It was called "college." If you think of college as the best years of your life, it's largely because your friends were just *there*. Outside of college, there are still a few places, like Pearl Place, where cars aren't a necessity.

StuyTown—formally "Stuyvesant Town–Peter Cooper Village"—is an intriguing and complicated example of such a pocket of walkability. It's about twenty-five city blocks of Manhattan turned into two "SuperBlocks." Those blocks are, in essence, parks ringed with tall apartment buildings. This is immensely liberating for parents and their kids. "It was kid heaven even in the middle of the mean New York of the 1970s," David Brooks, the columnist and author, told me.

As a boy, young David thought there were way too many rules in StuyTown's public square, but ultimately "it provided me with a great childhood," because the safety and walkability were liberating. "Starting at [age] six or seven, my parents would just let me run out the door. My friends and I would wander from playground to playground."

StuyTown had its issues and still has them. Like a commune, there was central planning and plenty of strict rules—strict enough that Brooks called it "Singapore on the East River." Also, the development's history is rooted in segregation. "Tight-knit community" and "inclusive," sadly, do not often mix in American history.

But in one setting, racial and class integration go hand in hand with community cohesion. The most integrated neighborhoods in the U.S. are military bases[10]—and they're among the best places to raise kids.

Tim, a middle-class African American grandfather in the D.C. area, lived on Army bases in his twenties. His son is now raising kids on a Navy base. "There's no better place," Tim tells me. "Like-minded people. You're all engaged in a common purpose." The "common purpose" includes serving your country in the military, but it also includes raising kids. Sure enough, many of the counties in the U.S. with the most babies per capita are counties with military bases. Geary County, Kansas, and Liberty County, Georgia, are two of the most fecund in America. Liberty County houses much of Fort Stewart, and Geary County includes much of Fort Riley—both large Army bases.

Housing at a military base is centrally and intentionally planned, but it's pro-family in a way that's reminiscent of unplanned, old-fashioned village life. The military explicitly accommodates families with children—particularly by giving them a safe, *walkable* place to entertain themselves and explore the world on their own and with friends.

"My father's childhood spent on military bases truly resembled that of a wayward Tom Sawyer," wrote planner George Foster. "Wandering around with friends finding the next fun spot to play until he made his way home for dinner. On any given day, he might pedal off to a ballfield on his banana seat bicycle, or perhaps mosey over to the Exchange to buy a pocketknife with money he'd made selling lemonade."[11] Foster was lamenting that walkability on military bases was in decline because bases were expanded without walkability in mind. This loss of walkability is far truer of our cities and suburbs.

Central planners in the mid-twentieth century believed that the old, hodgepodge neighborhood was outdated and that modern man's life should be built around cars. So instead of mixing houses and shops on any given street, they built "rational," efficient central strip malls, to which people from many different neighborhoods could drive, park, and do their shopping. Then they could return home. It was downright *scientific*!

The inherently isolating architecture of the suburb—where each home is a castle—is a force of alienation. Just consider the term for many suburbs: "bedroom community." It's like a Holiday Inn Express, where you merely rest your head before heading out—but for thirty years.

You may live in a suburb where kids can ride their bikes safely, shout over the fence to the neighbor kids, and gather in self-organized pickup games. Those are rarer and rarer today, and they tend to come at a price. Increasingly, a kid is either being driven somewhere to some planned event by Mom or Dad, or he is sitting at home playing *Roblox* on the iMac. A more kid-friendly community is a walkable community. More kid-friendly communities would make parenting easier—and would probably result in more children.

If you want fecundity in the sheets, you need walkability in the streets. Few neighborhoods in America demonstrate that better that Kemp Mill.

Holy Days in Kemp Mill

"On Shabbos in Kemp Mill," longtime resident Seth Kaplan tells me, "you have no idea where your kids are."

The Kemp Mill neighborhood in Silver Spring is the most Jewish neighborhood in the D.C. area. The two major synagogues—Kemp Mill Synagogue and the Young Israel Shomrai Emunah (or YISE) around the corner—are modern Orthodox, which means Kemp Mill is chock-full of Orthodox families. It is, as a result, so densely packed with kids that you might lose yours in the crowd.

"I just had my sixth yesterday," Moshe Litwack reports with a distant, sleepless gaze from underneath a goofy Sherlock Holmes hat. His wife and new baby are still in the hospital, but Moshe and the other five kids are celebrating Purim at YISE. Purim is possibly the rowdiest celebration in Judaism, and Young Israel's community room is swarming with kids dressed as Spider-Man, Waldo, Cinderella, Kobe Bryant, and a hundred other characters. It's the same loud, kid-filled, costumed scene over at KMS.

Bouncy castles, dance floors, pizza, carnival games, some hard liquor at YISE, plus, of course, *hamantaschen*—the official pastry of this celebration prescribed by the book of Esther—define this Purim

Night. On Purim Day, the alcohol will be more ubiquitous, and the kids—lots of them—will range freely through the neighborhood.

It's on these holidays, as on all Saturdays, that Kemp Mill is visibly different from the other suburban neighborhoods in Montgomery County. On Shabbos, at certain times of day, you'll see families—not infrequently families of six, seven, or eight—all walking to one of the Orthodox synagogues in Kemp Mill. At other times, you'll see kids of all ages, wandering free, often in small posses.

"Since this is an Orthodox synagogue," explains Joe, a father of three at KMS, "most of the people who belong to the synagogue don't drive on the Sabbath. Therefore, they have to live within walking distance of the synagogue. Therefore, there's this geographical community. That does make it easier" for parents. This constraint—the prohibition on operating machinery during the Sabbath—makes Kemp Mill the extraordinary neighborhood it is. G-d has issued a walkability mandate here, and thus created a parent-friendly community.

Think of where you might walk—to your bus stop, your kids' elementary school, your neighborhood playground. Now imagine that these places are also where you see old friends, make new ones, receive spiritual guidance, celebrate holidays, educate your children, and even dress up and get a bit drunk once a year while your kids bounce around you.

Consider the ripple effects. Your children will have dozens of friends in walking distance, and those friends will have parents with very similar values and worldview to you. Your life is easier, because, as Seth said, you don't need to know where your kids are.

"When people move in here," says Jeff Lawrence, who came to Kemp Mill with his wife, Donna, in 1978, "they never leave."

The tight-knit community all in walking distance means you don't need to keep track of your own children. You can outsource that to the broader community. "Everybody knows everybody's kids," Jeff says, "which gives a sense of freedom and security. . . . If your kid falls, not only will someone help them, that person will probably *know* them."

Joe's wife, Ava, says that living in Kemp Mill makes raising kids easier, as she doesn't have to entertain them constantly or drive them to activities "because they have lots of friends in walking distance." Ava and Joe moved to Kemp Mill from Olney, a town a bit up north. "We moved here because this was where our kids' friends lived."

Crucially, the kids all get together without needing Mom and Dad to plan it. "I'll never forget, when we moved in," says Ava, "there were so many kids that were just popping in on a Saturday afternoon."

Banning cars one day a week may not pass in any town council, but some planners are seeking other ways to help more families live in places built for actual humans rather than for these wheeled machines we own.

Governments Need to Build for Kids

The "fifteen-minute city" is one idea that urbanists tout. Elementary schools, playgrounds, and corner stores should be at most a fifteen-minute walk from one's house. I would add churches, synagogues, and mosques, too. High schools, big parks, coffee shops, and the workplace should be a fifteen-minute bike ride. Anywhere else you want to go, including downtown or intercity trains, should be a fifteen-minute trip by public transit.

You don't have to share the car-phobia of most urbanists to sign up for some variation of this idea. For many parents, the ideal "fifteen-minute town" would include all that important stuff in walking and biking distance, plus a fifteen-minute drive to work.

Competing concepts of walkability float around the urbanist debate. One distinction I like is "kid walkability" versus "hipster walkability." I picked up this distinction from a friend of mine named Mike, a dad of five, introverted, not typically found in coffee shops or neighborhood bars. Mike lives in the suburbs. He cannot bike downtown or walk to the Metro. And he takes his coffee in his own kitchen, thank you very much.

But Mike wants his kids to be able to walk up and down the block, or ride their bikes to friends' houses, ballfields, and the burger joint. He's happy to live in a bedroom community from which working parents have to drive. It's ideal as long as Mom and Dad don't have to constantly drive the kids everywhere. This sort of "kid walkability" is more attainable today for families than is total walkability, and it does most of the work. Especially if you have avoided the Travel Team Trap, most of what you need for your children is friends with whom they can play without needing a driver or having to run across six lanes of traffic.

Daybreak, a community in South Jordan, Utah, aims for something like "kid walkability." You could also call it family-focused urbanism. It's not *urban*, but it relies on density to make sure everyone is within a quarter mile of a park or a trail.[12] Parents there mostly drive to work, but on evenings and weekends—and for the kids, throughout summer vacation—the community tries to make life more car-free.

Debates over parenting and how to make America more family friendly often rest on disagreements over the proper role of government. *Is it government's job to support families, or is it the job of business and voluntary institutions?* These are good debates, but we don't need to have that debate here, because we have generally agreed that streets and sidewalks are the purview of local governments. The city of South Jordan voted to allow the Daybreak community to build more densely than was otherwise allowed. That's great. It's a crime against families that so many local governments deliberately make walkability impossible.

The unwalkability of my former neighborhood was the fault of the Montgomery County government. It was the politicians and government planners who decided that Randolph Road should be three to five lanes in each direction. It was the county government that decided it didn't need to build sidewalks the length of my street. It was the county government that zoned the neighborhood around our first Maryland home so as to outlaw all commerce, thus making it illegal to open a barbershop, coffee shop, or corner store within walking distance of my house. (The only retail available on my 1.25-mile walk to the Metro was the vending machine at my physical therapist's office.)

Keep in mind, Montgomery County's governing class prides itself on being progressive. "Climate Action" was a centerpiece of the county executive's reelection campaign in 2022. Yet the county continues to build in a way that forces residents into cars. When your bike trails have parking lots every few miles, it tells you that walking and biking are for exercise, and actual *living* requires four wheels.

Making a place kid-walkable and kid-bikeable isn't that complicated, but it requires overcoming certain modern biases in favor of efficiency. *Efficiency* has become a religion among the governing class, which has led to massive consolidation of everything from retail to high schools. Smaller, more local schools might not perfectly reap economies of scale, but they would allow kids to walk to school and, when school's out, run to the ballfields and playgrounds.

Sidewalks should be wide. Roads should be narrow. Speed limits should be low. Long blocks should be interrupted by cut-throughs that work for strollers and tricycles. That is, we should build places for people. As of now, much of America is built for cars rather than for people, and so we're getting more cars and fewer people.

Some parents really do value the walk to the coffee shops. For others it's the basketball courts that should be steps away. For many, though, the most valuable thing to have within walking distance might be Grandma. And to help parents make this happen, the problem isn't a lack of sidewalks—it's a lack of affordable homes, which is yet another fruit of government failure.

House-Poor

Housing and childcare are the costs that loom largest in the discourse over parenting and over family policy. It turns out both could be addressed in one fell swoop if local and state policymakers wanted to become aggressively pro-family.

The best way to make childcare more affordable is to make it easier for new parents to live next door to Grandma and Grandpa. Although the media sometimes make Grandma out to be a desperate last option in childcare—where Mom turns only if there's no professional day-care available—the data tells a different story.[13] In general, parents love it when their own parents look after the babies.

Informal childcare by family and close friends who live next door and can watch the baby on a moment's notice is one of the most valu-able things a parent can have. Many, like the Amish or the families of Kemp Mill, build their lives around this. Others stumble into it and find it of immeasurable value. But millions of parents find such ar-rangements impossible because of high home prices and scarce housing options. If a government wants to make childcare more affordable, that government should make sure a lot more housing is built.

High home prices and rents are the single biggest cost obstacle to family formation. They make would-be parents feel locked out of start-ing a family because they are locked out of owning or even renting a decent home. Those who do buy a home end up house-poor, with monthly payments that take up too much of their income.

Some social science draws a link between high housing costs and family formation. A creative study in England showed that when fam-ilies' mortgage payments dropped due to falling interest rates, those families had more babies. The authors, Fergus Cumming and Lisa Dettling, found that "a 1 percentage point reduction in the monetary policy rate . . . leads to a 5 percent increase in the birth rate among families on an adjustable rate."[14] Likewise, economists found in 2014 that when rents go up, renters have fewer kids.[15]

The U.S. government could make a limited but real difference by selling off a small portion of its landholdings to allow developers to build homes. One bill, the HOUSES Act, would result in an estimated 3 million new homes by selling off about 0.1 percent of federal land-holdings located in or near population centers.[16]

Most of the action would have to be on the local level, though.

"Starter homes" used to exist. Like the 990-square-foot brick co-lonial where my wife and I welcomed our first five children, modest and affordable no-frills homes—duplexes, or bungalows, with a small yard or at least a patio—are exactly what a couple needs for starting a family. But they are vanishingly rare. Some of the problem is market dynamics. Much of the problem is regulation.

A *New York Times* piece on the disappearing starter home explained that "communities nationwide are far more prescriptive today than decades ago about what housing should look like and how big it must be. Some ban vinyl siding as too cheap-looking. Others require two-car garages. Nearly all make it difficult to build the kind of home that could sell for $200,000 today."[17] Sure, vinyl siding isn't great, but far worse is the impossibility of finding a reasonable two-bedroom within ten miles of your family.

"In Portland, Ore.," Emily Badger of the *Times* explained, "a lot may cost $100,000. Permits add $40,000–$50,000. Removing a fir tree 36 inches in diameter costs another $16,000 in fees." Developers say they want to build smaller, more affordable homes, because the demand for them is steadier. Government rules—environmental rules, safety mandates, aesthetic regulations, or simply antidevelopment rules—get in the way.

"You've basically regulated me out of anything remotely on the affordable side," one home builder said. The result is a much higher ante, to use a poker term—a barrier to entering the family-rearing stage of life.

A big problem is that a lot of local political leaders don't really want families moving in. "Businesses mean revenue. Families mean costs," Tom Weisner, the late mayor of Aurora, Illinois, once told me. Families mean schools, playgrounds, sidewalks, and social services, all of which cost money, and none of which bring in revenue. Businesses mean sales taxes and greater property taxes. Childless young professionals have the most disposable income to spend downtown. If you see the world as a revenue officer sees it, you have no incentive to make a community more family friendly.

Local governments should do everything they can to encourage more homes, including homes for young families. Zoning laws and building regulations get in the way of more housing, meaning they make it more expensive to start a family or grow one.

One common regulation in the U.S. is to require big front yards.

"Minimum setback" rules combined with minimum lot sizes make it illegal to build a dense cluster of modest family homes, but that's exactly the sort of development pattern that could make kid-walkability or family-focused urbanism affordable.[18]

Many cities and counties outlaw the granny flat: a second small unit on a single-family lot. These small units sometimes mean rental revenue for a homeowner, and sometimes—as the name indicates—they mean a place where grandma can live, which is good for Grandma, Ma, Pa, and Baby.

A passionate group of urbanist architects are obsessed with another U.S. regulation: the two-staircase requirement. Any apartment building over three stories is required in many states to have at least two staircases. The justification is fire safety: if fire blocks one stairway or the path to that staircase, then the residents are trapped in a towering inferno. As with many regulations, the two-staircase rule has survived without any proof that it makes apartment dwellers safer. And as with many regulations, this rule has negative and somewhat surprising consequences.

The result is a "case study in anti-human engineering," declares architect and single-staircase advocate Frank Zimmerman.[19] Requiring two staircases accessible from every apartment all but requires a long central corridor through the middle of the building with stairwells at either end. Because the corridors are wasted space, developers make them as narrow as allowable. They end up airless, lifeless, and very unlikely places for anything resembling neighborly socializing. Also, a central corridor with apartments on each side makes family-sized apartments unfeasible. Every bedroom needs a window, but each apartment (except for maybe corner units) has only one exterior wall—apartments must be lined up long and narrow, each unit like a book on a bookshelf.

A "point-access" building with a single core of stairs or an elevator allows for more attractive common areas (imagine a central lobby on each floor or a large, open central stairwell with a skylight, as opposed to a long, dreary corridor). Most important, such deregulated building allows for more variety of apartments—and this is what allows families to grow and connect. One-bedroom, two-bedroom, three-bedroom, and studio apartments all on the same floor means more of every type of housing in a city, and it means more intergenerational mixing. It means more opportunity for an apartment building to be communal, and nothing feeds family formation like community.

To be sure, single-staircase point-access buildings will not suddenly make America family friendly. But this is just one example of measures that would, if implemented, make family formation a bit more feasible. Government is in the business of regulating, mandating, and zoning neighborhoods and homes. Given that, all existing and new regulations ought to be reviewed in light of this question: Does this make home-ownership and family formation unduly hard?

It's not merely lawmakers and regulators who should be asking how they can make family formation easier, though. That question should be at the front of mind for every employer.

What Employers Can Do

Right after 9/11, corporate America got all patriotic. After George Floyd was killed, corporate America went woke. As Millennials and Gen Z are finding parenthood unattainable, there's an obvious opening for Big Business to weigh in to the culture wars today: corporate America needs to go *pro-family* now.

Companies need to adopt policies and instill a culture that make it clear to employees, and even customers, that they are on the side of helping people have kids.

Why would they do this? For starters, millions of Americans want children but don't feel they can afford them, or want more children than they have. (The average American woman wants more than 2 children and has 1.7 children.[20]) If employers want the best talent, they will try to give women (and men) what they want. The most profound thing they can do is make it easier for twenty- and thirty-somethings to have more children. Employers are in the best position to help parents and would-be parents because what all parents need is money and time, and your job is both the principal source of your money and the primary devourer of your time. Helping parents spend time with their children helps make them happier workers, which makes them better workers. Studies reflect this intuition.[21]

Many big employers have made progress in this area. Lactation rooms, where nursing mothers can pump their breast milk in privacy, are standard in many workplaces (though they are often windowless, unventilated storage rooms). Large companies concerned about recruiting and reputation grant generous paid maternity and paternity leave. Still, employers could do a lot more to make America more family friendly.

Health insurance premiums are a good place to start. Employers who provide health insurance often cover part of the monthly premium and leave the rest to the employee. The cost of insurance coverage—and therefore the premium—rises as a family gets bigger. A pro-family company should take this into account and try to cushion the increase in premiums when a child or three are added to a policy. Ideally, the family plan would resemble the cost of covering a childless couple, and each family member after three would add nothing to the employee's premium. Many employers do exactly this, but it should be standard, so that no parent needs to ask if a second or third child will increase her premiums, and thus reduce her paycheck. The result would be, in effect, childless or empty-nest workers subsidizing their colleagues with kids at home, and the biggest families would be the most subsidized—which is exactly the point.

Creative employers could come up with a hundred small ways to communicate the pro-family, pro-natal message to employees. Here's one: own a couple of Snoos. The Snoo is a magical "smart" bassinet that, according to every parent I know, is extremely effective at getting babies to sleep and keeping them that way. As such, it is the most effective tool for helping new parents sleep, and thus keeping them nearly sane. The Snoo also costs more than $1,500. Some parents buy a used Snoo. Others rent one, which is sensible, because you only use it for a few months per kid. An expensive item that is incredibly valuable for a short time (and a bit burdensome to store) is a perfect item for a "sharing economy." Employers should own a Snoo or two (or a lot more for bigger employers) and loan them out to their employees for a baby's first months.

Also host a springtime company picnic or Christmas party that is legitimately family friendly. Part of the point of the company picnic should be to give parents an opportunity to unwind while their kids have fun. That might mean hiring entertainment or babysitters to keep an eye on the playground and the bounce house.

Every little policy that says "family comes first" helps shift the culture. Many employers, for example, give workers a day off to volunteer for a charity or nonprofit. Likewise, it should be clear company policy—written clearly in employee manuals and repeated in HR memos—that flexibility is built in for family obligations, or for coaching little Jackson's soccer game. No parent should feel it's extravagant to ask to get off early in order to catch Sophie's ballet recital or Madeline's pre-K graduation. Even more, each kid's birthday should be a free "personal day." No, an extra day off isn't going to convince anyone to have an extra kid, but it can help signal that you are an employer who wants to employ happy parents.

Beyond Maternity Leave

So much of the debate over work-life balance begins and ends with paid maternity leave, which is a shame. That is way too small a discussion. Helping working parents actually requires thinking bigger.

Paid parental leave is good because in its absence, moms often leave their babies and go back to work far too early for both mom and baby. But government-funded or government-required paid leave for new parents has not delivered either the career or family benefits supporters have hoped for. Pro-family employers and policymakers will have to get more creative than simply paying moms and dads to take a few months off after birth.

For starters, the benefits of government paid leave are unproven. In 2004, California began paying new moms 60 percent to 70 percent of their salary for the first six weeks after birth. As a result, more California mothers took leave, which counts as a success in itself—mommy-baby time is objectively good for both. But the second-order effects didn't materialize. Economists in 2019 used tax data to check in on the women who took advantage of this program when it launched, and compare them to similar women who had babies just *before* California launched this benefit. They found no evidence that this paid leave helped women's careers. In fact, six and ten years after giving birth, the women who took the state paid leave were earning less than their counterparts who didn't have that option.[22] This paid leave program also didn't seem to help women achieve the family size they wanted, as the economists found no evidence of higher birthrates.

What they found was that two classes of women were more likely to take paid leave: wealthier women and married women. These women used that leave to spend more time with each child—which is good—but it all turned out to be neither pro-natal nor pro-career. Pro-natal, pro-family reformers need to think bigger. What parents need is not merely a few weeks or months before returning to work. What we need is job flexibility that allows moms and dads to spend time with their kids rather than at the office—we can imagine other company policies that could support parents.

Consider why *paternity* leave is generally not used as fully as *maternity* leave. For starters, the way adults and babies are wired, physiologically and psychologically, means that Mom is the primary parent for a newborn in most cases. This is about nursing, postpartum hormones, and a million other things. Dad is of course necessary here, and for some couples it's awesome to have Mom and Dad both home for the first few months. But it's not as valuable for other couples. If Mom is staying at home for a while, she may need her husband around only for the first few weeks—especially if it's the first baby, or if older siblings are already in school.

After Katie gave birth to our first, I was back at work within two weeks. Katie loved the quiet days alone with the baby, and if I had six weeks of paternity leave, Katie would have kicked me out of the house and told me to get a second job. Right now, however, I would love to take a week or two leave to spend canoeing or camping or driving cross-country with my oldest—and so here's another idea for innovative pro-family policy.

Call it puberty leave: a new parent can take any portion of his or her parental leave at any time in the child's first eighteen years. Imagine a one-on-one camping trip, or a week away, every summer in high school. That would be more valuable for some parents, particularly fathers, than a few extra weeks without work while Mom is also home with a newborn. I suspect that tons of parents—especially caring dads—would claim those weeks around the onset of adolescence, which would be helpful for kids, too. Social science shows repeatedly that girls who spend more time with their fathers have better outcomes. They are less depressed, less sexually active as teenagers, do less drugs and alcohol, and are more likely to finish school.[23] Around thirteen, cracks often appear between dad and daughter, and that's exactly when daughter needs contact with dad the most. A puberty leave would make it easier for them to have that time together.

To help mothers' careers, we also need to take the idea behind maternity leave—help women keep their jobs while spending time with the baby—and expand it. Here's a more sustainable and lasting change a thoughtful pro-natal company can do: cultivate more "new-mom jobs."

Imagine a young employee announces she's engaged. She'll marry by the end of the year and hopes to have children. She plans to take maternity leave, but afterward, she'd love to work part time from home and not rely on a daycare center. With this multi-month notice, she and her boss can craft a position that would be indefinite in length, remote when possible, and generally less than forty hours per week. Maybe she takes on tasks that are less time sensitive and less reliant on in-person contact—better for getting done from the laptop on the back porch when the baby is napping. Companies should cultivate these roles, and begin training would-be parents or parents hoping to expand a few months before the baby arrives. While these new-mom and new-dad jobs would be indefinite in duration, many parents would want to return to full-time work, likely after the kids begin pre-K. Many would ramp up from twenty hours at home to thirty hours, as long as they are done with work in time to pick up the kids in the afternoon. Making this the norm in a company would palpably build loyalty and connection by respecting and promoting family.

Moreover, these new-mom jobs could help address an awkward dynamic with many employers: not infrequently, a new mom decides after a couple of weeks of paid maternity leave that she has no desire to return to the office full time. Yet maybe her company's policy states that maternity leave is only for workers who are coming back. If the boss suspects his worker will never return, he nevertheless might be constrained from seeking a permanent replacement because there might be something inappropriate about calling to ask, "Are you actually coming back here, or will you work the bare minimum to justify the maternity-leave pay you took, and then go back to being a full-time mother?"

All this awkwardness can be avoided by an explicit employer-paid Baby Bonus. If you're about to have a kid, and you decide to "retire" into full-time parenthood, you get a one-time check equal to some portion of what you would get from full parental leave. If you make that decision partway through parental leave, you tell your boss and cash out some portion of your remaining leave pay as a partial Baby Bonus.

Here's a simpler alternative: give a bonus to every employee who is expecting or adopting. Some companies are beginning to experiment with this idea. Public Square, a tech company, for example, announced a five-thousand-dollar Baby Bonus in 2022.[24]

The Breadwinner Bump

As long as we are talking about companies paying new parents for having babies, we should fess up to the Breadwinner Bump. It's already a thing, even if often not acknowledged out loud: when a worker has a kid—the first, second, or whatever—and as a result the worker's spouse leaves the workforce, that worker sometimes gets a pay hike. Why? Maybe an employer just wants to promote family. Often, though, it's simple supply and demand.

If you have a really enjoyable job—say you teach Honors English at a small high school—you are likely taking a discount in your pay compared to a job in consulting or law. Part of your compensation is the fun of the job. But taking that pay discount for the sake of enjoyment becomes more difficult as your family's economic needs grow. *"Honey, I understand that Stella could use shoes that fit, but can I tell you about the stimulating conversation on Hawthorne in the teachers' lounge today?"* As a result of this familial pressure, a boss will need to pay a breadwinner parent more money to keep him or her than he would pay a singleton or a married worker with no kids. Making this Breadwinner Bump more explicit would be a radical pro-family move.

This may set off alarm bells. *Discrimination! Patriarchy!* But wages already discriminate in favor of those more willing to walk away. That's the way market pricing works.

A Breadwinner Bump should, of course, be gender neutral. You may object that, in reality, we know more men will get this pay raise, because women are more likely than men to become stay-at-home parents. But that is just an objection to human nature and societal preferences. Demanding strict, bean-counter-level equality of outcomes results in inhumane policies. This sort of nondiscrimination absolutism would logically reject parental leave, because parental leave discriminates in favor of parents. But the entire point of going pro-family is dropping neutrality and taking a side: we want people to build more and bigger families.

What's in it for the employers? Well, pro-family employers find that being pro-family helps the institution. This is most obvious at religious employers.

"They pretty much said that here your first focus is family." Noelle was a new professor at Brigham Young University–Idaho and had just completed orientation. "They encourage that if, say, your son has a baseball game, you should leave work early to go to the baseball game. If your wife needs to take a child to a doctor's appointment, leave work to be there for them. And they really emphasized that you will be a better employee if you're happy in your family life." This is part of the reason Madison County, Idaho, has the most births per capita.

As with sidewalks, we are talking here about bringing humanity into an area where we often forget humans. Treating employees as *people* pays off in the long run for employers. For most adults, that means seeing your employees as, above all, spouses and parents, and understanding that work is crucial but it's not the most important thing. I have been lucky to work at conservative, pro-family institutions throughout my career. One boss, whose children were grown, told me, "Tim, you may accomplish a lot in your writing career, but nothing—I mean *nothing*—will compare to the joy of raising your children and seeing them become adults. Nothing."

This should be part of every company's mission statement.

Taking a Side

You may ask, *Why is it an employer's responsibility to promote family?* After all, isn't a job merely an exchange of labor for money? If the employee chooses to spend his money on diapers and labor and delivery bills, that's her choice, right?

Likewise, it may seem unfair for a boss to privilege family over other things. Why should we accommodate Sophie's ballet performance more than my own desire to take in the Arsenal-Chelsea match from the pub during work hours? Granting paid family leave but not paid puppy leave, or paying a Birth Bonus, is, in a strict sense of the word, "discrimination." But it's every employer's prerogative to say that some things are more important than others. Our culture is currently not family friendly enough, and so it's right and just for employers to scrap neutrality here and say "we are pro-family."

Likewise, development and zoning debates often pit various legitimate interests against one another. A homeowner who worries that a new development will change the neighborhood isn't out of line for wanting to preserve the local character of his community, but his interests need to be weighed against the interests of the would-be homeowners who desperately want a townhouse in which to start a family. Aggressively building more apartments and starter homes for young families is taking a side, and local policymakers should be unabashed in saying "we take the side of people who want to start a family, even if that is undesirable to those who want to maintain current housing density."

And increasing walkability and bikeability will often come at the expense of those who want to drive fast with more, wider lanes, fewer crosswalks, and fewer stop signs. It will also mean throwing some concrete sidewalks down on people's front lawns. Trees will die if we build more sidewalks. But again, we should proudly take the side of kids over trees and cars.

The bigger point here: raising children isn't simply some adults' lifestyle choice. Without demeaning the childless or the child-free-by-choice, we can say that starting your own family is a natural part of adulthood.

Our institutions—local governments, employers, industry—have a duty not only to the present but to the future. If you care about the future, by definition, you should want to help people have and raise children.

Thus we can say that the duty of raising kids is not merely the parents' duty, but the duty of society.

CHAPTER 4

It Takes a Village

In the course of five weeks my wife and I had potty-trained our sixth child, taught three kids to ride bikes (yeah, we had fallen behind on that one), and built a tree house. I had relearned algebra and the first declension in Latin in order to semi-homeschool my middle schooler, and my wife, in a brilliant and entertaining diversion, had ushered the kids through planning and preparing family menus with cuisine from France, Mexico, Italy, and (if I remember correctly) Texas.

During dinner on Italian night our six-year-old, with all sincerity, asked, "Dad, can tomorrow be Family Day?"

I laughed—and cried into my homemade spaghetti. We'd had *nothing but* "Family Day" since March 13, when "flatten the curve" and "social distancing" and "stay-at-home orders" began to flow in. Thankfully we had a great backyard and plenty of woods nearby, but we were all well past the "cabin fever" stage. My wife had removed the seats from the minivan, which we converted into my office—a rare place to find privacy.

The weeks of lockdown in 2020 had some upsides, for sure (I finally conquered the bamboo patch in the corner of the yard!), but it was emotionally stressful, academically subpar, and socially stultifying. The introverts in our family were desperate for alone time, and the extroverts were desperate for more humans to talk to.

Our single biggest saving grace was that we had, built into our household, our own little platoon. We were eight people and two dogs, which meant more playmates, more variety in conversation, and less boredom.

My friends who fared best in the lockdown, though, did it by slightly breaking the rules and tweaking the definition of a "household." On Pearl Place, four families counted themselves as a single household. Soon it was five and then six. The best way to spend those weeks was in a "pod."

Katherine, a mom of two in D.C., was pretty clandestine about her pod, because she worried that her neighbors in a liberal, wealthy, rule-following neighborhood of the District would report her or something.

She and her husband had across-the-street neighbors whose two children matched their two in age. For all "stay-at-home" purposes, these two families from two homes considered themselves a single household. In those early and terrified days, podding required agreeing on rules about what sort of COVID-risk-taking was allowed. (Supermarkets were fine, Katherine and pod agreed; parties were not.)

They did their quasi-homeschooling together, the kids played together, and the adults socialized together. Like me, Katherine now had a "family" of eight—only her family was 50 percent adult.

Katherine and her podmates were surprised by the advantages this conveyed. You could schedule who would be in charge of schooling or simply watching the kids in a way that allowed you to get work done. If something unexpected came up—a work disaster or deadline—your backup was a hundred feet away. And having three adults to hang out with, rather than just one, made life more enjoyable.

Thousands of Americans formed pods in those weeks. Many loved them so much that there was talk of keeping them, even when school reopened and social distancing was a bad memory.

These parents had discovered that even in normal times, four hands are not enough to raise children. In order to be healthy families, families need other people.

Having your own subrational and extremely needy roommates puts you in need of adult connection even as it makes that very connection more difficult to achieve. This became clearer than ever during the lockdowns, and polls found parents more likely than non-parents to feel lonely in those days.[1] Sometimes the loneliness surprises new moms or dads.

"I hadn't foreseen that motherhood would turn our home in the suburbs, a Dutch colonial with a box-hedged yard, into a site of solitary confinement,"[2] wrote one *New York Times* writer, Judith Shulevitz, who was curious enough to visit "co-housing" developments in which buildings and communities are structured so as to trade out some familial privacy for some companionship.

While marriage and parenthood are great guarantees that you will spend less time alone (for better and for worse), modern parenting can paradoxically be a terribly isolating experience. Yes, in the long run, a spouse and children are the best inoculation against loneliness, but while the children are young, Mom and Dad are often depressed and solitary.

Parental loneliness is a big problem in itself, but this isn't simply a mental health story—it's a story of cultural illness. Parents' feeling of loneliness or isolation is a signal—a warning sign—that we are treating a communal undertaking as if it were an individual enterprise. This isn't inevitable. In fact, it's not normal.

However novel "pods" and "cohousing" sound, they are mostly just reviving older ways. Whatever "pull yourself up by your bootstraps" maxims you may have heard evoking our rugged and individualistic ancestors, isolated, atomistic living is actually a modern innovation, not a tradition of our past. In order to create a more family-friendly society, we have to build a society where parenthood is connective, not isolating. How do we do that?

The answer is not in filling up the adults' social calendar, or arranging more kids' playdates. It's something like the opposite, in fact. The cure to parental loneliness and family isolation is planting the family in an ecosystem that's different from the one typical in much of America—an ecosystem where "playdates" are replaced by running around the neighborhood, and cocktail parties give way to impromptu front-porch beers. This is a world where an empty social calendar doesn't mean boredom and isolation, but it means less planning and more fun.

The Forgotten Virtues of Community

"To be a young homeowner in a suburb like Elmhurst in the 1950s was to participate in a communal enterprise that only the most determined loner could escape," Alan Ehrenhalt wrote in his 1996 book, *The Lost City: The Forgotten Virtues of Community in America*: "Barbecues, coffee klatches, volleyball games, baby-sitting co-ops and constant bartering of household goods, child rearing by the nearest parents who happened to be around, neighbors wandering through the door at any hour without knocking—all these were devices by which young adults who had been set down in a wilderness of tract homes made a community. It was a life lived in public."[3]

This communal enterprise is largely lost in America today, especially for parents. For Katherine in D.C., the pandemic pod meant more than the scheduled division of tutoring/teaching/supervising duties. It also meant regular adult company without any planning or travel times—something parents deeply need.

"Contrary to what one might think, the loneliest people in America aren't the elderly," writes Judith Shulevitz. "They're young adults (close to two-thirds of them, according to the Harvard survey) and mothers of small children (about half)."

That's how Shulevitz became interested in "co-housing" communities—intentional, family-focused housing developments that paired the privacy of a single-family home or apartment with infrastructure and community expectations that would bring families out from behind their four walls and create a network of mutual reliance.

"If there is an adage that informs life in co-housing, it's *treat thy neighbor as thy family,"* she writes. "Thy extended family, that is, assuming it's a happy one."

This means communal "sharing closets" full of travel cribs, wagons, beach gear, or anything expensive and bulky that you only use a few times a year. Life becomes cheaper if you can use this stuff without having to own and store it all.

Co-housers share maintenance and cleanup days. They eat meals together. There are other formal shared responsibilities. But the most important might be the *informal* shared responsibilities. That includes keeping an eye on the children. Alternatively, some co-housing communities pay for formal daycare, Shulevitz reports. It's all about building a support structure around the nuclear family.

This is what I saw when I traveled to a kibbutz—a planned neighborhood, built around a school, with small, quiet streets—in the Golan Heights region of Israel. The dads I met there said they would not want to raise their children anywhere else. Yoel, an armed jeep driver and professional tough guy, smiled like a schoolboy when he told me he was a new dad. He grew up here, and wouldn't have had it any other way: "You have a lot of freedom in the Golan Heights."

He was speaking broadly of the rural mountainous region, but also specifically of the kibbutz where we were standing. Ilan, an older neighbor, made the same point more emphatically. It's so safe on the kibbutz that "you don't have to take care of your children."

Most of us do not live on a kibbutz or on Pearl Place, or anything like it. This is central to our family-unfriendly culture, and the growing perception that raising kids is unaffordable. "With fewer built-in communities to support and encourage parents through the challenges of raising a healthy family," writes scholar Angela Rachidi in a study on family affordability, "the weakening of our core institutions has likely helped shape evolving views of family life as burdensome, contributing to an overall perception of affordability challenges."[4]

Part of the problem is the built environment and the shape of suburbia, binding us to cars. Part of it is the modern economy, putting us all farther from our extended families. Some of it is technology, which loosens our bonds with our physical place.

Another part of this parental alienation is our culture's view of children as a lifestyle choice—like owning a boat. Maybe you'll be nice and help your neighbor with his boat maintenance, but you certainly have no duty to relieve him of the burden he brought on himself by buying a boat.

"Children are a personal choice and therefore a personal problem, many people seem to believe," writes parenting columnist Stephanie Murray. The prevailing attitude is "Have as many as you want—just make sure they don't bother the rest of us."[5]

It's very American in a way: *Live and let live. You do what you want, but don't expect me to pay for your choices.* This attitude is common on the American right and left. It's also inhumane. Yes, the nuclear family is the fundamental unit of civilization. Yes, parents are the primary educators of their children and have ultimate responsibility for them. But no, parents and siblings are not sufficient for raising kids.

Parents need other parents as role models, sounding boards, and sanity checks. Parents need other adults as their kids' teachers, coaches, and mentors. And parents need neighbors—physically proximate human beings—to play with their kids, help their kids keep out of trouble, or get them out of trouble.

What's more, being a parent often means having your hands literally full—or a baby strapped to your chest—while you try to do the things other adults are doing with empty hands and unburdened torsos. I can't count the number of times someone opened a door for me while I pushed a stroller, or how many times I helped a mom with a baby and toddler load her groceries in the parking lot. A mom carting little kids around is like a person recovering from shoulder surgery—she can't quite get by without the help of kind strangers.

"[P]arenting is an inherently social occupation," Murray explains. "Trying to cram it into an individualist framework, where the costs and consequences of children fall on parents and no one else, distorts the whole endeavor."

To continue with Murray's vaguely economic language: Children—when brought into public—necessarily have *externalities*. Babies cry and sometimes smell unpleasant. Little kids have tantrums, even at the hands of the most adept parents. And slightly older kids often have too much energy to be contained calmly for the duration required. These traits of children spill over and affect non-parents.

Murray tells of the time she realized midflight that her fourteen-month-old was chewing a tube of Chapstick found in the seatback pocket. Her only two options were (a) let her child eat an entire stick of petrolatum, paraffin wax, and some stranger's lip detritus, or (b) trigger a screaming fit on a crowded airplane. Other passengers on that plane might now be thinking "or (c), don't bring your one-year-old on a plane, lady."

Which is exactly the problem. There's pressure "for parents to avoid public life altogether," as Murray put it, but parenting isn't something that can be done in private.

When the logic of capitalism and autonomy rule the social sphere, the old-fashioned family doesn't thrive. That's why some thinkers argue we need a replacement for the old model.

"The Nuclear Family Was a Mistake," wrote David Brooks in a 2020 essay in the *Atlantic*. The essay discussed "chosen families" that embody the painted sign from Home Goods one might hang in a kitchen: "Family isn't always blood. It's the people in your life who want you in theirs; the ones who accept you for who you are. The ones who would do anything to see you smile & who love you no matter what."[6]

A pandemic pod was a chosen family. Co-housing is something like a chosen family. But you don't have to buy into this commune-like aesthetic as a solution to acknowledge the problem it is trying to address, and to understand why "intentional communities" of parents have cropped up in modern America from time to time. You just have to look around at the cultural trends of the past sixty years.

The story of America from the 1960s to today is largely a story of family breakdown. Marriage rates collapsed, divorce became commonplace, out-of-wedlock births skyrocketed, and eventually marriage and children themselves came to be seen as forces of oppression. What Daniel Patrick Moynihan identified in the 1960s as the disappearance of fatherhood in black inner cities showed up over the next few decades in the working class of all races. Modern America seems designed to dissolve the family through welfare policies with bad incentives, the sexual revolution, and modern capitalism.

But there's another way to look at the crumbling of the American family: it's only partly a story of novel anti-family forces emerging; it's largely a story of traditional supports of the family crumbling.

This is the lesson of late-twentieth-century America, Brooks argues in his *Atlantic* essay: "[T]he story of the family, once a dense cluster of many siblings and extended kin, fragmenting into ever smaller and more fragile forms."

Suburban sprawl, television, the car, and finally the pandemic have taken something absolutely crucial and wonderful—the nuclear family— and isolated it in an environment where it lacks the requisite support.

"We've made life freer for individuals and more unstable for families," Brooks correctly states. "We've made life better for adults but worse for children." Brooks's headline—"The Nuclear Family Was a Mistake"— was deliberately provocative. It would be like saying "the human heart was a mistake." Your heart cannot keep you alive without lungs bringing in oxygen, ribs for protection, and a vascular system for distribution.

The nuclear family needs a support system. It needs community. It needs to be embedded in an infrastructure of extended family, and friends, and clubs, and schools, and churches, and playgrounds, and libraries, and coffee shops, and diners, and just plain neighbors. It's hard to have neighbors, though, if you eliminate the neighborhood.

Neighborhood Effects

Zaheer Hasan, an immigrant physician, used a funny image to explain to me why he gave up much greater income in Pakistan to raise his three sons in Perrysburg, Ohio, a suburb of Toledo. Were he to make millions in Pakistan, he told me, the norm would be for him to buy a gated mansion, manned by lots of household staff including tutors for his children. His wealth could provide him with a self-contained compound that would be cut off from the bustling world outside.

He far preferred his Perrysburg four-bedroom: "I'd open the door and I'd find thirty sneakers in the house—and no food left. And our kids would be somewhere else." The whole block was raising the Hasan children. "Kids in the neighborhood adopted my kids," Zaheer told me. "Everybody watched over everybody else's kids."

Yet this sort of block—this *village* that, a former first lady once reminded us, is required to raise a child—is not the norm in twenty-first-century America. One mom of four in D.C. described her isolation this way: "If I had just *one* other mom on our block I could rely on and turn to, it would be life-changing."

Running to the store or running in the park while the kids nap is no big deal if your husband or wife is home. It's easy if you can just flag down your neighbor and say, "I'll be back in an hour. There's a bottle in the fridge if Maria wakes up."

Throughout much of history, and still today in some parts of the country, this is taken for granted. Consider Imogene or Smullton.

Imogene, Iowa, is my idea of heaven. It's a tiny town with about three things: an Irish pub, a Catholic church, and a softball field. Imogene's population is about thirty, but these fabled institutions—the Emerald Isle, St. Patrick's, and the annual Shamrock Days softball tournament—bring in folks from all the surrounding towns. Chris Hernandez is a mom of four, and she doesn't believe she's raising them all on her own. Some of her friends are her kids' "auntie-mommas," she explains, and neighbors are "extended siblings."

Parenting isn't an individualistic undertaking for her and her neighbors. "We all kind of have the same philosophy," she explains to me before her softball game, while her kids slide down a hundred-foot slip-and-slide made out of agricultural plastic sheeting and a garden hose. "If your kid is being a jackass, and you're not there, I'm going to say something."

An Imogene neighbor in a separate conversation put it more delicately: "You can critique someone else's kid," she said. "Not be a jerk about it, but be like, 'Hey, knock it off.'

"If we were going too fast down the gravel road, sometimes people would call Mom and Dad and tell them. Or if they saw us somewhere we probably shouldn't have been, they would call 'em."

Smullton, Pennsylvania, is by some measures even smaller than Imogene. It might not even show up on your map. It's the part of Rebersburg that is south of Elk Creek. Rebersburg in turn is part of Miles Township, which is in Centre County, in the center of Pennsylvania. Smullton and Rebersburg are Amish country. Powered by horses, donkeys, and their own backs, the men and women of Smullton plow their fields to feed their families and communities. They also operate Mammy's Donut Shop.

Elizabeth, aged about twenty, sold me coffee and a chocolate-peanut-butter donut there one fall morning in 2021. She explained how attached she and her family were to their community and the land. Their ways are centuries old.

Elizabeth is the youngest of five children, which isn't extraordinary in Amish country. I asked her what her community did to make big families more feasible. The question puzzled her—there wasn't anything specific she could think of, other than that all the kids pitched in on work.

Oh, also, her brother who was married with kids lived next door. "Does he often rely on you and your parents to watch the kids?" I asked. Nothing formal, most of the time, she said, but a few times a week, he or his wife asks Elizabeth or Grandma to watch the kids for a bit—typically at a moment's notice.

If you are a parent, this possibility sounds amazingly liberating and valuable. Maybe you pay tens of thousands of dollars a year for a nanny who gives you something similar. Maybe you would if you could afford it.

Our car-centric lives mean we're less likely to even know the people who literally live next door. Meanwhile, the friends we're closest with are more likely to live a drive away. Most apartment buildings are just as isolating.

Our alienation from our neighbors has become so normal that, just as Elizabeth didn't think anything of her closeness with her brother, we don't think there's anything weird about being near-strangers with the guy over the fence or the couple around the corner.

While most Americans said they were happy with their neighborhood in a 2019 survey by my colleagues at AEI, there were telling details in that same study.[7] Only half of respondents said they spoke with neighbors more than "a few times a month," and nearly two-thirds said that they and their neighbors "rarely" or "never" help one another out. That is, we're happy with our neighborhoods only because we're not expecting enough from our neighbors.

The connections were even weaker for those in the study under age forty-five—that is, for those who are (or could be) raising young children. American family life is isolating—not everywhere or among everyone, but in most places and for most people.

It's not just cars and walkability, though. The problem goes back to our vicious tendency to schedule, plan, and run everything in kids' lives—it means there's way less unscheduled time and unstructured space. Fields and courts, which would normally provide those spaces for kids to play without structure, shouldn't be constantly held for folks with a permit or scheduled activities. If Little League doesn't have a game, let the kids take over the diamond. You may, right now, be picturing some kids tearing up the infield. Hall of Fame slugger Harmon Killebrew had a great story he told about this, involving his dad.

When Mr. Killebrew would play ball in the yard with Harmon and his brother, Mrs. Killebrew on some occasions objected, "You're tearing up the grass." Mr. Killebrew's response: "We're not raising grass. We're raising boys." Nobody wants a ruined field, but keeping kids from playing in order to preserve a local field reflects a fundamental error. Kids need to be set free to explore and occasionally to mess stuff up a little bit.

It's harder to break out of the Travel Team Trap, when the Man won't let your kids play pickup sports. "They get in trouble if they play pickup football," said one high school friend who raises her boys in our old hometown. The town and the school district crack down on boys "messing up the field."

While kids need liberty and adults need to not have to worry about kids, it's also important for adults and children to mix, which is more likely to happen in neighborhoods than in schools. Our society is increasingly built to keep children in their own age cohort all day, every day, supervised by formally assigned adult authority figures such as teachers or a coach.

But if you look back at your own childhood, you probably learned some of what it means to be a grown-up from informal interactions with adults other than your parents or teachers. A neighborhood with playgrounds, schools, and corner stores, but also offices and factories, is a neighborhood in which a kid might bump into a former coach, a friend's mom, or an uncle. This intergenerational, informal mixing has been the norm in human history for millennia, and in the twenty-first century it's rare. Both children and adults lose out.

Finally, if we want parents to let their kids go free, neighborhoods need to have fewer perils of all sorts. High-crime neighborhoods obviously make free-range parenting less feasible. If a kid might run into violence, drug use, or other criminal activity, a conscientious parent will keep that kid home more often.

If you're trying to raise a kid, it's a lot easier when the neighborhood is helping you, rather than hurting you.

Back to Family

"It takes a village to raise a child," which Hillary Clinton made famous, has its roots in an African proverb.

The modern ear might miss something in this saying: historically, that "village" wasn't the town you choose after an extensive real estate hunt, or the soul mates you chose for your co-housing commune. The village typically meant extended families—cousins, second cousins, siblings, in-laws, and grandparents.

This runs contrary to the current discourse in elite circles, where *family* is equated with *trauma* and where we are all expected to craft our own bespoke lives. Nevertheless, it's true: extended family is still the best support network for most people.

This is the reality today for Elizabeth and the Amish of Smullton. It's the reality for the thousands of Americans who in recent years have jumped on the rising tide of multigenerational housing. It's the reason so many young parents who are blessed with the means to do so are buying a house next to or across the street from their brothers, sisters, or, best yet, parents.

There is no support group like family. There is no better partner in family formation than the family in which you were formed. This is a bit old-fashioned to say. David Brooks, in his essay on the inadequacy of the nuclear family, waded into the notion that the extended family could be replaced. "[T]he new families Americans are forming would look familiar to our hunter-gatherer ancestors from eons ago," he wrote. "That's because they are chosen families—they transcend traditional kinship lines."[8]

It's wonderful when friendships grow so tight that they feel like family. But there's always something suboptimal about the "chosen family." Chosen families "have extremely fluid boundaries," anthropologist Kath Weston wrote in the book *Families We Choose*. But what makes unchosen family indispensable may be precisely how *unfluid*— how *concrete*—it is. Many cultures in many places in many times have been too rigid, too tribal, too loyal to the extended family. (See, for example, Afghanistan or mafioso-run Sicily.) But American culture today has the opposite problem. We are a culture of free agents with commitment issues.

We are all paralyzed by the infinite choices offered for every aspect of our lives. Far from being shackled by rigid life scripts like a heroine in a nineteenth-century novel, today's young adult in America is left to write her own life script from beginning to end. We are each charged, in the words of one momentous text of the 1990s, with "defin[ing] one's own concept of existence, of meaning, of the universe, and of the mystery of human life."[9]

Or as Taylor Swift put it to the New York University class of 2022, "I know it can be really overwhelming figuring out who to be, and when. Who you are now and how to act in order to get to where you want to go. I have some good news: It's totally up to you. I also have some terrifying news: It's totally up to you."[10] Young single adults, young married couples, and new parents could all benefit from fewer choices and more givens. What's more, we could all benefit from having more people whose presence in our lives is not contingent—more people who cannot give us up without it being an extraordinarily big deal. Less fluidity.

Remember Kim Brooks, the anxiety-ridden mother who faced prosecution for leaving her son in the car at Target for a few minutes? On that very trip, Brooks's mom tried to talk her into moving back to Virginia. "It's hard to live far away from family when your kids are little, I remember," Brooks's mother remarked.

But getting far away from family is precisely the aim of modern, enlightened Americans who like to think they have outgrown their benighted small-town upbringing. For many of our elites, success in life is moving away from your hometown, and getting beyond the reach of those old forces that shaped you as a child. Americans with graduate degrees are the least likely to live near extended family.

Kim Brooks's life had been propelled by an urge to grow beyond needing her mom. "My parents had tried, for eighteen years, to give me everything I needed in order to make me a successful human," Brooks wrote, "and the mark of their achievement toward my success would be my not needing them anymore, not even now, with small children of my own to raise."

There it is again: you can call it a hyperindividualism, a worship of autonomy, a cultivated alienation, or a deliberate severing of ties. *I'm going to raise my kids my own way, away from the prying eyes and lecturing voice of my parents*, says the woman—for this burden falls unevenly on women—who spends all her free time sweating over parenting books and websites.

But Brooks, like so many liberated, modern, independent young parents, found herself wishing she had her kids' grandma and grandpa nearby.

My wife and I relied heavily on her younger sisters to babysit our oldest kids. Now those sisters rely on our oldest kids to babysit their own. Yes, babysitters can be hired on the free market, but nothing beats family—and there's data to prove it.

The closer you live to your parents and siblings, the sooner you start a family, and the sooner you give your first child some brothers and sisters. That was the finding of European demographer Bastian Mönkediek, who was surprised by the result. (Many demographers believe "strong family" cultural norms lower birthrates.) Instead, Mönkediek found that women who live closer to siblings and parents have kids younger, and that the age gap between children was smaller for more physically proximate families.[11] Dutch parents were more likely to have another kid if they got help from their own parents in raising the most recent baby.[12]

Another European sociologist in 2011 examined how women changed their attitudes toward family size based on the sort of support they received. Studying German families, the research found that giving women money to pay for daycare or hire a nanny did nothing to make a woman want more children. The only thing that really worked: having family nearby that could informally help out. "[H]aving received help from the informal family network," the study found, "shows a significant positive effect in women's childbearing intentions."[13]

Parents and kids aren't the only beneficiaries of having more family around. The empty-nesters and the childless benefit, too.

"A society that cuts off older people from meaningful contact with children, a society that segregates any group of men and women in such a way that they are prevented from having or caring for children," feminist anthropologist Margaret Mead wrote, "is greatly endangered."[14]

That is, we *owe* it to our parents to let them care for our kids. We *owe* it to not-yet-married twentysomethings to have them look after little tots. We *owe* it to the never-married or those who couldn't or didn't ever have children to leave them with some part of caring for the children of the community. This cuts against the contemporary thinking on the feminist left and the capitalist/individualist right.

"Think Twice, Grandma, Before You Become the Nanny," was the headline at Bloomberg News. "The biggest losses from taking care of grandchildren are what economists call opportunity, or indirect, costs," the liberal economist Teresa Ghilarducci wrote. Most important: "You forgo the opportunity to earn money."

"There may be health risks to consider, too," she added. "While there could be other benefits to interacting with children, such as keeping depression at bay and staying mentally sharp, grandparents spending time with young children could be exposed to more germs."[15]

Got it? Taking care of your grandkids may be good for your mind, your soul, your children, and your grandchildren, but it could reduce your income and possibly expose you to germs. Seeing kids as *opportunity costs* and *germ bombs* is, sadly, not limited to economists writing at Bloomberg News. It is part of a broader epidemic, especially among our college-educated elites. Too many of our tastemakers and policymakers see children—with the inevitable demands they impose on parents and society—as something akin to parasites.

Our public places are becoming places where kids are not welcome, and this will only accelerate. Our family-unfriendly culture is resulting in fewer families—less marriage, more childless adults, and smaller families. After a decade and a half of falling birthrates, the number of children in America is shrinking every year.

Fewer children every year means more people will go through more days not seeing children. This means more places at more times will become places children aren't found, and thus places where children eventually don't belong. It's a vicious spiral that's caused a historic Baby Bust.

CHAPTER 5

What Killed the Second Baby Boom?

My first night as a dad is seared in my memory. I remember collapsing into a blue maternity room recliner and bawling my eyes out, overwhelmed by the dizzying mix of terror and gratitude that only parenthood brings. I was in awe at the physical feat my wife had just performed in delivering a human, but that was a small part of it. I was also encumbered and elated by the sheer responsibility of having this human life placed in my care.

It is beyond my skill as a writer to describe my mental and emotional state that first evening, physically exhausted, engulfed by the burden of love. But one of my clearest memories is standing in the nursery at 4 a.m., gazing at that tiny, priceless, sleeping face, before the nurse gently informed me that my baby was actually two bassinets down and that I was staring at someone else's child.

My wife, our baby, and this strangers' baby were all housed in an overflow wing of Sibley Memorial Hospital. The hospital hadn't been able to expand yet in reaction to the surge of babies born in the area, which mirrored the nation as a whole.

Having a baby back then was cool. Frankly, Katie and I were riding a trend by having Lucy in the year 2006.

All the biggest celebrities in America had babies in 2006. Angelina Jolie and Brad Pitt welcomed a baby in May, the day after Gwen Stefani gave birth. Britney Spears had her second kid with Kevin Federline in September. Heidi Klum and Seal had a baby about a week before my wife and I did. And of course, Tom Cruise and Katie Holmes welcomed little Suri this same year.

Almost 4.3 million babies were born in the U.S. in 2006, the most born since the Baby Boom, and a big 3 percent jump from the prior year.[1] "A baby boomlet," the media declared. "[T]he United States has a higher fertility rate than every country in continental Europe, as well as Australia, Canada and Japan," explained the Associated Press.[2]

And then everyone hopped on the bandwagon, trying to emulate Tom Cruise, Brad Pitt, and me. In 2007, America broke the prior record, set in 1957, by having 4,317,000 babies.[3] The stars were aligned for it. Stefani, Jolie, Klum, and Holmes were all from Generation X, which had already proved a more fruitful generation than the Baby Boomers before them. Britney Spears was a borderline Millennial, one of the largest generations in American history, being the echo of the Baby Boom. The populous Millennial generation was just entering prime baby-making years. Could this be a second American Baby Boom?

It wasn't.

Inflation flared up. The housing market peaked and began to come down. When my wife and I had our second child in 2008, births were falling below 2006 levels. Then the bottom fell out. The banks all failed and the economy plunged into its deepest recession, sending millions into unemployment—10 percent of the workforce in 2009. The stock market lost half its value, demolishing Americans' retirement savings. Birthrates followed the market's downward trend.

Beginning in 2009, the economy began a recovery; birthrates did not.

In 2013, the Dow Jones Industrial Average surpassed its previous 2007 high. That year, Miley Cyrus was MTV's Artist of the Year—her singles "Wrecking Ball" and "We Can't Stop," songs celebrating decadence and depravity, went big. Cyrus went on to explain her intention to never have kids.

"We're getting handed a piece-of-sh*t planet," she told *Elle*, "and I refuse to hand that down to my child. Until I feel like my kid would live on an earth with fish in the water, I'm not bringing in another person to deal with that."[4] Cyrus said she was speaking for all Millennials in proclaiming, "We don't want to reproduce because we know that the earth can't handle it."

When Katie and I welcomed our sixth child in 2016, we were no longer doing something cool. The whole having-kids fad had flamed out. Angelina had filed for divorce from Brad. Tom and Katie were already split, as were Seal and Heidi. Gwen Stefani was no longer a celebrity coach on the show *The Voice*—her seat was now filled by Miley Cyrus.

The economy continued to improve. The market doubled again from 2013 to 2019, and unemployment dropped to near-record lows. Yet the birthrate plummeted as fast as it had during the Great Recession.

In 2019, only 3.75 million American babies were born, way down from the 4.3 million in 2007. All this happened as the second-largest generation in American history—the Millennial generation—entered its prime years of family formation. We had more potential parents than ever before, yet we were getting fewer babies from them. Then things got really bad: the pandemic hit and birth numbers fell further, with 2020 clocking the largest one-year drop on record, down 4 percent to 3.61 million.

For a moment back in 2006, we stood at the cusp of a second Baby Boom, with Suri Cruise, my daughter, and that other random baby at Sibley as the pioneers. But then the Millennials came in like a demographic wrecking ball and knocked us off a cliff—an unprecedented Baby Bust.

How did we go from Baby Boomlet to Baby Bust? The economics and policy we touched on in chapter 3 matter here. But we should start with Miley Cyrus and her belief system: "We don't want to reproduce because we know that the earth can't handle it."

Where did the Millennials get this notion?

They've been hearing it since grade school.

Breeding Like Rabbits

"No problem facing the Earth looms larger than the growth of the reproductive rate of the human species," opined William A. Burley in the *New York Times* on April 29, 1990. "Virtually all . . . human suffering can be attributed to the crushing effect of a population that is too numerous for our planet."[5]

The op-ed, illustrated with a swarm of baby rabbits devouring the Earth as if it were a head of cabbage, didn't pull punches. "The belief among many cultures that children are the equivalent of wealth is a bankrupt social and economic theory. In the last decade of the twentieth-century, fewer children mean a better life and a healthier environment."

Burley was not merely trying to reach the readers of the *New York Times*. He was trying to reach their kids. His op-ed argued that this dark truth about the harms of children must be taught to young children. He was in position to do just this, because as the op-ed page noted, Burley was the principal of the John Pettibone School, a public elementary school in New Milford, Connecticut.

Burley's students at the time were Millennials. Today he would be teaching the children of Millennials, but the John Pettibone School closed in 2015 due to low and falling enrollment.

"It was heart-wrenching," the school board chairman told the *Litchfield County Times*. The board took no joy in its decision, which forced some local kids, accustomed to walking to school, into taking a twice-daily fifty-minute bus ride. But the leaders of New Milford keep facing exactly this sort of heart-wrenching decision.

A few years earlier, New Milford Hospital had closed its renowned "Family Birthing Center." "Declining Birth Rate, Cost of Running Center Led to Decision," the local paper's headline declared. Again, heart-wrenching, but once again, it was just a matter of numbers: "In 2009, 343 babies were born at the hospital. By 2011, the number had dropped to 263 babies. The rate during the first three months of 2012 shows a continuing decline."[6] The drop continued, in the surrounding area, and among New Milfordians in particular.

The population shock that closed Principal Burley's old elementary school in 2015 soon hit New Milford High School. I was there for the Green Wave's final football game of the 2021 season. The scene was lively, but longtime residents saw a fading town. "When I was in high school, New Milford was huge," Dylan McIntyre, a local cop, told me on the sidelines. Since 2007—when New Milford High School was graduating the students born in the months before Principal Burley's cri de coeur—student population has dropped by 15 percent.[7] Surrounding towns are doing even worse. "Some of the schools we played combined varsity and freshman teams and only fielded fifteen kids," one football mom told me.

Across town, the old John Pettibone School is now the John Pettibone Community Center. "Gentle Adult Yoga" was the main event when I visited in 2021. In the shadow of the former school building that Sunday, volunteers hosted "Howl O Ween," in which the robust dog park community provided treats and giveaways while locals dressed up their pups in costumes.

"I don't have kids," explained Melissa, in charge of community affairs at Candlewoof Dog Park. "I have a dog. That's my kid." Melissa, a married woman in her late forties, was not complaining. "I have two nephews and a niece, and I love them. But I get to sleep in and do what I want." The other two people at Candlewoof on Friday night were a man named Fabien and a woman named Darcy. Darcy has two children, and Fabien has one.

Melissa, Fabien, and Darcy are all friendly, conscientious, pro-family, and (as evidenced by their volunteer work at the dog park) pro-community. These three, representing three married couples and thus six adults, have a combined three children.

New Milford's adults aren't replacing themselves. The only reason the town isn't shrinking is that adults from smaller dying towns are moving here, thus depopulating their own hometowns even faster. New Milford isn't extraordinary in this regard. It may just be ahead of the curve.

Baby Bust by the Numbers

Any way you count it, the United States is undergoing a baby drought.

The Baby Bust began in 2008. That means the average American kindergarten began shrinking in 2013. The average middle school began shrinking in 2019. The Baby Bust hit high schools in 2022, and soon will make impact on college campuses and then the workforce.

We have not only fewer babies; we have fewer *children*. America was home to 74.2 million children (ages 0–17) in 2010.[8] That number dropped to 73.6 million in the 2020 census, and then fell by another million over the next two years.[9] People in their sixties in 2020 outnumbered children under ten.[10]

Here's an even more depressing way to measure our demographic trajectory: Do more people exit your local hospital in a baby carrier or in a body bag? That is, do you have more births or deaths?

New Milford residents had 396 babies in 1994, just a few years after Principal Burley's op-ed. That year, 190 New Milfordians died. By 2008, the numbers were not too different: 337 births to 197 deaths. After that, births plummeted and deaths steadily rose. Come 2016, New Milford welcomed 227 babies, and said goodbye to 250 of their neighbors.[11]

Zoom out and you see deaths outnumbering births on a larger scale, even before the pandemic. West Virginia lost 23,000 residents in 2019, while only 18,000 babies were born.[12] Deaths also exceeded births in Maine, New Hampshire, Rhode Island, and Vermont in 2019.

This is a lot of numbers, but the most important one is the Total Fertility Rate.

This usage of the word *fertility* is not specifically about the biological or medical ability to have children. Instead, Total Fertility Rate (TFR) is a statistical tool used by demographers that begins with the number and pace of births and calculates the average number of babies a woman is expected to have over her lifetime.[13] It's a useful number because it captures long-term trends better than the other birthrate data do, by weeding out ebbs, flows, and other confounding factors. The TFR is the most useful way to compare births across time or places, and so hereafter, where I say "birthrate" I mean "Total Fertility Rate," unless otherwise specified.

The magic number here is 2.1, known as the "replacement" level. A birthrate of 2.1 indicates that a population will naturally remain flat. Below-replacement birthrate indicates a population will, in the long run, shrink. Above 2.1, and a population will grow.

(Why 2.1? Well, it's 2 babies as opposed to 1 because men can't have babies, so women, as usual, need to pick up the guys' slack. The extra 0.1 is mostly due to the fact that a portion of babies will not survive until childbearing age. Some argue that 2.2 ought to be considered the real replacement level.)

Most of Europe, along with China, Japan, and South Korea, is well below replacement. The birthrate is falling in almost every country in the world, and experts predict that in a few decades, almost all countries will be below replacement.

In 2006, the U.S. was one of only a few wealthy countries above replacement. Since then, we've fallen way below the waterline. The United States, before the pandemic, was nearly half a baby below replacement.

If our birthrate decline doesn't reverse, the United States will join South Korea in having a shrinking population year after year.

Following the history of America's birthrate reveals something about how we got here, and how we might turn things around. Specifically, the tale of the post–World War II Baby Boom gives us a hint about the current Baby Bust, and how to create an America that is family friendly enough to give us our next boom.

Over the first 150 years of American history, the birthrate steadily fell from about 7 to about 3.1. Then it accelerated downward, dropping below 3 in the 1920s. Births didn't rebound during the Great Depression, and during World War II, America's birthrate dropped to 2.1.

When the men came home from World War II, birthrates famously went through the roof and stayed there for well over a decade. The U.S. birthrate spiked above 3.5 in 1960, higher than it had been in fifty years. And then almost as quickly as the boom began, it collapsed. The Pill and the sexual revolution brought the fertility rate below replacement for the first time in American history. For most of the 1980s, '90s, and aughts, the birthrate hovered right below 2.1 babies per woman. Next came the "baby boomlet," as the American press called it, arriving just a few years into the new millennium. That's when Tom, Brad, and I had babies.

Then the Great Recession hit and things collapsed. The U.S. birthrate fell from about 2.1 in 2007 down to 1.7 in 2019.

Were you to plot the birthrate across U.S. history, you would see two interesting details in the middle of the last century. What is *not* exceptional is that after men returned from the war in 1945, their wives started having babies. What *is* exceptional, what shocked demographers, is that the boom wasn't just a makeup for four lost years. It was a decades-long, unprecedented, and totally unexpected reversal of the centuries-long trend of falling birthrates. Birthrates in wealthy countries always tended downward, and there had never been a massive, decades-long reversal of that trend.

Then look at the Great Recession. What's unexceptional is that a collapse of the economy caused birthrates to fall in 2008 and 2009. What's surprising to some is that they never rebounded.

The last years with birthrates significantly above 2.1 were in the 1960s. Now the oldest Baby Boomers are pushing eighty, and they're the ones we're burying today. The pandemic in 2020 and 2021 disrupted death figures and births, but by 2023, births were back on their pre-COVID downward trajectory.

Even without the deaths and foregone births of the pandemic, our population would already be dramatically shrinking if not for immigration. According to the Congressional Budget Office, deaths will consistently exceed births by 2043 in the U.S.[14]

The rest of the wealthy world is a few steps ahead of the U.S. in this flight from fertility. Not a single country in Europe was at replacement level in 2019. Spain and Germany are below 1.5 babies per woman.

Over in Asia, some nations are far worse. South Korea's fertility rate hit 0.92 in 2019.[15] That is less than one child per woman, a recipe for a rapidly shrinking population. China's population shrank by more than 800,000 people in 2021, as 10.4 million Chinese died while 9.6 million Chinese babies were born.[16]

India fell below replacement level around 2020, following the same trajectory that South Korea did as it developed economically[17]—except India's birthrate is far lower than South Korea's was at this stage in its economic development.[18] Indeed, if you had to pick a single factor to predict whether a country was having enough babies to replace itself, wealth would be the obvious choice—with one exception (more on that later), poor countries are the only ones above replacement.

But poorer countries' fertility rates are falling, too. The world's birthrate was about 5 babies per woman in 1964. Since then, it's been a pretty steady fall, and by 2019, it was less than 2.5 babies per woman. Mexico, which had nearly 7 babies per woman in 1970, fell below replacement level in 2017. Brazil, Malaysia, and Vietnam are among the still-developing nations with below-replacement fertility. Even the still-fruitful are all on downward slopes. Nigeria went from 6.1 babies per woman in 2000 to 5.2 in 2021, and this trend is accelerating.[19]

The world's birthrate will fall below replacement around 2070, the Pew Research Center calculated in 2019.[20] The odds are that we will turn that corner even earlier.

The demographic story of today is that a wealthier world is having fewer babies, and the wealthiest countries are having the fewest. This makes for a bit of a puzzle, considering that the number one answer given when you ask an adult why they don't have kids, or more kids, is "we can't afford it."

The Money Excuse

"We don't want kids," Nicole told me.

I was walking around the Lower Avenues, a neighborhood in Salt Lake City that looks like it would be the perfect place for a young family.

The streets are lined with modest single-family houses with small yards. The sidewalks are shaded with trees, and the neighborhood is peppered with schools and playgrounds. But the only couple I ran into on a lengthy morning stroll was Isaac and Nicole, and they had no interest in raising children here. Why not?

"We can't afford it," Nicole said.

I pressed the couple on what made kids so expensive.

"Everything," Isaac began. "Health care—but honestly, it's just selfishness," he confessed. "I joke with Nicole, 'Some people are watching *Teletubbies* and cleaning up vomit, and we're going to be drinking margaritas in Paris.'" Moments later, a neighbor greeted the couple, pushing a double stroller through the Avenues—the passengers in the stroller were two Chihuahuas.

Pondering this surreal scene later on, I realized that Nicole and Isaac had concisely stated the two most common explanations I get when I ask ordinary folks why America is undergoing a Baby Bust. And I wondered whether we could fairly pin our Baby Bust on cost or selfishness.

Both of these explanations have an appeal, but they have the same fatal flaw. Yes, both cost and selfishness deter people from having kids or having more kids, but neither explains *the change* in the birthrate over the past generation. You can no more blame selfishness for a decline in birthrates than you can blame a rash of plane crashes on *gravity*. Selfishness is as old as Adam and Eve.

Blaming *cost* almost makes sense. After all, the Baby Bust began in earnest in 2008 and 2009 with the Great Recession. And yes, birthrates seem to fluctuate inversely to *housing* costs. We will discuss the costs of parenthood, and how government policy can make parenting more affordable, in a later chapter.

First, though, we need to wrestle with the *difficulties* of blaming unaffordability for the Baby Bust. The first difficulty is that birthrates are lowest among the people who can most afford births and babies. Poorer countries, remember, generally have higher birthrates, while wealthier countries have lower birthrates. In the U.S., households in poverty had a crude birthrate of 74 babies per 1,000 women. Households with income at least twice the poverty level had a crude birth-rate of 44.[21] Keep going up the income ladder, and the birthrate keeps dropping. The richer you are in America today, the fewer kids you have on average (until you get to the very rich, who have more kids).

A closer look at the timing also upends the economic explanation for the Baby Bust. The birthrate was far lower in 2019 than it had been during the Great Recession. From the trough in 2009 to the end of 2019, the stock market nearly quadrupled.[22] Unemployment went from 10 percent in late 2009 to a startlingly low 3.5 percent in late 2019.[23] The last time Americans had a job picture as pretty as 2019 was in the heart of the Baby Boom.

Contrary to their self-perception, Millennials are exactly as wealthy as the previous two generations were at their age, when adjusted for inflation. The Millennial generation had the same per capita wealth in 2020—when the median millennial was thirty-two years old—as Gen X had in 2007 when the median Gen Xer was thirty-two.[24]

In a million other measurable ways, America's wealth seems to make the case that we should be having more kids, not fewer. Cars are safer, information about nutrition for pregnant mothers is better, more Americans can afford more calories of food than ever before. Yet we're having fewer kids than ever before, and the trends are all in the wrong direction.

So why do so many people say it's become unaffordable to have kids? It's not a made-up complaint. Raising kids has become tougher and in ways that at least make it *feel* more expensive, thus driving down birthrates.

The Baby Bust is the result of the cultural shifts discussed in the earlier chapters that have made America less family friendly. Neighborhood youth sports have been replaced by time-consuming, money-sucking travel sports. The "good public schools" where upper-middle-class parents make sure to send their kids are in neighborhoods where the home prices and the property taxes are prohibitive for many. The culture demands more "enrichment," more hovering, more helicoptering of our children, as paranoia of stranger-danger creates a rule that *good* parents are constantly afraid.

Demographers talk about the current "demographic transition": a shift to high wealth and low birthrates as we "increase investment" in each child. We now take "quality" over "quantity," sociologists say. "Investment" in our children means driving ourselves crazy, and while it does reduce the quantity of children we have, it doesn't actually help us or the children we do have. If it did, we wouldn't see the record rates of childhood anxiety and depression that have defined the twenty-first century.

Of course we have fewer kids when the time demands of parenting have skyrocketed.[25]

Crucially, we've all become less connected to our neighbors and our communities, turning children into an individual burden rather than a community responsibility. Isaac and Nicole's view of their world didn't include extended family and family-friendly community. If they wanted support raising children, they would have to pay for it. To be sure, there are some who think the Baby Bust is a good thing. And they have plenty of backup from the stories our culture tells.

Idiocracy

At the aging playground of the former John Pettibone School, I met a couple pushing a two-year-old in a swing while grandpa sat on a bench watching the baby in a stroller. They said that New Milford is a good place to raise kids, but explained, "We're done at two. We don't want anymore."

I wondered: If New Milford is a good place to raise kids, why were so few babies being born here—so few that the high school was shrinking, the elementary school closed, and the birthing center shuttered, all while the senior center expanded and the dog park grew? So I posed the question to the couple.

That's when Leigh, from the next bank of swings, piped in. "Have you ever seen the movie *Idiocracy*?"

Idiocracy, a pointedly satirical film, opened to a limited release during the Baby Boomlet of 2006. The dark comedy tells the story of a future populated only by drooling idiots, after the smart, well-educated people stop breeding. "Evolution does not necessarily reward intelligence," the movie's narrator intones in the first minute. "With no natural predators to thin the herd, it began to simply reward those who reproduced the most, and left the intelligent to become an endangered species."

"That's what I believe," Leigh said. A woman in her late thirties, Leigh was proud to say she didn't have children of her own. Like the dog park folk, though, she loves kids, and she even cares for foster children—which explained her presence at the playground. Of the adults of the species, though, she has a lower opinion—particularly the breeders among us. *Idiocracy* was the framework through which she viewed parents. "You know, one man has six kids by age thirty, and treats them like property." She said this just a few minutes after I had told her that I have six kids.

Whether I am an idiot for having six kids is a fair subject for debate. But what about the other half of the story in *Idiocracy*—the yuppie couple that never reproduces? They come across as anxious, controlling, overeducated, and ultimately isolated even from each other. So, if Leigh was worried about the dysgenic fallout of us country rabbits and our breeding, then how did she explain the declining reproduction of the urbane and sophisticated?

"We are financially responsible," Leigh explained, "and we have these massive bills because we are more educated, and we have these massive debts because we went to school where it was tens of thousands of dollars a semester." By her sociological framework, you can tell whether a couple is educated—or not—by their brood size: *You shall know them by their fruitlessness.*

"Too many people are having too many kids," agrees Jesse, a twenty-nine-year-old bartender in Greenville, South Carolina, who describes himself as "a feminist." Jesse mentions his unhappily married or divorced family members. He points to kids messed up by bad parents. He is resolved to avoid those same mistakes, and he has structured his romantic life accordingly.

"I use Tinder. I use Bumble," he explains, naming the popular dating apps. "I never really get very much, because I'm picky. But I'm honest. I don't really do *dating*. I don't do relationships," he says. He finds "a lot of women who are into that because they've been in possessive relationships." Is a happy marriage a possibility? Nah. "Everybody's miserable, but there's a contest" on social media, he explains, "to see who can make their life look more perfect."

Jesse, who openly rejects his "conservative Baptist upbringing," has a simple idea of living the good life: avoid making a big mistake. It's a complementary mindset to Leigh's *Idiocracy*-informed worldview. The problem, as they see it, is that too many people are making big mistakes—namely, having kids they are unfit or unwilling to raise.

Demographers and economists make a more sophisticated version of Jesse's argument: the Baby Bust is a sign of progress.

"Maybe there are fewer babies right now," explained University of Colorado demographer Amanda Jean Stevenson, "but people are able to live the lives they want to, and that's a profound thing."[26]

When Brookings Institution scholar Melissa Kearney authored a paper suggesting that changes in student debt, housing costs, childcare costs, or other economic factors couldn't explain the collapse in fertility after the Great Recession, writer Lydia DePillis summed it up this way: "Interesting survey paper on fertility trends finds little evidence to support the usual economic/social explanations for declining birthrates, concludes (surprise surprise!) that younger women might just want more out of life than children."[27]

"Here's the answer," according to *Washington Post* columnist Petula Dvorak: "choices. For the first time in human history, women truly have them. A lot of women don't feel pressured to have kids they don't want."[28]

"It's a sign of better access to education and employment opportunities," Business Insider explained in 2021, "a rise in individualism and women's autonomy, better sex education, and a shift from religious-based to more secular values."

Low and falling birthrates, in this way of seeing things, are signs of autonomy, prosperity, and happiness. In that light, who would lament the Baby Bust other than backward religious conservatives who want to control women's bodies?

Likewise, some environmentalists cheer lower birthrates and our coming population decline.

"[C]onsidering that overpopulation is quite literally killing the planet, what does it matter to you that the birthrate is down?" That's how liberal journalist Laura Bassett responded to my concern about the Baby Bust.

"Having children is one of the worst things you can do for the planet," feminist attorney and writer Jill Filipovic wrote.[29]

"Procreation is becoming a global public health concern, rather than a personal decision," feminist writer Kristen Pyszczyk stated when home improvement stars Chip and Joanna Gaines announced they were expecting. "So when people do irresponsible things like having five children, we absolutely need to be calling them out."[30]

"[H]aving many children is wrong, or at least morally suspect, for standard environmental reasons," a bioethicist wrote at NBC News in 2017: "Having a child imposes high emissions on the world, while the parents get the benefit." Parents are responsible for their children's emissions, the author argued, just as much as a jailer would be responsible if he were to "release a murderer from prison, knowing full well that he intends to kill innocent people."[31]

DePillis again made the point even more starkly. "[F]or the foreseeable future," she wrote, "the biggest thing you can do to shrink your footprint is *have fewer kids.* Arguing otherwise is fantasy. No amount of buses or energy-efficient appliances or diet changes will outweigh the impact of AN ENTIRE HUMAN LIFETIME of consumption."[32]

It's not just liberal feminists and environmentalists celebrating our collapsing birthrates. "America's so-called 'baby bust' signals a glorious future for its workers and the U.S. economy more broadly," argued John Tamny, a pro-capitalism writer, in a 2021 letter to the *Wall Street Journal*.[33] Still other economists believe that we'll simply adapt to fewer people with technology. "A paradigm shift is necessary," German demographer Frank Swiaczny told the *New York Times*. "Countries need to learn to live with and adapt to decline."

"[T]he economic case for pro-natalism is really weak," explained liberal economist Paul Krugman. Perhaps an aging workforce can cause economic stagnation, "but you can also use fiscal stimulus—and low interest rates mean debt is not a serious problem." In other words, any economic costs of an older population can be paid by more government borrowing and spending.[34] (If interest rates get high or inflation rears its head, maybe we need to reconsider, but what are the chances, right?)

So are the sociologists, feminists, Jesse the bartender, and economists correct? Does a world with fewer babies mean more happiness?

CHAPTER 6

We Can't Afford a Baby Bust

Anywhere you turn, you can find well-spoken folks—feminists, environmentalists, capitalists, liberal economists—cheering the Baby Bust, or at least dismissing those of us who worry about it. But we *should* worry about it. For all the parents who say they can't afford to have kids, as a society we need to understand that we can't afford to have so few kids. The costs of below-replacement birthrates are economic, personal, and cultural.

First, the Baby Bust is bad for the economy. The inflation and supply chain disruptions of the early 2020s are a preview of the economy in a shrinking and aging population.

Second, the Baby Bust is bad because women still want 2.5 babies but are getting 1.6 babies. Worse, I talk to many women who tell me that they want a big family but conclude "it's not in cards" for all sorts of reasons.

Third, having kids is actually good for us. Despite the media reports telling you otherwise, children actually make us happier.

Finally, the Baby Bust is bad because it reflects something broken about us.

More babies are good for the nation, good for families, and good for parents. They're not burdens on society—they *create* society.

Let's begin with the hoary myth, from the likes of Principal Burley, that the world is overpopulated.

The Population Bomb That Wasn't

"The battle to feed all of humanity is over," scientist Paul Ehrlich wrote in his bestselling 1968 book, *The Population Bomb*. "In the 1970s hundreds of millions of people will starve to death in spite of any crash programs embarked upon now."

Ehrlich became a celebrity preaching the gospel of population control and promising fire and brimstone. The overpopulation alarm sounded constantly throughout the 1970s, '80s, and '90s. Ehrlich and the alarmists turned out to be fabulously wrong.

We are not overpopulated, and our population growth is not too rapid. Yes, people like Ehrlich might feel the planet is too crowded for their tastes, but that's a subjective judgment. Objective measures show that we are not taking up too much of the planet.

Begin with Ehrlich's measure: food availability per person. The population of Earth more than doubled from 1968 to today, and the calories available per person increased by nearly 30 percent in that same period, with growth in every continent.[1]

What's more, we are producing this greater food supply from less and less land. At some point in the last generation, humans reached peak agricultural land use. Sometime around the 1990s, the combined acreage of farms and livestock land began shrinking, scientists say. The decline in total land use for agriculture has been rapid.[2]

The world population will begin shrinking in the 2060s, according to the Institute for Health Metrics and Evaluation at the University of Washington.[3] Others put the date a decade or two later, but the general consensus is that in the lifetime of today's children and young adults—including many of Principal Burley's former students—the world population will peak.

Ultimately, if you believe that 8 to 10 billion people is too much, the data won't change your mind, but in general, the panic about overpopulation has proven, over the past fifty years, to be unfounded.

Now let's talk about the dangers of a Population Bust.

Too Few Workers

The *easiest* warning about the Baby Bust regards the fate of Social Security. But the *best* story to tell is the one about how you couldn't buy a car in 2021, why your favorite restaurant stopped serving lunch in 2022, or how ambulance wait times rose in 2023.

Let's work up to the supply chain and labor market issues by starting with the simple math of our federal retirement system:

Social Security is not a savings account. The checks for today's retirees are coming out of the paychecks of Gen X, Millennial, and Gen Z workers today.

Here's the problem: we have fewer workers today than we used to. Some of that is due to people dropping out of the workforce, but some of it is due to demographics. America's working-age population flatlined in late 2018, and will fall for the foreseeable future.[4] A greater share of the population is retirement age than ever before, and that share is growing at an accelerating rate.[5] When you consider how much old folks rely on working-age adults, this becomes a problem.

Currently, there are about three retirement-age Americans for every ten working-age Americans. By 2050, there will be four retirees for every ten workers. This ratio will keep rising because each year we will have more old people and fewer working-age people. The Social Security Administration raised the alarm about "a declining worker-to-beneficiary ratio" and the need to reduce benefits, increase taxes, and increase the retirement age in 2005, *back when the birthrate was at replacement level.*[6]

This story scares a lot of people, but it is just a *reflection* of the real threat: we will, over the next couple of decades, have fewer people to do productive work.

Let's take a step back to think about what money means and what wealth is. We are all used to measuring wealth, whether of an individual, a family, or a whole economy, in dollars. But those dollars are just a symbol of a deeper reality. Social Security, for instance, could always keep benefits where they are because the U.S. government can produce dollars at will. But while dollars generally *represent* wealth, they don't *equal* wealth.

Wealth is really *resources*: materials, equipment, processes, and most of all *humans* who can do work. Fewer teenagers today means fewer workers a decade from now. That means less work done in a decade than would otherwise have been. That means fewer people to care for the elderly, to repave roads, to wait tables, or to supervise the transfer of a shipping container onto a truck.

Here's an illustration of what that means in practice:

One day in 2021, I thought my geriatric Toyota Camry was dying. My oldest daughter was approaching driving age, and so while the car was in the shop, my wife and I spent a day looking for used cars. It was a nightmare. Prices were 25 percent higher on average than a few months earlier, and for SUVs, trucks, and vans, the increase was even greater. Friends who had bought a used car in 2018 found the car was worth *more* in 2021 than they had paid for it. You know something is wrong when used cars are appreciating.

The specific causes of this disruption in 2021 were manifold, most stemming from the pandemic, and God willing they will never happen again. But the morass was all a foretaste of what happens to an economy when the number of young people is shrinking. Things don't get made or delivered without people to make or deliver them. Automation can relieve some of the pressure but not all of it. Fundamentally, you only have the stuff you have because some other human expended labor in making it and delivering it.

By 2022, the manpower shortage was present everywhere in the economy. I showed up at Ireland's Four Provinces, a venerable local pub in Falls Church, Virginia, one day for lunch, to find out they now don't open until 4 p.m. Clothing stores shut the changing rooms because they couldn't hire enough staff to man them. Small businesses that couldn't find help closed altogether.

Lunch at the pub or trying on a pair of khakis may be no big deal. But when your local government can't staff its ambulances, police departments, and dispatch services, you have a problem. Montgomery County, Maryland, a wealthy suburb of D.C., in 2023 reported that in its emergency call center, 65 of the 198 jobs were unfilled, which resulted in considerably slower emergency-response times.[7]

Saving a million dollars for retirement does you no good if there's nobody you can pay to fix your leaky pipe. "[T]hese savings only matter to the extent that young workers are ready and willing to take your money," economist Alan Cole wrote in 2022. "Neither private saving nor government pension schemes work unless there are enough workers to meet the needs of older Americans. No amount of financial wizardry will conjure them into existence."[8]

The Great Demographic Reversal, a 2020 book focused on the challenges facing China, has warnings about an aging society that apply to the U.S. as well. As life spans extend and the population ages, dementia and Alzheimer's disease will become much more pressing issues for our society. "The costs of such diseases are bound to grow rapidly," the authors write, "partly by diverting a growing proportion of the available workforce into care for the dependent old. Even then, the availability of properly trained carers will probably be insufficient, leading to a greater burden for the affected old and their families."[9]

An economy with fewer working-age adults but more goods-and-services-consuming old people is an economy with higher prices, more scarcity, longer wait times, and ultimately lower quality of life.

Fewer People Means Less Prosperity

In general, fewer people is bad for the economy. But even economists have gotten this wrong throughout history.

You may have heard the word *Malthusian*. Thomas Robert Malthus was a British economist about two hundred years ago whose explanation of birthrates and economics dominated demographic and economic thinking (and still holds sway today). In particular, Malthus's model was based on scarcity and productivity.

When a society is poor, people naturally restrict births because they fear spreading their limited resources too thin, Malthus argued. As people reduce their reproduction, wealth per person increases. As time goes by, productivity increases. Eventually people are rich enough that they can ramp up the baby-making again.

Malthusianism, in short, holds that lower birthrates cause greater wealth. In the short run, it's reasonable to consider that resources are finite, and more people means fewer resources per person. Each extra kid who shows up at Billy's birthday party means a smaller slice of cake for everyone.

Malthus's model, however, omits the *ultimate resource*, to use the term of environmental economist Julian Simon. The *ultimate resource*, of course, is the human mind.

More people, in the long run, makes us wealthier because *more people* means more creativity and more innovation, which means more cakes for everyone. History has proven this again and again. Human life is better today than it was five hundred years ago, when it was better than it was five hundred years before that. The arc of human existence bends toward the less nasty, the less brutish, and certainly the less short.

What's the cause of this slow, steady improvement of human life? It's not climate change. It's not space aliens or lizard people. The obvious cause of progress is other humans. It's not that every human makes the world better, but it sure seems like *on net* people make the world better. To borrow the economists' terminology, the expected value of each new human is positive.

The reason we have more calories per capita today than we did when Ehrlich was on his *Population Bomb* tour is that some of those excess humans devised better seeds and farming techniques. Most notably, a human named Norman Borlaug spurred the so-called green revolution that massively improved crop yields. Borlaug wasn't a mere "lifetime worth of consumption," as the overpopulation-worriers de-scribe people.

If you wanted a more systematic look at this, you could try to com-pare places with greater and lesser populations, and measure their economic growth. The problem, of course, is that there are a million "confounding" factors, a million reasons Place A might be more eco-nomically prosperous than Place B. For example, wealthy and growing places attract more immigrants because there are more jobs. This obvi-ously doesn't show that population growth *causes* economic growth, but rather the converse. Alternatively, poor places with few well-paying jobs could have greater population growth simply because the opportu-nity cost of parenting is lower.

It's difficult to separate these variables, and it would be immoral to run a controlled study. We wouldn't, for example, randomly relocate people against their will to various parts of a country to measure the effect of growing populations in a place's economy.

Lucky for us, history already conducted this unseemly but enlight-ening experiment, and a Yale economist crunched the numbers.

The occasion of the natural experiment was the aftermath of World War II. Ethnic Germans had spread throughout Eastern Europe before and between the world wars. Following the end of Nazi occupation, many countries wanted ethnic Germans out of their midst. After the Potsdam Conference in 1945, the victorious parties took up the work of moving those Germans back to Germany without their input.

Between 1945 and 1948, about 8 million people were forced from their homes in Poland, Czechoslovakia, and the rest of Eastern Europe into new homes in Germany. Crucially, they weren't homes of their choosing.

"Upon their arrival in West Germany," wrote economist Michael Peters, "the refugees were not free to settle where they wanted to but their assignment was organized and implemented by the Military Governments of the US and the UK."

Notably, the refugees were not distributed evenly across Germany. "[S]ome counties received hardly any refugees and other counties re-ceived so many that their population almost doubled," Peters explained.

That's where the natural experiment occurs: What happens to the economies of places that suddenly get booms in population?

Peters compared the economies of the counties who got almost no new Germans to the economies of the counties that got many. (The resettled Germans didn't appear to move too much after resettlement, Peters found.)

In the short run, the German counties whose populations grew rapidly didn't look that different economically than other German counties. But after about fifteen years, the places with larger population growth saw a significant rise of income per capita. Peters concluded, "an increase in the share of refugees by 10% increases income per capita by roughly 5–6% after 15 years."

That is, faster population growth seems to have made the pie so much bigger that each individual's slice was larger. Having more members makes a community healthier and happier.

Some scholars see an easy solution here: "Let's Have More Immigrants, Not More Babies," wrote Brookings Institution scholar Isabel Sawhill.[10] Surely on some scores immigrants can fill our gaps, but importing the people we are not creating is not a sustainable solution. For one thing, the rest of the world has a falling birthrate, and the top three sources of U.S. immigrants—Mexico, China, and India[11]—all have birthrates below replacement level. Secondly, immigrants to low-birthrate countries gravitate toward that lower birthrate. Third, and most importantly, solving your labor shortage by importing large numbers of foreign workers sets up the sort of racialized class dichotomy that underlies so much ethnic tension in Western Europe these days.

Immigration will help the U.S. deal with labor shortages, but there's no getting around our need for more babies.

The True Shape of the Bust

Admittedly, the Baby Bust didn't look so bad at first. Starting in the 1990s, teen births fell. Then twentysomethings began having fewer babies, but thirtysomethings started having more.

It seemed that American women were having fewer unwanted babies and were merely having babies later, yielding all kinds of benefits: more education; later, stronger marriages; and happier, more stable families. I call this the Happy Planning Story, and for a while, it appeared to be true.

But as Millennials entered their thirties, the story unraveled.

The average thirty-five-year-old American woman in 2020 had just above 1.5 kids, which is the lowest number on record. Women turning forty in 2020 also had fewer kids than their counterparts at any time over the preceding decade. The Millennials aren't simply having babies *later*, it turns out. They are having *fewer babies* than prior generations. Again, the gap between desired number of children and the actual number grew.

To some extent, the falling birthrates since the Great Recession reflect fewer big families, but they mostly reflect the spread of childlessness. From 2007 to 2019, first births fell by 21 percent, significantly more than second births (down 16 percent), or third or later births.

As a result, only about half of American women in their late twenties have children. This is a huge departure from the not-too-distant past. In 1975, it was 70 percent.[12] Now that Millennials are entering their forties, we can foresee that a larger share will exit their fertile years with no kids at all.

There are fewer families with children at home—not merely as a percentage, but in absolute terms. The number of families with children under eighteen years old, which steadily rose from 1950 until 2007, is now steadily sliding, down 3.3 million families, or 9 percent, from 2007 to 2020.[13]

Again, this isn't merely a story of women waiting longer to have babies. The share of women who are childless from age 30 to 34 nearly doubled from the 1970s to the 2010s. And the currently childless increasingly expect they will never have kids. In 2018, 37 percent of non-parents aged 18 to 49 considered themselves unlikely to ever have kids. By 2021, it was 44 percent.[14]

Importantly, the drop in baby-making is *not* mostly a white-people problem. Hispanic women, African American women, Native American women, and Asian women all had birthrates well below replacement in 2021,[15] with the most rapid drops among Hispanics.

"Hispanic women, who once had by far the highest fertility of any major racial or ethnic group, have had the single largest drop in fertility of any group, more than a third since 2007," the *New York Times* reported in 2021. "In Arizona, Hispanic women made up approximately 60 percent of the total decline in births in the state since 2007."[16] The number of black babies and toddlers living in the U.S. fell by 8 percent in the decade before the pandemic.[17]

The Baby Bust is, in part, an abortion rebound. After dropping for a generation, abortion rates began climbing nationwide in 2018, and the available data suggests they climbed even more throughout the pandemic. Abortions increased by 2 percent in 2019, even while pregnancies decreased, so this isn't a case of abortions increasing with the total number of pregnancies. Rather, put another way, the *abortion ratio*—the share of all pregnancies ending in abortion—increased by 2 percent.[18] In Michigan, the state that provides the most granular abortion data, the abortion ratio and the abortion rate (abortions per woman of childbearing age) have both been climbing since 2009, the year the Great Recession ended.[19]

The shifting demographics of abortion also push back against the Happy Planning Story. This isn't about "freedom of choice" saving high school girls from being "punished with a baby," in the words of President Barack Obama.[20] No, teenage abortions have been steadily falling since the 1980s, and there were 70 percent fewer teenage abortions in the U.S. in 2019 than in 1990. American women in their early twenties had 40 percent fewer abortions in 2019 as in 1990.

The abortion increase in the decade-plus following the Great Recession has occurred entirely among women in their thirties. Married women and mothers who already have children account for a growing share of abortions. In short: the babies who are *not* being born, increasingly, are being *not*-born to married women at or around age thirty.

Maybe those women just don't want children, critics argue. But the data doesn't bear that out. Abortion and childlessness are always presented as "a woman's choice," with the implications that this world of fewer babies is the world women want. But in general, the Baby Bust is a story of women not getting what they want.

Women Want Babies

This cannot be emphasized enough: the collapse in births is happening while women still say they want two or more children.

Pollsters and researchers have asked men and women, married and unmarried, parents and non-parents, different versions of the question, and the answers have changed over the years. But a basic pattern is clear: American women want more than two children on average.

"Women born in 1995–1999 wanted to have 2.1 children on average when they were 20–24 years old," an Ohio State University study in 2023 found, "essentially the same as the 2.2 children that women born in 1965–1969 wanted at the same age."[21]

"What is the ideal number of children for a family to have?" Gallup has asked since the 1930s. The sexual revolution and the advent of birth control knocked this average down from 3.5 to 2.5, but it has rebounded in recent years and hit 2.7 babies in 2023.[22]

This tells us something that might not be obvious depending on your social circles or your media diet: Americans generally think two to three kids is optimal, while Americans generally end up with fewer than two kids.

But if you want to limit the question to women of childbearing age, the General Social Survey allows you to do exactly that. The GSS asks, "What is the ideal number of children for a family to have?" Women ages 15 to 50, since the late 1970s, have given the same answers as the general public: about 2.5 babies per family.

In 2018, demographer Lyman Stone collected the results of every survey he could find about ideal family size and performed his own analysis of the GSS data and found that "every single estimate of ideal or desired fertility, including our hardcore minimum estimate from adjusted GSS data, is way above actual fertility."

This is true even for Millennials and Gen Z. When polled in their twenties, members of these two generations stated "on average, that they wanted to have at least two children," the *Wall Street Journal* reported in 2023, "just a fraction less than members of Generation X and the youngest baby boomers when they were surveyed at the same age."[23]

The *Journal* went on: "by the time women born in the late 1980s were in their early 30s, they had given birth, on average, to about one child less than they planned. That is roughly double the size of the shortfall for women born two decades earlier, and it is likely too large to be erased by a spurt of childbearing in their late 30s."

By any measure of what American women think is the ideal family size, they're getting less, and the gap is growing between the number of babies women want and the number they end up with.

The subtle differences in wording across polls reveals a nuance that's easy to miss. Some polls have asked women how many children they *intend* to have, while others ask how many they *expect* to have. These surveys, Stone has found, show that "intentions" and "expectations" generally fall short of "ideal" family size. On the average, women *want* more than 2 babies, *intend* slightly more than 2 babies, but end up with 1.7.

A small portion of women in their thirties are child-free by choice, according to a study in the *European Journal of Population*. This study found that the largest group of ultimately childless adults "consists of individuals who initially wanted to have children or at least did not definitely reject having children, but postponed family formation and ultimately remain childless for different reasons."[24]

That is, life got in the way.

There are a hundred reasons a woman might fall short of her own ideal number of children. Infertility is the most obvious. Divorce or never getting married are two more. This has happened throughout human history. The data suggests, however, that this group is increasing in number, which tells us that *our culture is increasingly hostile to family formation.*

The key nuance here is not only are American women not attaining their ideal, but a growing number are *choosing* not to attain their ideal. This may sound self-contradictory, but if you think about various aspects of our lives, we often *choose* to not attain our ideal, because we perceive that our *circumstances* are not ideal. My ideal home would have a wraparound porch and three stories above ground. Under current circumstances, including sky-high mortgage rates and my extended family and job being planted in the very expensive D.C. region, attaining my ideal would involve sacrifices that I am not willing to make, and so we will settle for something smaller.

American women are clearly making these sorts of compromises when it comes to family: even if their ideal is two or three kids, many know that the most they can really hope for is something less.

Nobody is promised their ideal life, of course, and we shouldn't fret that not everyone has a wraparound porch. But when Americans, as a rule, are falling short of their ideal in such a meaningful thing as *family*, it deserves our attention.

On family size, American women intend less than they want, and then they get even less than they intend. Both of these shortfalls reflect poorly on our culture, our economy, and our governance. Some of the shortfall can be explained by relationships, biology, and luck, but the fact is, many couples are lowering their expectations, and then missing even those lowered expectations due to societal factors. If couples see having a child, or another child, as simply too daunting, there is something deeply wrong.

Some will tell you that there is no problem here. Women now have more choice, and when given a choice, fewer people want to be parents because, so the story goes, parenting is the pits.

Parenting Is Hard

"Oh, come on, millennial women. Just look at us," pleaded *Washington Post* columnist Petula Dvorak, facetiously. "Frantic and apologizing, overwhelmed between staff meetings and gymnastics, shamed for bottle-feeding, booted for breast-feeding, passed over for promotions, denied on the day-care list—isn't this what you've always dreamed of?"[25]

"Since about the 1960s, we've had pretty clear evidence that being a parent doesn't make you happier than not having children," explains Professor Jennifer Glass of the University of Texas at Austin. Glass and others compiled all sorts of studies in which adults were asked how happy they are. They tried to control for various factors—such as income, age, and education—and they calculated that in the U.S., parents are 12.7 percent less happy than non-parents.[26]

Often, parenting is miserable. Never let anyone tell you otherwise.

I have on occasion shouted unrepeatable obscenities at children who were too innocent for a PG-13 movie, because I was overwhelmed with frustration and anger. I have also walked past my baby's nursery once, as she was being rushed to an intensive care unit—and wondered if I had the heart to take down the furnishings if she never came home.

Taking on another kid is taking on a burden of labor and worry unmatched in the rest of your life. Comedian Jim Gaffigan has offered a vivid description of having a fifth child: "Imagine you're drowning. And someone hands you a baby."

Raising kids is arduous and often terrifying. The "joy" of parenting is often deeply unhappy. Sure enough, for decades, the data suggested that parents are less happy than other adults. The childless don't change diapers. They go out to dinner when they want. They don't have irrational miniature humans screaming insane and logically impossible demands at them daily. As Isaac and Nicole like to say, the childless don't clean up vomit while watching *Teletubbies*. And they don't have anxiety about the safety or uncertain future of vulnerable people for whom they feel deep responsibility.

Of course parents are less happy, the reasoning goes.

Exhibit A in this account is typically a 2004 study by Nobel Prize–winning economist Daniel Kahneman. In a book titled *All Joy and No Fun*, author Jennifer Senior explained Kahneman's findings this way: "Child care ranked sixteenth in pleasurability out of nineteen activities."[27] If you have tried to get snow boots on a five-year-old or have sat through a "play" written on a summer afternoon by a seven-year-old, you probably wonder which three activities were less pleasurable.

Well, one of the things that bring less pleasure than parenting, according to this oft-cited study, is *work*. Another is *commuting*.

That changes the meaning of this study, now doesn't it?

The items on Kahneman's list that brought *more* pleasure than parenting included sex, eating, drinking, socializing, praying, and cooking.[28] Parenting, I grant, often interferes with these fun things. But the activities that brought more pleasure than parenting are almost all diversions or pastimes. Unless you are a minister or a chef, none of them is a calling or an occupation. If you filled your whole life with "relaxing" or spent twelve hours a day watching TV—not just on college football day, but seven days a week—do you think you would still find much pleasure in that?

Of all the activities in Kahneman's study, only two could form the foundation of a life and possibly provide meaning to the women interviewed: working and caring for kids. Of these two, caring for kids was considerably more enjoyable than paid work.

There's another telling detail in that study: Parents were asked how happy they were after interacting with different people. Interactions with friends, girlfriends, boyfriends, spouses, and siblings all brought more happiness than interactions with kids. That's no surprise, as interactions with kids are more likely by far to involve screaming or cleaning up bodily fluids. But get this: mothers in the study ranked time with their kids higher than time with their boss, coworkers, and clients.

"If the Kahneman study has a big social message," concluded Bryan Caplan in *Selfish Reasons to Have More Kids*, "it's not that kids are a disaster for happiness. It's that women enjoy taking care of their children more than working outside the home."[29] There's the hoary old joke in which a friend asks a man, "How's your wife?" and the man replies, "Compared to what?" Ask a parent "How are your kids?" and the most truthful answer might be "Compared to what? *Work?*"

So the whole "parenting makes you unhappy" story, which obviously has grains (some days, silos) of truth, has always been overblown. In fact, the "happiness gap" as recorded in past decades no longer exists, according to a 2015 study by economists Chris Herbst and John

Ifcher. "Parents are becoming happier over time relative to non-parents," they reported, after studying data sets of more than 100,000 American adults.[30]

In 2021, seventeen years after the Kahneman study, the Institute for Family Studies and the Wheatley Institute fielded a poll asking adults—both childful and child-free—about their lives. Do you find life lonely? Do you find it meaningful? Are you pretty happy? *Very* happy? On all of these scores—even considering the isolation of modern parenting—parents looked happier and more fulfilled by statistically significant margins.[31] Some of that happiness advantage for parents came from the fact that parents are more likely than non-parents to be married. But even isolating that variable by looking only at married folks, the result holds up: those with kids were happier than those without.

Kids Are Good for Your Health

I spoke with a woman named Cher and her husband, Ben, in Utah one day, as their four children played for at least fifteen minutes on an escalator. "The Baby Bust is a potted-plant boom," explained Cher, who worked in the floral industry.

If you buy a ficus from Kroger or Trader Joe's, you may be buying from Cher's family business. "The plant industry is booming, because it's human nature to want to care for and love something. Plants and pets are the new babies," as Cher put it. "It's kind of sad."

Community, belonging, and connection are three rapidly dwindling commodities in America today. Modern American life is alienating. On average, we know our neighbors less. We belong to fewer things. We are a more secular and disenchanted society, meaning we believe in less. Social trust is falling. Isolation is growing. Political polarization and radicalism are increasing.

Modernity "liberates" us by taking away our "scripts." Most of us, it turns out, can't pull off a lifelong improv act. Our culture expects a person more and more to handle life on his own, stripped of the support, guidance, expectations, and meaning traditionally provided by religion, community, and extended family. This supposedly "liberating" modernity makes life a lot harder. Alienation and loneliness make marriage harder and make parenting more daunting. They also make marriage and parenthood more crucial.

Herbst and Ifcher, in the study that showed the increasing happiness of American parents, found that "non-parents' happiness is declining absolutely." Their research suggests that "children appear to protect parents against social and economic forces that may be reducing happiness among non-parents." Those forces include the side effects of liberated modern life: "the decline in community and political involvement, growing disconnectedness from family and friends, and the growth in economic insecurity."[32]

Family has always been the best bulwark against alienation. It's not that marriage and parenthood free us from needing community support—quite the opposite, in fact. The work of marriage and parenthood requires community support more than almost any other undertaking. It takes a village, after all, to raise a child.

But it also takes children to make a village. "Families help keep neighborhoods stable," writes Will Austin, founder of the Boston Schools Fund. "As children move from early education into early adulthood, families are some of the most predictable long-term renters, taxpayers, and consumers. Whether you have children or not, kids make a neighborhood."[33]

Being a parent thrusts you into social institutions or occasions, sometimes against your will. You find yourself at a library story hour just for something to do with Tanner and Emily. You enroll your children in school or daycare. You end up talking to strangers because both of your kids are climbing on the same jungle gym. Then someone ropes you into coaching kindergarten basketball in the local rec league.

That is why, as Herbst and Ifcher put it, "parents have not experienced the growing social disconnectedness and economic insecurity to the same extent as non-parents." Early-twenty-first-century American alienation exacerbates loneliness for a million reasons, ranging from iPhones and social media to pandemics and drinking habits. That makes safeguards against loneliness, like marriage and children, all the more valuable.

Parents aren't the only ones who benefit from children. Children benefit from having other children around, and the best way to ensure your kids have playmates is to give them brothers and sisters. "A large household is associated with fewer mental problems in children," concluded a study out of Norway.[34] The effect was especially large on girls. When we recall that teenagers—especially teenage girls—in the U.S. are facing record amounts of depression in 2010s and 2020s,[35] we have to wonder whether the Baby Bust, which has given these girls and boys fewer brothers and sisters, is a contributor.

An only child is more prone to being a lonely child,[36] and people who experienced loneliness as children are more likely to feel lonely as adults.[37]

Even if you don't ever have kids, you should want your neighbors to have kids. "Parenthood changed me" is a cliché, but it's also corroborated by the research. Parents were less likely than non-parents to commit crimes, University of Chicago economists Maxim Massenkoff and Evan Rose found in a 2022 study.[38] That's no surprise. But the researchers found something very interesting: arrests of both men and women drop precipitously when they are expecting a child. As the authors put it, "pregnancy triggers sharp declines in arrests rivaling any known intervention, supporting the view that childbirth is a 'turning point' that reduces deviant behavior through social bonds."

Kids are not only the building blocks of tomorrow's society; they are the catalysts for today's society.

It turns out that all people—including non-parents—are *better* when kids are around. That was the finding of psychologists in the United Kingdom who conducted experiments and a public study on various main streets. They quizzed more than two thousand adults about how much they aspired to be helpful, generous, socially conscious, honest, forgiving, et cetera, alongside questions of how much they intended to pursue power, wealth, or influence.[39]

Before asking these questions, though, the researchers primed the subjects. Some of them were given tasks that got them thinking about kids—say, describing a day at school—and others were given prompts that were about adult life. Still others went in unprimed. These experiments consistently showed that these gentle prompts had a small but significant effect. Making adults think about kids makes adults a bit more helpful, generous, honest, and forgiving. It also makes them a bit less concerned with power, wealth, and influence.

The same study also did some street research: Do adults give more to charity when children are around? The researchers set up stands to ask for donations (for a charity that had nothing to do with children, by the way) on shopping streets. They recorded the donations per two-minute increments, and measured them against the number of children on the sidewalk in each two-minute block of time. More kids meant more donations, and this was true for parents and non-parents.

We become our best selves when little humans are underfoot—even when they're not our own. Put another way, a childless society is a meaner and sadder society.

Since this is a societal problem, not a personal one, it deserves a societal response. As a culture, we need to somehow abolish the Travel Team Trap, stop normalizing and demanding helicopter parenting, pave sidewalks, build more playgrounds, and make workplaces more family friendly. But the political debate these days focuses on the bottom line—the affordability question. So the question at hand now is this: If we want more babies as a society, should we subsidize families?

CHAPTER 7

Should Uncle Sam Subsidize
Mom and Dad?

E xpensive."
　　 Joshua, an eighteen-year-old black man in Ohio, was asked for a single word that popped into his mind when he thought of having children. *Expensive* was the word.

Joshua didn't have a full-time job yet. He was working a few gigs here and there but still relied on and lived with his parents. He was unsure about having kids, even though he knew he wanted kids. In fact, he regarded raising kids as "part of the American Dream"—he just believed he could never afford this part of the American Dream.

Raising kids costs too much these days is the standard explanation for America's Baby Bust. "We can't afford it" was Nicole's answer in Salt Lake City. This echoed what I heard from dozens of other Millennials while researching this book.

Joshua said only one thing could convince him to have kids: "Just having a lot of money, and being able to provide children with the best life they can have."

It's a reasonable and simple story: *I'd have kids if I could afford it, but I can't.* This implies a simple solution: *To make parenting more doable, the government should spend more providing free daycare, paid maternity leave, and other parental subsidies.* Is that simple story true? Are there economic problems we can actually fix in order to make parenting easier and more common?

It's complicated, it turns out. Some interventions help. Some don't. Ultimately, the data shows there's only so much government and money can do—which confirms once again that money doesn't really explain why Millennials and Gen Zers are avoiding marriage and baby-making.

Still, the questions of tax credits, paid leave, and childcare subsidies are at the forefront of every debate about the topic, and they're worth taking seriously.

Joshua was part of a focus group I organized to figure out why many young men are apprehensive about having kids. These men all dismissed the official cost estimates of having kids as too low (the U.S. Department of Agriculture, for instance, estimated, before the recent inflation, that a kid costs $250,000 to raise). The guys in our focus group didn't want to give their future children just the bare necessities—they wanted to make sure their kids had "the best."

Sure, these official estimates cover the cost of clothing and daycare, but what about building memories through family getaways or giving my kids the best chance to succeed by giving them music lessons and tutoring?

These men were not wrong that parenting has hidden costs. Personally, I was caught off guard by the immense quantity of *destruction* children bring about. In a four-week span, one of my sons lost his bike at a local playground, forgot his brand-new baseball bat and a glove at the ballfield, left my deluxe illustrated copy of *The Hobbit* out in the rain, soaked a flip phone in the local creek, and lost a scooter. Another son has a knack for unscrewing tiny pieces from his toys or my tools, losing that tiny piece, and thus rendering the whole thing useless. Such has been the fate of two telescopes, an electric tire inflator, a woodworking jig, and a deep fryer. (My "Never. Unscrew. Anything. Ever. Again!"

moment belongs with "No wire hangers ever!" from *Mommie Dearest* in the parenting hall of fame.)

I half joke that raising children inculcates the virtue of detachment. You learn not to love any physical belonging too much, because you know it might be destroyed any minute. More broadly, you come to think of everything you have—including your savings and future income—as the components of a massive sacrifice to be immolated on the altar of family.

Daycare is the most terrifying cost for would-be parents. "I did not have children," wrote liberal *Washington Post* columnist Monica Hesse about her late twenties and early thirties, "because day care where I live costs an average of $24,000 per year, and renting a two-bedroom apartment can cost upward of $30,000, and in my childbearing prime my salary ranged from $37,000 to $45,000."[1]

Millions of young adults want kids but aren't trying to have them yet; most of them cite insufficient funds as the reason why not. In a pre-COVID survey by financial institution SoFi, 60 percent of the *I-want-kids-but-not-yet* cadre said their savings were too low, and half said they wanted a higher salary before bringing new humans into this world.[2]

This is all reasonable, but once again, the *cost* of raising children can't explain the *decrease* in making children since 2007 or since 1980, because the cost of raising children hasn't really gone up. While that USDA estimate of the cost of raising a child has been going up, it has been going up slower than wages have. The estimated cost was a lower portion of wages in 2022 than at any other time since 1980, according to research by scholar Jeremy Horpedahl.[3]

The cost of college is blamed in two ways: young adults have too much student debt to start a family, and the cost of raising a kid "right" includes unfathomable tuition costs. The unfathomable sticker prices of college are also not real: basically nobody pays full tuition, and while list prices for tuition are skyrocketing, average tuition paid has been basically flat for twenty years, according to data from the College Board. In fact, the average tuition check in 2020 was lower than it was back in 2004.[4]

To be fair to the Millennials and Gen Zers, there is a way in which it's more expensive to raise kids today—but it's not about daycare or destruction of property. It's about the *opportunity cost* to having kids, which is greater because women today have greater opportunity to earn.

Women have always been more involved in the whole gestating-and-rearing-children process, and so they have always had more trade-offs to make between family and work. As women find it easier to make more money and build better careers, it becomes more "expensive" for them to take a step back or dial down their work for the sake of family. Greater economic and professional opportunity for women isn't a "problem to fix," in most common understandings of the phrase. Children and career will always compete for our time and attention, and not many people want to undo the economic gains made by women.

So, if we want to address the problem of "kids are too expensive," we're going to need to get creative. We have to study what has worked and what hasn't in order to better understand the nature of the family-affordability problem. Let's begin with a few of the areas in which Uncle Sam tips the scales against family: Social Security and taxes.

Family-Friendly Social Security

Social Security was conceived partly as a replacement of community bonds. "Where heretofore men had turned to neighbors for help and advice," President Franklin Delano Roosevelt said on the third anniversary of Social Security, "they now turned to Government." It was also understood as a replacement for the venerable notion of raising children who in turn care for us in our old age.

As one would expect, then, Social Security curbs baby-making. Comparing across many countries, three researchers writing in Cambridge University's *Journal of Demographic Economics* found that when a government ramps up its retirement benefits, birthrates fall. They noted that "an increase in the size of the Social Security system on the order of 10% of GDP is associated with a reduction in TFR of between 0.7 and 1.6 children."[5]

Social Security takes spending power away from people in their prime years, reducing both the ability and the incentives to raise children. Social Security, in its current state, is very anti-natal. Congress obviously won't shrink Social Security, but they could make it more fair to families.

One proposal in Congress would help new parents take time off work by tapping into Social Security early. Senator Marco Rubio proposed a bill to allow a new parent to take parental leave on Social Security's dime: upon the birth of a child, a parent could draw on three months of Social Security benefits, in exchange for postponing retirement benefits for six months. For married couples, one parent could give his or her months to the other parent. The net result would be six months of paid maternity leave at no fiscal cost to taxpayers or employers.

Here's another idea: because Social Security is funded by today's workers, maybe those who contributed more to today's working-age population by raising kids should get larger Social Security benefits. Think of it this way: Social Security determines your benefits based on your work history; it should also take your *parenting* history into account. Years spent as a full-time parent should be credited to Social Security work history. This would increase the retirement benefit for seniors who had spent many years as stay-at-home parents. Considering that women do a vast majority of unpaid child-rearing work that Social Security currently counts as nothing, this would be a massively feminist reform.

The alternative to making Social Security benefits more family friendly is making the Social Security taxes less family unfriendly. For two-thirds of taxpayers, payroll taxes take a bigger bite than income taxes.[6] The Social Security tax doesn't care if you're a bachelor whose entire income stays with you, or if you're a mom of four who feeds a small army on a single income. No matter your family situation, FICA (the Social Security payroll tax) takes 6 percent of your first dollar and every dollar up to about $165,000. A pro-family tax reform would fix that.

One parent—whether a single parent or one of two earners filing jointly—should be exempt from FICA up to the poverty line multiplied by his or her family size. The mother of four under this reform wouldn't pay Social Security taxes until about $35,500 in earnings.

Parents, by raising children, are keeping Social Security healthier and subsidizing the retirement of the childless. It's only fair to exempt parents from paying the Social Security tax until, at the very least, their family's basic needs are met.

Pro-Natal Tax Reform

The U.S. income tax code has plenty of family-friendly aspects, but it can still be reformed to be more family-friendly. Pro-family tax reform starts with eliminating taxes and tax breaks that make life more expensive for families.

The mortgage interest deduction is a good place to start. This tax break, a golden jewel of the real estate and banking lobbies, subsidizes houses in a way that drives up home prices. In the long run, for a homeowner, this is probably a wash, because the added cost he pays at purchase is recouped through the tax break and when he sells. In the short term, though, this distortion increases the cost of buying a first home, effectively forcing homeowners to tie up more of their capital in their house until they sell. In other words, the mortgage interest deduction shifts wealth from the family-building stage of life to the retirement stage of life. This is the opposite of pro-family. A pro-family reform would scrap the mortgage deduction. It might make sense to use that extra revenue to create a first-time homebuyer tax credit offsetting some of the purchase costs.

One dastardly up-front cost of buying a house is the "transfer tax" states and counties charge. This tax and others like it are not user fees that cover the government's record-keeping costs. This is the government acting as a sneaky middleman, pocketing a few grand because the buyer or seller might not notice a couple thousand dollars while making a transaction of a few hundred thousand. These wretched taxes add yet another barrier to entry to families trying to buy a home. Localities ought to repeal them, and state legislators should ban these government barriers to homeownership.

Marriage is also discouraged by parts of our tax code. The Earned Income Tax Credit and Child Tax Credit, for instance, both have marriage penalties—two adults see their credits shrink if they get married. These marriage penalties deter thousands of low-income mothers from getting married.[7] Since marriage is pro-child and pro-natal, abolishing these marriage penalties would help families form and grow.

Puppies Versus People

Those are the easy reforms, because they amount to removing government disincentives to family formation. The thornier question is whether government should *promote* family through the tax breaks or monetary benefits.

The first difficulty: it's not clear which "pro-family" benefits actually promote family. There's also a fierce debate over whether promoting family is a proper role of government.

When the Republican tax cut in 2017 expanded the Child Tax Credit to $2,000 per child, some free-marketeers cried foul. "In a free society, the government would be completely indifferent as to whether anyone had children or not," argued libertarian Laurence Vance at the Future of Freedom Foundation.[8]

"What will tax reform do for puppies?" young conservative opinion writer Adam O'Neal asked wryly in a *Wall Street Journal* op-ed during the 2017 tax cut debate. "Congress is preparing to maybe even double the Child Tax Credit. But what about couples who opted for dogs instead of children?"[9]

The *Wall Street Journal* writer wasn't seriously promoting a doggie tax credit. He was objecting to a child tax credit. The premise: raising children is a consumption choice—like raising cocker spaniels—and ought not be privileged by the tax code. "The Child Tax Credit," O'Neal wrote, "exists to transfer wealth to a preferred group (human families) from an undesirable one (childless superconsumers)." And a real conservative ought to "just to eliminate all the exemptions and credits and cut tax rates accordingly."

When it comes to subsidies for consumption, O'Neal's or Vance's argument holds: rather than give a tax carve-out for electric-car owners, just cut everyone's tax rates a tiny bit. But their argument against a child tax credit fails because it ignores a simple fact: children aren't consumption; children are humans.

Babies aren't objects. Babies are subjects. Objects—electric cars, homes, coffeemakers—are contingent goods. They are good insofar as they improve the lives of humans. Babies are the opposite of consumer goods. They are *that for the sake of which* we build societies, and thus governments, and thus tax codes. A tax code should favor toddlers over terriers or Teslas, because man-made law should favor people over nonpeople. A government should be partial toward children, because a government should be partial toward humans. Ours is a government *for the people*, not *for the puppies.*

That still leaves us with the question, though, of whether the government can effectively promote childbearing through spending or tax breaks.

Subsidizing Babies

"Pregnancy and childbirth are bloody, messy, flesh-tearing endeavors after which American women are discharged from the hospital with no codified support." This, along with the cost of daycare and rent, was columnist Monica Hesse's personal explanation in the op-ed pages of the *Washington Post* for why she never wanted to have a child in her "childbearing prime." This was also her sociological explanation for why the birthrate in the U.S. was plummeting: the lack of "codified support" for parents.

She is right that American parents are insufficiently supported, and that this makes women less eager to have babies. That's what this book is about. But here's the thing: Hesse, like many American mothers, had tons of support, as her subsequent parenting columns would lay out. First of all, she has a husband, which is the most important support that mothers need. Hesse also has her in-laws from whom she could spend months "mooching child care," as she put it.[10] Her employer gave her paid maternity leave, plus the freedom to work from home afterward.

It wasn't *support* the columnist claimed to lack, but "codified support." Sure enough, support is more valuable the more it is visible and reliable. But Hesse's column made it clear that she specifically meant *government support*.

"No free Finnish baby boxes containing all necessary baby gear," she explained. "No free British midwives, dropping by your home to check on the mental and physical well-being of the new parents. No free Swedish lactation consultants, no German hebammen. No mandated paid maternity leave as exists throughout Europe and in other countries like South Korea, Israel, Mexico, Chile."

The baby boxes and midwives aren't "free," of course. They are paid for by the Finnish and British governments. The proposition here is that more Americans would have more babies if the federal and state governments provided more subsidies, more taxpayer-funded support, and more government-mandated benefits.

You see this argument every time a conservative brings up the retreat from marriage or falling birthrates: *If parenthood matters to you, then pony up your tax dollars and pay for what parents need.*

It's certainly worth investigating. The U.S. government can do a lot of things, as can the governments of California, Delaware, Utah, and any other state. Can government spending help us start and grow families?

The People's Republic of China provides an instructive reminder of government's power to affect birthrates—and the limits of that power. China's Communist government curbed birthrates starting around the time of Paul Ehrlich's *Population Bomb*, and then accelerated this process in the 1980s with the introduction of its one-child policy: a combination of free birth control, penalties for having a second child, and forced sterilization and abortion.

Chinese women averaged more than 6 babies each in 1968. By 2000, that birthrate was down to 1.6.[11] (It was above 1 baby, because some party officials skirted the rules, some wealthy people simply paid the fines, and rural women were typically allowed a second child.) Beyond the horrors and injustices of its enforcement, this policy caused predictable problems: "They have too many men, too many old people, and too few young people," reporter Mei Fong told *National Geographic* in 2015. "They have this huge crushing demographic crisis as a result of the one-child policy. And if people don't start having more children, they're going to have a vastly diminished workforce to support a huge aging population."[12]

Beijing began to loosen the one-child policy in urban areas in 2013, at first allowing two children to parents who had no siblings. In 2016, the government allowed *anyone* to have two children. This became a three-child policy by 2021, and later that year, China abolished all of its curbs on family size. At the same time, the central and local governments began offering Birth Bonuses alongside the state-funded benefits one would expect in a socialist state.[13]

What followed? Continued collapse. Fewer babies were born in China each year following 2016, and the government's *official* birthrate remained below 1.7, though it's widely assumed that the real rate is closer to 1.2.[14] From nearly 18 million births in 2016, China dropped to 9.6 million in 2022.[15] In 2022, amid government efforts to boost births, China's population shrank by 1 million people.[16]

It seems that an autocratic government was able to *deter* its subjects from having more than one child, but when the government tried to reverse this policy and *encourage* baby-making, it failed.

That's a standard experience worldwide. Singapore, after decades of suppressing births, has spent twenty years subsidizing, encouraging, and begging people to have babies. Their birthrate is closer to 1 than to 2.[17]

European countries are the models that progressive critics point to when accusing the U.S. of being relatively unfriendly to families. Hesse, in her *Post* column, implied she would have had children earlier if the U.S. had the sort of "codified support" offered in countries like the United Kingdom, Finland, Sweden, and Germany.

But most of these social welfare states have lower birthrates than the U.S. does, fewer babies than women say they want, and steadily falling birthrates like ours. Whatever the virtues of British midwives, Swedish lactation consultants, and German *hebammen*, they aren't giving women the families they wish they had.

Some American conservatives view Hungary as a model of pro-family, pro-natal governance. Through marriage promotion, baby subsidies, and more, the Hungarian government has tried to reverse the birthrate slide—with mixed results. Birthrates did rebound from their 2011 trough of 1.23 to 1.55 right before the pandemic, but that simply mirrors the increase in neighboring Czechia (1.43 to 1.71) in those same years. Slovakia's birthrate climbed by the same 0.22 babies from its 2012 trough to 2019. Romania's prepandemic trough-to-peak saw a 0.23-baby increase.[18]

"Hungarian fertility rates performed no better than, indeed somewhat worse than, the fertility rates of nearby countries," noted demographer Lyman Stone, who concluded that Hungarian prime minister Viktor Orbán's pro-natal campaign "was a flop."[19] Those are harsh words, but it does seem that intensive pro-natal policies are not great at elevating birthrates up to what women want or even up to replacement. A lot of government interventions don't work at all.

That's not to say other family-friendly policy (including spending) cannot work. The French, for example, seem to have made modest but real—and maybe even lasting—improvements in their birthrates.

Piles of Cash

Year after year, France has the highest birthrate in Europe. Contrary to one popular simplistic explanation, that's not just because of immigration. Yes, France has plenty of immigrants, and yes, French immigrants are much more fecund than the native born. But if you don't factor in the immigrant population, France would still have the highest birthrate in all of Europe. Immigrant women in France averaged 2.6 babies each in 2017, while the native-born population averaged 1.8 babies.[20] That same year, the European average was 1.59 babies, and the second-most-fertile European country was Sweden at 1.78.

French fecundity, then, isn't mostly about Algerian or Moroccan immigrants. It's something about France. Katie and I had a particularly lovely evening in Montmartre once, and I can tell you that the trope of Paris being romantic is true. But a more material suspect in France's high-for-Europe birthrate is its simple—but aggressive—program of pro-family spending.

When French parents have a baby, they get a $950 Birth Bonus. (It's double for adoptions.) Then the government starts paying a monthly allowance of about $185. Those add up to about $7,600 over a child's first three years.

On top of that money comes government-paid and protected parental leave. French labor law guarantees the right of a new parent to suspend his or her employment contract for one to three years upon the birth of a child. France's social security system pays a "stay-at-home parent" benefit for up to one year for a first child and up to three years for younger siblings.

This massive system with multiple overlapping benefits ends up transferring huge sums of money to parents, particularly parents of young children. And here's the key: all of the benefits mentioned above come in the form of straight cash, which parents can spend how they please.

This seems to boost baby-making. Summing up the research on the effects of this cash, Stone wrote, "France's historically generous tax and benefit treatment of families contributes to its anomalously high birthrate for Europe." Poland also saw large birthrate increases in the years after instituting a large cash grant to parents.[21]

Hungary learned this same lesson, eventually. "After five years of trial and error," Stone wrote, "Hungary has found a policy that works: throwing a massive pile of no-strings-attached cash at families to help them have kids."

Spain had a universal child benefit from 2007 to 2010. Within months of its introduction, births increased—thanks to both fewer abortions and more conceptions, researchers found. When the government ended this benefit, abortions rose and conceptions fell.[22]

Here in the States, Alaska's state government brings in royalties from leasing out oil and gas drilling rights on state-owned land. These royalties are automatically kicked back to state residents, through the Alaska Permanent Fund. Because royalties vary, and thus the size of the APF varies, economists suspected this was a good natural experiment. One 2022 study found that years with larger APF payments are followed by years with higher birthrates in Alaska.[23]

Many want to take this sort of program national through a Universal Basic Income. Others push a benefit more targeted at parents. In 2021, a Democratic Congress and President Joe Biden increased the tax credit to $3,600 for each child under six and $3,000 for older children, paid out in twelve monthly installments regardless of work status. This Biden version was not really a tax credit, since it was delivered through a monthly check and was paid regardless of tax liability. It was a $300 or $250 monthly *child allowance*. This monthly allowance expired at the end of 2022. Many Democrats wanted to restore it, while others preferred childcare subsidies. A few Republicans, led by Senator Mitt Romney, pushed their own version of a child allowance or tax credit. The debate here is one worth following, and it is a contentious one.

Let's start with the $2,000 child tax credit created in the 2017 tax cut bill. While *Wall Street Journal* writers objected to the credit as some sort of social engineering scheme or special-interest tax break, it was really just a fairness measure. It's simply an acknowledgment that a family of five is actually five human beings, and thus needs more money than a single free agent.

Let's examine this by comparing two hypothetical households.

Imagine two homes in the suburbs. In one, a married couple lives with their three teenage children. Next door is a bachelor pad: five buddies who live together and hold jobs as baristas or Uber drivers.

If the married couple has a slightly higher-than-median income for a family of five, they earn about $125,000 after commuting and work-related expenses. In our bachelor pad next door, the roommates each net $25,000. These two households have the same aggregate take-home pay of $125,000. How are they treated at tax time?

In the bachelor pad, each roommate gets a $13,850 standard deduction, and so his taxable income is $11,150. This puts each bro in the 12 percent tax bracket with a federal income tax bill of $1,136 per dude. On aggregate, this household pays $5,680 to Uncle Sam at tax time.

The married couple next door gets a standard deduction of $27,700, which leaves a taxable income of $97,300. This puts them in the 22 percent tax bracket. Without the Child Tax Credit, their tax bill would be $12,646—more than twice the household tax bill of the bachelor pad next door, which has the same income and same number of people.

The $2,000-per-child tax credit brings the family of five down to a $6,646 tax bill—which is still a bit more than the dudes pay on aggregate. This illustrates that a child tax credit at around $2,000 is simply a way to take into account the fact that larger households need more income to achieve the same standard of living. (Prior to the 2017 tax bill, this reality was captured by the personal and dependent exemptions.)

That's the case defending the current credit. The next question is whether we should expand the credit—and if so, by how much. Common sense and fairness dictate some minor reforms and expansions. For starters, the credit should be adjusted for inflation, just as the standard deduction and the income tax brackets are.

Then we expand the credit in the ways proposed by Senators Mitt Romney and Steve Daines: other family benefits, such as the Child and Dependent Care Credit and the Earned Income Tax Credit for parents, should be abolished, and their value folded into making the Child Tax Credit a bit larger.

Then the tax credit should apply to all children, rather than cutting off kids the year they turn seventeen as it currently does. In fact, eighteen-year-old dependents should qualify as children for tax credit purposes until they finish high school.

On the other end of childhood, without changing the long-term price tag much, Congress could make the same credit more valuable by allowing parents to reap more of the credit's value within a child's first five years—basically transforming some of the tax credit into a Birth

Bonus. Why? For one thing, this is when many parents have their highest daycare expenses. Also, parents of young children tend to be younger themselves, and so they tend to earn less, which means shifting a tax credit forward to the parents' late twenties is basically just smoothing a family's income. Also, providing a bigger income bump for new parents creates a more tangible incentive.

None of these changes embraces the idea of a massive pile of cash. They just preserve the tax credit as it now stands, but reform it so that it makes a little more sense.

If we consider bigger expansions, though, thornier issues arise, along with many more objections—some more valid than others.

Conservatives have a bad habit of worrying too much about the undeserving poor spending money on the wrong things. This is excessively paternalistic and insufficiently merciful. If we want to support families, it will cost money. We can either put the government in the position of telling people what to spend money on, or we can give out money knowing that some of it will be frittered away.

A more legitimate concern from the right is that large child allowances could discourage work: paying people for nothing makes it easier for people not to have a job.

The first response to that objection: paying people *regardless* of whether they work is less anti-work than many federal welfare programs, which pay people *not to work*. A child allowance is different from those means-tested benefits, because starting a job doesn't decrease your child allowance in the way it could decrease your unemployment benefits, your disability benefits, or your food stamps. Republican child allowance proposals often aim to replace those other, work-discouraging (and marriage-discouraging) federal aid programs with a single unconditional check.

The second response: discouraging work isn't always bad. If a married couple gets a large child allowance and that helps one parent stay at home, or at least dial down to twenty hours a week, that's a good thing. Conservative policy scholars like Scott Winship, my colleague at the American Enterprise Institute, don't mind this outcome. Instead, they worry about the environments where *most* children are raised by a single mother: Appalachia, inner cities, collapsed and alienated former industrial towns. For all the family-level upsides of helping a mom stay home with her kids, there's a downside at the broader community level: children who grow up in an environment where the adults in the community don't work are not apt to absorb the notion that work is part of adulthood, the worry goes, and this is a driver of intergenerational poverty.

"[W]hile we should always want to reduce hardship," writes Winship, "reducing short-term poverty through unconditional cash transfers can come at the expense of expanding opportunity if those transfers incentivize behaviors that will impede children's upward mobility."[24]

Most important, the biggest impact of large piles of cash may not be to help couples expand their families. Rather, data suggests these payments could contribute to single motherhood: when the Alaska Permanent Fund payments increased, lifting birthrates along with them, that increase in birthrates was—statistically speaking—entirely due to unmarried childbearing.[25]

As you see, this theoretically simple solution—give parents piles of money—quickly becomes a complicated thicket.

Preventing child poverty is a basic moral duty. Alleviating the stresses on working-class and middle-class parents is good. A large child allowance does both of these things. It may also make it easier or more appealing for young adults to start families or increase the size of their families.

At the same time, a large child allowance could harm families by discouraging marriage or discouraging work. Children benefit from having married parents, and history has shown that children suffer if they are raised without a clear example of earned success. Intergenerational poverty is largely a story of children raised by single mothers without the models of present fathers or parents earning a living through stable work.

It's a devilish problem: direct material aid to parents can indirectly harm some of those parents, their children, and their children's children.

There's no perfect or simple answer here. Ideally, fathers would take responsibility for their children; ideally, couples would wait until marriage to conceive; ideally, civil society would provide all the benefits that families need without government having to step in. We do not live in an ideal world. We live in a fallen world, and so we need to search for the best of many flawed policies.

A good compromise—which maximizes aid to families while minimizing bad incentives—adds a modest work requirement to a modestly increased Child Tax Credit. Romney and Daines, in their 2022 bill, tried to strike exactly that balance. Their bill would create a $350 monthly allowance for young children (double the current tax credit) and a $250 monthly allowance for school-aged children (50 percent higher than at present). But Romney and Daines would not simply expand the Child Tax Credit as President Biden did in 2021. The Romney-Daines proposal would also require at least one parent to work: only parents with $10,000 or more in earnings would be eligible. (This is about one-fourth the median earnings for a high school graduate with no college experience.) This work requirement is also a marriage incentive, as it applies to the family unit, not to the individual. The proposal would also scrap marriage penalties and reduce earnings penalties that exist in other federal aid programs. And to avoid juicing inflation or the deficit, the Romney-Daines bill offsets its added costs by scrapping the tax deduction for state and local taxes—a deduction that overwhelmingly benefits high earners.

Would this solve our Baby Bust or eradicate child poverty? No. But it would probably address both issues without creating many of the unintended problems that current policy ignores.

Money Can't Buy Love

Ultimately, government spending can spur only modest increases in birthrates. And no amount of aid to parents will make America into a family-friendly country.

Hungary and France were able to apply slight upward pressure to their birthrates with massive spending, but neither country's birthrate is back up to replacement level. To get the U.S. to 2.1 babies per woman, according to the best estimates, it would take a child tax credit of about $5,300 per child per year, on top of all other benefits currently available to parents.[26]

Underneath all the data and social science is a stubborn fact: money, on its own, cannot increase family formation or family size. Marriage and having kids are far too intimate to be determined simply by cash. Money, of course, indirectly affects both, but being richer doesn't make people have more kids, and being poorer doesn't make people have fewer kids.

If the cost of child-rearing was really the primary obstacle, then child-rearing would become more common as people accumulated more money. But statistics indicate otherwise. High-income people in America have fewer kids than middle-class people, who in turn have fewer kids than poor people. For households earning more than $200,000 in 2017, the birthrate was under 44 babies per 1,000 women. For those earning between $50,000 and $100,000, it was about 52.5 babies. For those earning under $50,000, it was more like 60 babies per 1,000 women.[27] This is historically typical. "Where real incomes have risen fertility has declined," demographer Enid Charles wrote in 1934. "The more prosperous classes have the fewer children."

Millennials and Gen Zers told researchers for SoFi that they would have kids if their income or savings went up. But there are reasons to doubt this claim. That study showed that in every single income bracket, from $25,000 to $200,000, about 45 to 50 percent of young adults were choosing to delay kids. Those earning more than $200,000 were just as likely to be delaying children as those earning $50,000 to $100,000.[28]

The timing of our Baby Booms and Busts casts further doubt on the simple money story. Our current Baby Bust began with the Great Recession in 2008, yes, but the downward trend never stopped, even after the economy rebounded and climbed—often at record pace—for a decade from 2009 through 2020.

It's the same story throughout history. Birthrates in the U.S. fell from the end of World War I from 3.3 children per women until they bottomed out at 2.1 in 1932. The steepest part of this drop was in the early and mid-1920s, and this birthrate collapse happened in Europe, too, just as the economy was booming on both sides of the Atlantic. The "decline of fertility during the 1920s occurred in the face of economic prosperity and its downward course was not markedly accentuated by the depression," noted demographer Jan Van Bavel. "In fact, the downward drift of fertility . . . was actually . . . stabilized in the depths of the depression."[29]

Yes, in the short term, poor economic conditions like high unemployment (or in 2020 the closure of every Main Street in the world), drive down birthrates temporarily. But the general trends do not paint a picture of wealth causing more babies or poverty causing fewer.

"[T]he mid-term fertility trend, in contrast to the short-term ups-and-downs, was not governed at all by unemployment or by the growth of the economy," Van Bavel wrote about the interwar period. "For example, all countries exhibit declining fertility, during the 1920s, irrespective of the level of unemployment in industry and the growth of GDP per capita. And in all countries, the decline of fertility halted in the latter part of the 1930s, irrespective of the severity of the economic crisis."

Geography also undermines the "affordability" explanation for the Baby Bust. Together with two colleagues, economist Melissa Kearney studied changes in birthrate by state over time. They then compared those changes to other changes, such as the increase in childcare costs, or the increase in average student debt loads. Changes in "unaffordability" didn't really correlate with changing birthrates. States where student loan debts were growing the most didn't have bigger Baby Busts, and the places where childcare costs grew the most actually saw slightly smaller Baby Busts. Kearney's overall conclusion: "we are unable to identify a strong link between any specific policies or economic factors and the declining birth rates." Instead, she attributed falling birthrates to "*[s]hifting priorities* among more recent birth cohorts."[30]

A final telling detail: our Baby Busts in the 1920s and the 2000s started in the upper class and then spread to the middle class, and then to the poor.

Trickling down from the upper class to the middle class and below is a feature not of economic need, but of *cultural* trends. Our Baby Bust, as Kearney's findings suggest, looks less like a matter of economic necessity than a cultural phenomenon.

Again, this doesn't mean money is irrelevant. Sending piles of cash directly to parents seems to result in more children. But all experience suggests that money acts through an intermediary. Government benefits help people get the families they want only if those benefits in turn change the culture. That's because culture, more than politics and economics, determines how people live.

And the model here for building a family-friendly culture is not France or Sweden. It's Israel.

CHAPTER 8

Israel

The Fruitful Garden of the Wealthy World

At the end of the day in the middle of bustling, dense, and very modern Tel Aviv, ten or twelve families are relaxing around a small patch of green—one half grass and the other half Astroturf.

The young children run all over, while the parents (both moms and dads) sprawl on the grass with their babies.

The play of a few tutu-and-leotard-clad six-year-olds spills over into the capacious sidewalk patio of a coffee/ice cream/snack shop that seems like a mixture of a WaWa and a cafeteria.

Four dads on this patio relax over coffee and seltzer, one holding a baby, another sitting next to a stroller. Nobody, exactly, is watching the children.

This is "picking the kids up from school"—or from ballet, or from daycare—but without the agonizing car lines, and with a lot more hanging out.

I looked with envy on these parents, socializing, at ease, in the public square. I approached one dad to learn more about the institution anchoring this block—the Mina and Everard Goodman Educational Campus—and about the family friendliness of Tel Aviv, and Israel more broadly.

"Israelis have more children than the people in Europe or the U.S.," I began, before this dad, Ezra, cut me off.

"I know! It's horrible. It's not here in Tel Aviv," Ezra defended himself, pointing eastward toward Jerusalem while kicking a soccer ball back and forth with his four-year-old son. "It's the very religious in Jerusalem. The women there all have eight or nine kids," he said, pointing at my notebook, insisting I write this down, while his wife walked up and handed him their newborn.

What a country! I thought. *The anti-natal secular urban guys have two kids!*

And the idyllic scene on this fall evening was no accident. The city of Tel Aviv had hired architects to design such a family-friendly public square in the middle of a crowded neighborhood. The first piece of this yearslong project was a kindergarten, which is typical of development in Tel Aviv. In fact, Tel Aviv was built around a school building, which was the very first building erected back in 1909.

More than one hundred years later, Tel Aviv is still visibly a *family* city. Babies are everywhere—in the cafes, the restaurants, the theaters, the workplaces.

The story of Israel's extraordinarily high birthrate is much more interesting than the one Ezra tells. It's a story about how infrastructure, expectations, and ultimately culture can avert low birthrates in the modern, wealthy, highly educated Western world, and so it undermines the demographic tale told by the media and academia in the U.S.

American commentators tend to reduce the Baby Bust to either a simple cause or a simple solution. *Oh, a wealthy, educated society will always have fewer babies* is the simplistic explanation. *If you want to help couples have more kids, you need a bigger welfare state* is the simplistic solution.

Neither response is false, but both are totally inadequate, as Israel shows. Yes, women with more educational and professional opportunities have fewer children—all the demographic scholarship tells this story. Yes, you can help people have more kids by making poverty less of a threat—data from France, Alaska, and unemployment insurance programs establish that.

But no, this doesn't mean that we have to choose between gender equality and replacement-level fertility. And it doesn't mean that the solution to the Baby Bust is a massive welfare state.

Israel is a very educated population with high gender equality and below-average welfare spending. Yet Israel, by far, has the highest birthrate among wealthy countries.

Israel is about twice as fecund as Europe, and has many more babies per capita than the U.S.—and it's not just because of the ultra-Orthodox. Ezra is no exception: secular Jews in Israel have a birthrate higher than any country in Europe.

"Well, Israel is different," the response goes. Yes, of course it is. But if the question at hand is *why is America's birthrate below the replacement rate*, Israel's story gives the lie to the explanation of "all rich countries have birthrates that low." And when the question at hand is *how do we help Americans get the family sizes they want*, Israel pokes a huge hole in the claim that we mostly need much more government aid.

Yes, Israel is different. But we should be very precise in explaining *how* it is different. This, too, does not allow of a simplistic answer.

Israeli Numbers

First, the numbers:

Israel has a social welfare system with plenty of benefits targeted toward parents and children. Still, its welfare state is skimpy compared to the average wealthy country.

Israel spends 18.3 percent of its gross domestic product (GDP) on social spending, well below the 21.1 percent average of nations in the Organisation for Economic Co-operation and Development, a coalition of wealthy nations.[1] If you narrow it down to family benefits, Israel is also below the OECD average, spending less than 2.1 percent of GDP, compared to, for example, Sweden's 3.5 percent.[2]

Meanwhile, the factors that supposedly make low birthrates inevitable—widespread wealth and education—are very present in Israel. Israel might be the most educated country in the world. Its government spends 25 percent more on education than does the average wealthy country.[3] What's more, a majority of college graduates in Israel are women.

At the same time, Israel has a birthrate well above the replacement level, and far beyond anything any other wealthy country could dream of. Israeli women averaged 3.01 babies in 2019. The numbers dropped a bit during the pandemic, but still remained around 3.

Again, the birthrates by religious group are more complex than Ezra's standard account would suggest. Israeli Muslims historically had higher birthrates, but as of 2019, Muslims and Jews were both right around 3. Jews in Israel are very diverse, and so are their birthrates. Ultra-Orthodox Jews average more than 6 babies per woman. Other religious Jews have between 3 and 4 on average. Unsurprisingly, secular Jews have the lowest birthrates in Israel besides atheists. But here's the most interesting part: secular Jewish women are having 1.96 children each, higher than any European country.

There's something going on in Israel.

Menachem W. was pushing a double stroller down the ancient and confusing streets and alleys of Jerusalem's Old City when I intercepted him for an interview.

The sand-colored limestone paving this historic neighborhood can be treacherous for the small wheels of the standard stroller, and the little rain gullies in the middle can easily catch an edge. Menachem, his wife, and their two young children were running late for a family photo shoot outside the synagogue. It takes serious skill to maneuver these streets so fast, and he had no interest in slowing down to give an interview.

Luckily, I am a New Yorker, so I could keep pace. My question was this: Why do Israelis have so many babies? For Menachem, an Orthodox Jew in his late twenties, the answer was easy: "Religion."

Many secular Israelis agree. Tal, thirtysomething years old in Tel Aviv, described herself as not religious at all. She explained Israel's high birthrates this way: "First of all, I think it's a religious thing. Because religious Jewish people have more kids. And it's a—" Here Tal paused and asked her sister in Hebrew, "How do you say *mitzvah*?"

Tanya, Tal's younger sister, defined it for me: "It's like a thing that in God's eyes is a good thing to do."

Yes, Tal said, "It's like a *mitzvah* to have lots of babies."

Sure enough, "*Mitzvah!*" was the simple answer I got that morning from a Jerusalem shopkeeper named Oren, who is in his forties and a father of four. Wearing his kippah and enjoying a smoke break on a Sunday, he went on to explain, "In the Torah, it says we should have lots of babies."

The Hebrew word *mitzvah* is rich with history. Its most common usage is probably this religion-inflected idea of a "good deed." But its most literal meaning is "commandment." And any discussion of birthrates among Orthodox Jews is likely to begin with the word *mitzvah*. This is true in Israel, and it's true thousands of miles away, in suburban Maryland.

While it's true that *Israel is different*, it will be enlightening to visit some of the places in the U.S. that have echoes of Jerusalem.

America's Zion

"It's a commandment to be fruitful and multiply," Aravah Treister explained to me back in Kemp Mill. Treister and I were talking on the patio behind Kemp Mill Synagogue while dozens of families, many with four or five children, ate pizza, played carnival games, and celebrated the beginning of Purim.

Aravah was an only child. She and her husband, Yair, have five children. This is not abnormal at all here. I don't have demographic data on Kemp Mill, but having lived next door to this neighborhood for eight years, I can confidently say that families with four or five kids are far more common in Kemp Mill than in almost any other neighborhood in

America—and it is *certainly* much more fertile than the rest of Montgomery County.

If you want to find a place that, on the county level, makes lots of babies, head to Madison County, Idaho, which I visited because it had the most births per capita.[4] Here we see in better detail just how, as Menachem says, religion influences birthrates.

Stroll along College Avenue in Rexburg, Idaho, and one of the first things you'll notice is Mariah's Bridal Shop, followed a few doors down by Baby Swag, a boutique that sells used baby clothes. A block or two later, where College Avenue hits Main Street, you'll find Main Street Diamonds—they mostly deal in engagement rings. If you take a right on Main, there's a slightly higher-end bridal shop. The brand-new wedding venue is a few blocks away.

"That's why we call it 'BYU–I Do,'" explained the hostess at the Red Rabbit Grill down the road. She said the mattress store across Main Street does half of its business selling double and queen beds to undergrad newlyweds.

BYU–Idaho is the most important institution in Madison County, which is what makes Madison County, by some counts, the biggest exception to our Baby Bust. No county in America has more births per capita. Some of this advantage is due to the makeup of the adult population: Madison County is disproportionately made up of women of childbearing age. But what's more, these women—as the shops on College Avenue and Main Street indicate—get married and have babies much more than the average American woman. There are nearly twice as many births per woman of childbearing age in Madison County compared to the average U.S. county.[5]

So I went to Rexburg to see what was going on there.

The first two people I met were sophomores Hannah and Jonathan. "We just got married last week," they told me. Getting married in the first few weeks of your sophomore year wasn't abnormal, either. Rick Merrill, who owns Main Street Diamonds, told me that "the boys coming back from their mission" are his typical customers.

BYU–I students are almost all members of the Church of Jesus Christ of Latter-day Saints, and the men often serve a two-year mission after their freshman year. The mission is a rite of passage, and upon return, as twenty-one-year-old sophomores, these guys often pop the question.

What's happening in Rexburg, then, is simple: young Mormons are hitting the age when marriage and parenthood are normal in their subculture.

In most of twenty-first-century America, twenty-one is not the age to propose, nor is twenty-two the age to start having babies. The median age at first marriage in the U.S. is just about thirty for men, and around twenty-eight for women.[6] At "BYU–I Do," it's a live question whether you'll still be single by graduation.

There's no doubt that religious teaching plays a role here. I know of no religion where marriage and family formation play a more central role. Marriage in an LDS temple allows the couple to be sealed in marriage for eternity, the church teaches. The highest level of heaven, in the Latter-day Saints understanding, is reserved only for married people.[7]

The common thread from Jerusalem to Kemp Mill to Rexburg is religion—and this is what makes them exceptional in the twenty-first-century developed world. In fact, the entire Baby Bust after the Great Recession could be attributed to the decreasing religiosity of American adults.

Sociologists Sarah Hayford and S. Philip Morgan studied this question and found very strong correlations. Way back in 2001, before the Baby Bust, American women who called religion "very important" averaged 2.3 babies, while American women who called religion "not important at all" had 1.8 babies on average.[8]

Lyman Stone did a similar analysis in 2022 and found similar results. For instance, Catholics who attend Mass at least weekly were averaging nearly 2.6 babies, while the nonreligious were averaging half that many.[9]

My own family, and our social circle, are part of this story. My wife is one of eight children, and most of her siblings live in the D.C. area. At last count, our six kids have thirty cousins on Katie's side. The same demographics hold for our friends: when my daughter received the sacrament of Confirmation a few years back, we had about twelve families over to celebrate, and this meant about seventy-five kids. At the schools where we send our older children, families of twelve or more are not unheard-of.

These sprawling Catholic families, mostly Irish, Spanish, or Central American, mean sixteen-year-olds often learn to drive on twelve-passenger vans, as my wife did. It also means a single family can span more than a generation: my fourth-grade son has a classmate who is an uncle—of a sixth grader.

Our Catholic faith is absolutely the source of this extraordinary reproductivity. Many of these in-laws and friends go to Mass daily, and we mostly send our children to Catholic schools. For us, the very first *mitzvah* holds, and we take seriously the church's teaching that love, sex, marriage, and family formation are inseparable. As a result, we don't do the same sort of family planning the average twenty-first-century American might do.

Yet in the median Catholic parish, you don't see many families of eight or more. The average Catholic is as likely as any other American to use birth control. So there's something in addition to religion that explains the variations in birthrates among U.S. places and subcultures.

Yes, religiosity predicts fecundity, researchers have long known. The exact causal mechanism has been harder to nail down. Scholarship on religion and birthrates suggests, as one 2008 study put it, that "specific religious teachings about fertility-related behavior and institutional enforcement of these norms may be less important components of the relationship between religion and [birthrates]."[10]

For instance: Protestant denominations generally do not share Catholicism's teachings against contraception, yet, for more than a generation, there has been no real difference in birthrate between American Catholics and American Protestants.

The best clue to this puzzle is one I picked up back in Salt Lake City, in the Lower Avenues, the same neighborhood where I had met Isaac and Nicole (the couple who prefers the prospect of margaritas in Paris to the prospect of children) and had met the lady pushing a double stroller laden with two Chihuahuas. Just before that encounter, I had sat down with University of Utah demographer Natalie Gochnour, who told me something about Utah: it's not just Mormons who have lots of kids out there; Catholics in Utah have more kids than Catholics anywhere else.

If there's something about Mormonism that causes big families, the non-Mormons are catching it, too. The same is true in Israel, as we saw, because even the secular Jewish women there are having more babies than their counterparts elsewhere.

A Fertile Ecosystem

"God has nothing to do with our children-making decisions."

Tsachi spoke to me while pushing a stroller laden with kids down a Tel Aviv sidewalk. It was a few hours after my stroller-led conversation with Menachem over in Jerusalem. While Menachem and his wife hope to have many more kids, Tsachi said he and his wife are done at three—which is not surprising, given their secular worldview and their more secular city of residence.

What is surprising, compared to secular adults in the rest of the world, is that Tsachi has three children. But in Israel, this is perfectly normal.

"It's not a *mitzvah* for me," Tal in Tel Aviv told me. Tal also has three kids and also describes herself as totally secular. Tal's family and Tsachi's show us why secular Jews in Israel have a birthrate that approximates 2, which is higher than the U.S. or any country in Europe.

"Religion," which was Menachem's first explanation for Israel's fecundity, is therefore an inadequate one, but it nevertheless is central to the story. Just because Tsachi doesn't consult G-d in his family planning doesn't mean Judaism doesn't play a role. "We are a tribe," he explained. "You have to keep the tribe going," he said, smiling down on his children in the stroller.

You don't hear this sort of talk on American sidewalks. That's because most Americans don't have the history that the "Tribe" here has. From Pharaoh to Hitler, history has seen multiple credible efforts to eliminate Jews from the planet. If any people would reasonably see reproduction as necessary for survival, it would be the Jewish people.

Some Israelis put a finer point on it: in the Holocaust, Nazis killed six million Jews and reduced the Jewish population in the world by nearly 40 percent. Having one more child today can start to make up for one Jew killed in 1940. Some Israeli Jews aim for six children, one for each million killed.

What's more, Israel has historically been surrounded by enemies, and Hamas's murderous incursion in October 2023 was a hideous reminder of this.

Put these factors together—the religious, the tribal, and the national—and a clear explanation of Israel's exceptional birthrate begins to take shape. If you measured the effect on family culture of each of these factors, you still wouldn't have an adequate account of Israel's family friendliness. You need a more ecological view.

The best way to understand Israel's fruitfulness is to imagine a garden. The largest and oldest tree in the center is the tree of religion. Those who eat from this grand tree imbibe the teaching that children are a blessing, made in the image of God. They believe that a large family is beautiful in the eyes of God. They take to heart the first *mitzvah*, "be fruitful and multiply."

But there are other large trees in this garden. Jewish tribalism is another one. Zionism or Israeli nationalism is another large tree.

These three trees provide their own fruit, but they do much more than that. They create shade. They feed and provide homes for animals, who in turn fertilize the soil. They spawn an entire ecosystem, and that ecosystem is pro-child and pro-family.

"Here, children are much more trusting of strangers," Menachem explains in Jerusalem. Six-year-olds, for instance, "know they can't cross the street. They know they have to ask someone. You're always getting kids coming over and asking you to help them."

"There's an affection from bus drivers for little kids," is how Kemp Mill dad of six Moshe Litwack describes Israel's kid-friendly ecosystem.

The physical infrastructure also facilitates raising children. For instance, when a new housing development crops up, a kindergarten is typically one of the first things built. And while Israel's safety net is leaner than those of other developed countries, there *are* government benefits for parents, especially parents of young children. Parents in Israel do not bear any of the medical costs of having babies.

You can use this image of a fruitful garden to explain America's Zion, too. Family time receives extraordinary emphasis in the Church of Jesus Christ of Latter-day Saints. For instance, parents are encouraged to make one night a week (usually Monday) "Family Home Evening," reserved for prayer, dinner, and family activities. But spending time with family and neighbors isn't supposed to be a one-night-a-week thing for kids. So when research in recent decades suggested that homework had very little value for kids, it was natural that Utah schools were among the first to ban it.[11] BYU–Idaho is the only college I've visited that has "mothers lounges"—that is, nursing rooms—scattered around its classroom buildings for student use.

Ben and Cher from St. George, Utah, had triplets before having number four. They couldn't stop gushing about how family friendly their city is when I ran into them. The community is built to make it easy and affordable to entertain and educate your kids. "Great charter schools," Cher said. Kids ski for basically free at the local mountain. The city is rapidly expanding its bike trail network, which liberates kids and parents from Car Hell. It's easy to make camping and hiking your family vacations there, which makes life much more affordable than renting a beach house or staying in hotels in New York or Boston.

But the ecosystem isn't merely legal and physical infrastructure. Most of the ecosystem is the norms.

"It's normal" to have multiple kids, Tal explains outside the kindergarten in Tel Aviv. And it's normal to have them with you almost anywhere. At a shop called Pizza and Beer, in Tel Aviv's Dizengoff Square at 7 p.m. on a Sunday, you see little children. Slightly older children from two families sit at a large table at the sort of restaurant that, in the U.S., would be considered too nice for children.

Two middle school–aged girls walk laps and chat a couple of hours after dark around Dizengoff Fountain. In the Old City of Jerusalem, children as young as five walk themselves to school. Being a parent is easier here, because free-range parenting is more accepted. As Ilan in the Golan Heights put it—a bit inartfully—"You don't have to take care of your children."

A different man named Ezra from Tel Aviv, more pro-natal in his outlook, had his first child in his late forties. Now he's fifty, and his wife is expecting twins. "People here *like* children," he told me as his three-year-old son climbed up and down a stool in a crowded coffee shop. "Other people have kids, so it's normal."

When other people have kids, having kids helps your social life, or at least doesn't harm it as much as it might in New York or London.

And here's a fact about Israel that's probably worth more than any pro-family government benefit in Sweden: about 70 percent of Israeli parents get help from grandma or grandpa in caring for the kids—that's about twice the European average.[12]

Even if you don't eat from the trees of religion, nationalism, or tribe, you still live in a pro-child ecosystem—the norms, the expectations, and the infrastructure—those trees have created.

In the U.S., different parents have different experiences on this front. This came clear to me one Mother's Day, when it's a tradition for journalists to attack or mock the observance. One journalist-mom summed up the day thus: "Do a ridiculous amount of work with almost no societal support . . . here's a card and brunch."[13] My first thought was that in my own world, and in Kemp Mill, and at BYU–Idaho, the mothers have plenty of societal support for their ridiculous amount of work. In these religious subcultures, in these lively, fecund gardens, mothers are less likely to feel like they're going it alone.

But there's a pro-family force in these subcultures that is more elemental than the social infrastructure fostered by religion, and certainly less conscious than acceptance of dogma. Maybe there is a simpler metaphor than the garden to describe this dynamic; maybe it's like a virus.

Pregnancy Is Contagious

"It's in the air," is how Professor Gochnour put it from her office in Salt Lake City.

"Most people that I know in our age group have three or four," Ava told me during Purim festivities in Kemp Mill. "And then there's another group, and they all have five, and they're all friends with each other, and *five is a great number*. Five is just what they do."

For all the surveys and multivariate regression analyses that try to tease out what aspects of religiosity *cause* bigger families, Ava's description may be the best: "They're all friends with each other, and . . . five is just what they do."

At a birthday party for a kid in our parochial school years back, a couple of moms approached me and asked a question that clearly had been a topic of conversation in the St. Andrew's parking lot: "The five or six big families at St. A's on a given Sunday, do you all already know each other or something?"

I stumbled through an answer ("*Well, Katie did go to high school with Paula, and I think my brother-in-law went to college with Tim and Lori . . .*") before I settled on a simpler answer: "Basically, yes. Most of the families showing up to eight thirty Mass in Catholic Assault Vehicles"—that's what we call the twelve- or fifteen-passenger vans many of our friends drive—"are our friends, and their kids are friends with our kids."

Only after the party did I consider what was behind the question: *Are you guys some sort of fertility cult? Is this a competition?*

No cult. No competition. But there is causality going in both directions. Maybe we're friends because we have a key thing in common—a ton of kids. But we probably also have more kids than we otherwise would *because* we are close friends. The slightly older families showed us it was possible (not easy) to have a fourth, then a fifth, and so on. We saw how their oldest girls became second moms. We hired their oldest boys to mow our lawn, which in turn made lawn mowing more desirable to our own sons (for a couple of summers at least).

But more than any lessons we consciously learned, we all sort of absorbed a spirit: *Having a baby every eighteen to twenty-four months for a decade or more is something people do.* Needless to say, in most of the U.S.—including at most Catholic parishes and Jewish synagogues—having five or more kids is simply not something that is done. Less than one-half of one percent of U.S. households has five or more children at home.[14]

Those big families in turn lead to more big families down the line. My children by age twelve have all cradled babies to sleep, changed diapers, and mixed a bottle of formula. Whether caring for a younger sibling or cousin, babysitting within our friend circle, or just hanging around a backyard barbecue or Sunday Mass, our children grow up surrounded by babies.

Look at it this way: in my social circles, more than 80 percent of children have a younger sibling, and most of them have *multiple* younger siblings. That's not true in most of America.

But can the pregnancy bug spread outside one's social circles? In Israel, it seems it does. Menachem, the Orthodox dad in Jerusalem, gives his fellow Orthodox Jews credit for the bigger secular families in Israel. "It's not so foreign to them," he says. "You can see everyone else walking around with ten, you look at them like they're crazy. But think 'I can have three.'"

"There is an element of contagiousness," Yair Treister admits when I ask him why Kemp Mill had so many families, like his, with five children. "We live in these tight-knit communities where your neighbors are all having them. I guess a lot of women when they see babies, they get that urge."

Yair *exists* because of that contagion. When he was born, his sister was already thirteen years old and his brother was ten. His parents, before Yair came into the picture, had the standard American family: mom, dad, daughter, son. But then Mr. and Mrs. Treister moved. "They weren't planning on having any more kids," Yair explained, "but when they moved to Israel, everyone was having them, and . . ." He gestures, as if to say, *And so here I am, and my five kids, too!*

The contagion works the other way. At least a dozen times, I've spoken to immigrants to the U.S. who, upon learning I have six kids, expressed deep joy for me—tinged with sadness. "That's great. I always wanted a lot of kids, but when we moved here, we felt that to fit in in America we couldn't have more than two kids." *It simply isn't done*, these men and women concluded, *so we won't do it*.

Where big families become normal, as in Israel, the culture and the infrastructure adapt to accommodate those big families, which in turn makes big families more normal. When there are lots of kids running around the neighborhood, it makes it safer to let your kids run around the neighborhood, too. Here you see a typical second-order effect of religiosity in Kemp Mill. Religious families have more kids, which means more kids in the streets, which makes it easier to have more kids. Likewise, the religious families of Kemp Mill have more homeschoolers and more stay-at-home mothers, which means more eyes on the street.

Desire, Morality, and Culture

There's more to the contagion than norms and infrastructure. There's also values and morality.

"The mechanisms connecting religion and fertility are not clear," sociologists Sarah Hayford and S. Philip Morgan wrote. The two set out to parse just what it is about religious people in the U.S. that makes them more likely to have a baby or a handful of babies.[15]

Hayford and Morgan attempted to tease out of the data the *causes*. Very religious women had more babies, but this wasn't a result of more unwanted pregnancies carried to term or even of getting married younger, they found. The average age at first birth was actually slightly younger among the nonreligious at the time of this study. The biggest difference was what sociologists call "desired fertility." Religious women were having more babies because religious women *wanted* more babies.

The next question was, *why* do religious women want more babies? As with any "why?" you could ask, you'll get a thousand different answers. Part of it is contagion: people surrounded by bigger families tend to want bigger families. But Hayford and Morgan found that half of the difference in birthrate was explained by attitudes toward family and sexuality.

Religious women are more likely to value child-rearing (by both dads and moms) over career. Religious women are more likely to disapprove of premarital cohabitation and divorce. Religion, the sociologists found, makes women desire more kids mostly because religious people are more likely to hold pro-family views.

It should be obvious that one's views on premarital sex, divorce, and the importance of family over work are all spread socially. Our friends', families', neighbors', and colleagues' views on these issues will help shape our own views. Living in a very fecund community can cause people to want—and thus have—more babies.

As demographers put it, "People's demographic decision-making . . . is embedded in regional cultural contexts where fertility-related norms define whether individuals should or should not follow certain behaviors and provide 'cultural timetables,' on when specific behaviors should take place."[16]

Our low and falling birthrate tells us that in most of America, the "cultural context" is one in which the norms discourage, rather than support, baby-making.

What does this mean for efforts to become more pro-family and reverse our Baby Bust? The average American commentator prescribes something like "be more like Sweden." That's inadequate, but at least it sounds like a plausible course of action: *increase the welfare state.*

You can't so easily tell America to "be more like Israel." But you can begin to see that policy and economics are not the primary determinants of birthrates. No economic reality will restore our desire to build families or the belief that it's doable. No policy suite will reverse our Baby Bust. It's not even as straightforward as *religion*, either. It's something broader. It's *culture.* Our culture will need to change.

For this reason, cultural institutions—specifically religious institutions—will need to take the lead on making America more family friendly. Churches, local schools, employers, nonprofits, Little Leagues, and community centers can't pass the obligation off to state and federal government.

All the countries that have deployed subsidies, free daycare, or other policy fixes have failed to pull their birthrate above replacement. Some demographers see it as a law of nature that once you fall below replacement rate, you never come back up above that line. For the most part, that's true, and it's no surprise.

Georgia is the one country to fall well below replacement and then come back above it. How did this small country go from a birthrate of 1.6 in the early 2000s, behind its neighbors Armenia and Azerbaijan, to 2.2 in 2016, well ahead of its neighboring countries?

The explanation may come down to one man. Patriarch Ilia II of the Georgian Orthodox Church in 2007 announced that he would personally baptize every third, fourth, or higher-order child born to a married Orthodox couple in Georgia.

This jump-started baby-making in Georgia, especially third and higher-order children. And, unlike the government subsidies in places like France and Alaska, this stimulus was followed by an increase in *married* births, with no effect on unmarried births.[17]

Other religions may not have a charismatic beloved leader like Ilia II, but certainly every religious entity should be asking what it can do to reverse the Baby Bust.

If your ranks are shrinking, and there are no young people in your pews or on your membership rolls, don't curse our demographics—fix something. Churches, synagogues, and mosques, along with religious schools, in particular, should ask what they can do to make it easier and more attractive to have babies.

Start with material aid. Everybody in your congregation who has a baby should receive from the congregation a baby box, a bit like the ones Sweden's government gives out. The baby box should have diapers, bottles, a pacifier, onesies, and parenting pamphlets. It should also have spiritual books directed at new parents. As a Catholic, I'd include a crucifix and an image of the Blessed Virgin Mary for the nursery wall. And every wealthy congregation that does this should partner with a poor congregation to provide baby boxes to those mothers, too.

Many churches, synagogues, and mosques provide daycare and children's services during weekly services. Others provide a cry room

be happy in this lifetime," he said. "And we sort of came to the agreement that authenticity was the release from the shackles of fame." The Smiths' bottom line: "Marriage for us can't be a prison."

Monogamy is a prison, and its rejection is liberating authenticity. Although this belief is most eloquently espoused by Marxists like Sophie Lewis (author of *Abolish the Family* and *Full Surrogacy Now: Feminism Against Family*), it's actually a perfect expression of something that's not quite Marxism: the mindset that sees autonomy as the highest good, tradition or constraint as obstacles to happiness and justice, and the best sort of relations as transactional ones explicitly consented to.

As former New York City mayor Bill de Blasio put it in the *New York Times* interview announcing his separation/open marriage, "avoid attachments."[30]

All of these arguments trickle into popular morality. Most Americans don't see marriage as an important prerequisite to having kids, and the minority that does believe it is shrinking—down to 29 percent in 2020.[31] Only about half of Americans say it is always wrong for a married woman to have an affair (slightly more say it is wrong for a man to cheat on his wife).[32]

"I reckon if I ever find a girl who keeps me from thinking about other girls, I may consider it," Jesse says of marriage, as he mixes me a Sazerac. But he doesn't think that's going to happen.

Marriage, which used to be the centerpiece of adult life, is now another *if-you're-into-that-sort-of-thing* thing. It's a lifestyle choice, and not one—many argue—that ought to be privileged over other lifestyle choices.

Though some aren't even that tolerant of marriage.

Family abolitionists write that the old system of a mother and father bound to one another and their offspring by duty and love ought to be replaced by "the classless poly-maternal commune." The nuclear family headed by a married mother and father, Sophie Lewis maintains, is "an anti-queer factory for producing productive workers, rife with power asymmetries and violence."[33]

Most don't go that far, but a ubiquitous argument these days is not merely that Will and Jada are right to break the bonds of fidelity within their own marriage, but that marriage itself is an oppressive institution.

Marriage is sexist and racist, *Teen Vogue* explained.[34] "Historically, it has been a fundamental site of women's oppression," writes political philosopher Clare Chambers. "Currently, it is associated with the gendered division of labour. . . . Symbolically, the white wedding asserts that women's ultimate dream and purpose is to marry, and remains replete with sexist imagery."[35]

You cannot dismantle the patriarchy, the argument goes, until you dismantle marriage.

While Sophie Lewis, Jada Smith, Bill de Blasio, and bartender Jesse celebrate these trends, they haven't been good for relationships, sex, or family formation. The retreat from marriage is arguably the most important part of both our sex recession and our Baby Bust. But that's not the only way the sexual revolution has resulted in less sex.

Sexless Among the Ruins

My wife has prohibited any illustrative personal anecdotes for this section, so I will have to lead with bare facts: married people actually have more sex than do single people.

Unmarried adults under age thirty-five are seventeen times more likely to be sexless than are married people, and the married are 33 percent more likely to have sex at least once a week.[36] Contrary to the wry jokes at a bachelor party, the retreat from marriage on net yields a retreat from sex. If Will Smith is right that monogamous marriage is a prison, at least you get regular conjugal visits.

But what about the freedom of casual sex? Shouldn't that make up for the decrease in marriage? The data shows otherwise: young unmarried Millennials have less sex than Gen X did. Millennials' celibacy may not be *despite* our wall-less, only-one-rule sexual landscape, but *because* of it.

Recall that high schoolers date less today than they used to. Millennial adults date less than their elders did.[37] Why? Just ask them:

almost half of women say a date has pressured them to have sex, while one-third of women say a date has touched them in a way that made them feel uncomfortable.[38] Young women date less, perhaps, because dating these days implies sex.

"[W]ith sex generally understood to always be on the table and the etiquette around it unclear, genuinely low-stakes, positive encounters feel more out of reach," Emba writes. If the threshold for a date rises to equal the threshold for sex, a lot more guys and gals are going to be alone with Netflix on a Friday night. If more dates end in sex, fewer weeks will end with dates.

It gets worse. With all taboos abolished and porn doing an increasing share of young men's sex ed, sex itself—especially with a casual acquaintance or a stranger—is also getting scarier. This all makes the idea of accepting a date riskier. As sex researcher Debby Herbenick put it to the *Atlantic*'s Kate Julian, "If you are a young woman, and you're having sex and somebody tries to choke you, I just don't know if you'd want to go back for more right away."

Now swing around and try to behold this scene from the perspective of young men. They read in the *New York Times* that the smart Millennial way to date is to "have a sex interview with a person to see if they want to invest in a first date."[39] They believe it is progressive to have no rules beyond *consent*. They are afraid of being "possessive" or controlling by pursuing a serious relationship. And they also know that simply asking a girl out can be taken as "an unwanted sexual advance."

Fewer rules, norms, roles, and expectations mean more fear and apprehension. One man Julian interviewed had reentered the dating scene in 2014 after a lengthy hiatus and learned that "hitting on someone in person had, in a short period of time, gone from normal behavior to borderline creepy."

A sizable minority of adults under thirty—about 1 in 6 according to a recent poll—believe that asking a girl out is inappropriate. A man who knows this will hesitate to ask a girl out. As a result, most men (about 2 in 3 men under fifty) say that concern over sexual harassment has made it harder for men to know how to behave on a date or if pursuing a date.

The result is paralysis. "Men in their twenties are terrified," a New York City therapist told Emba. "These guys are just . . . not flirting, not even asking anyone out—not doing anything," another woman said. "They're just paralyzed with fear."[40]

Is a guy really going to ask Sarah from his softball team to dinner or Felicia from accounting to a musical if simply asking the question could be construed as a sexual proposition and result in his social media shaming?

It was simpler and less confusing when the norm was that a first date was a first date, and that sex wasn't an option. In that simpler world, we got more babies.

Less Marriage = Fewer Babies

On our wedding day, Katie was a month shy of her twenty-fifth birthday. Believe it or not, this was normal: twenty-five-ish was average for an American bride back in 2006.[41] By 2019, an American woman's average age at first marriage had climbed to twenty-eight. It was in these same years that the U.S. birthrate fell from 2.1 to 1.7.

Later marriages mean shrinking families. In a given society at a given time, the later the average age at first marriage, the lower the birthrate. How strong is the effect? One model found that in wealthy countries, an average marriage age of 24 predicted a birthrate of 1.8, while an average marriage age of 30 predicted a 1.55 birthrate. That quarter of a baby is most of the distance between the 1.7 birthrate in the U.S. today and the replacement rate of 2.1. Put another way, the drop in the birthrate since 2009 can mostly be explained by the delay in marriage.

When a woman gets married, the odds of her becoming a mom in given year increases fivefold.[42] Asked why they don't have children, adults' No. 2 answer is that they don't have a partner. One in three childless adults aged 20 to 45 cited this reason. The only reason cited more was the desire for more leisure time. Partnerlessness—chosen and unchosen—was a bigger reason than childcare affordability or simply not wanting kids.[43]

The Baby Bust is largely a matrimony drought.

Like the other cultural shifts that are bound up with our aversion to parenthood, the retreat from marriage is broadly harmful, even beyond its downward pressure on birthrates. The sex recession is the fruit of sexual confusion and fear stemming from sexual deregulation. It is likewise the fruit of the retreat from marriage.

The retreat from marriage, in turn, is connected to a growing population of men who feel pointless and a growing population of women who feel used and undervalued. Cultural alienation contributes to drug use, alcohol abuse, loneliness, political polarization, extremism, gang violence, and racism. Places with less marriage and more divorce are places with more of these cultural pathologies.

Policymakers or commentators who try to address our drug, violence, political, or racial problems without addressing falling marriage rates are spinning their wheels. It's unpopular to say that monogamous lifelong marriage is a necessary pillar of civilization and a key element in a happy life for most people. But it's true.

That NIH study fretting about the "historically underserved" population of swingers and people in open relationships found lots of data about such "consensually nonmonogamous partnerships" as well as "nonconsensual nonmonagamy" (a clinical term for infidelity, which has earned the acronym NCNM). One thing they found: "Participants in open relationships reported . . . lower relationship satisfaction than monogamous participants. NCNM participants reported more HIV testing and lower satisfaction."[44]

In other words, nonmonogamy means nonhappiness. Married adults are happier than unmarried adults, a study in summer 2021 found. Married adults with kids were the most likely to report being happy, and the most likely to be "very happy."[45]

Children also benefit from having married parents. Economist Raj Chetty has found this repeatedly. Most recently, in a 2022 study, Chetty once again provided evidence that one of the biggest predictors of upward mobility—the likelihood of a child born poor rising out of poverty—is the share of children in an area being raised by married parents.[46]

Economic inequality has grown in recent years, and the reason is that family inequality has grown. College-educated Americans are more likely to get and stay married these days. That wasn't true in 1960. Stable marriages are good for family stability for a hundred reasons, and they are especially good for children.

Working-class women are more likely than wealthier women to be raising children alone—and that gap is growing. These children, raised by one parent or unmarried parents, are less likely to go to college and less likely to get married themselves. This all exacerbates inequality, as Melissa Kearney laid out in 2022 research.[47]

America's retreat from marriage thus perpetuates poverty and privilege. "Between 1980 and 2012," wrote economist Aparna Mathur, "median family income rose 30 percent for married parent families, versus just 14 percent for families with unmarried parents." Boys, in particular, suffer from being raised without their father present in the home. They do worse at school and are more likely to be caught up in crime.[48]

That's not a happy story.

An Unstable Equilibrium

So how, again, did the sexual revolution get us a sexual recession?

Like this:

The sexual revolution liberated sex from marriage, baby-making, and sacrificial love. Severing these connections reduced the incentive for men to commit to a relationship, which reduced and delayed marriage. More important, removing the guardrails around sex created a dating environment that was scary, harmful, and unpleasant for women, and ultimately terrifying or inaccessible for many men. This led to less dating, which in the long run exerted more downward pressure on marriage.

Finally, the sexual revolution's commodification of sex created alternative outlets of sexual energy, including porn—a force that in turn harmed boys and men and made dating and partnering more difficult for them.

Less dating and less marriage naturally yielded less sex. "We've gone from being penned in to being free to roam," writes Emba. "But in the open field that now rolls out before us, everyone feels a bit . . . lost."[49]

Our sexually liberated society became a barren landscape. Getting rid of all the rules, the guilt, the shame, the taboos, and the norms temporarily thrust us into a sexual Wild West, but in the end, we found ourselves in a sexless desert.

Maybe those old rules, taboos, and guiderails weren't anti-sex forces after all. In a world with rough gender equality and a healthy disdain for sexual abuse, there may be only two possible equilibria: the porn-and-sexlessness equilibrium, and the judgment-and-family equilibrium. Bacchanalia can only be a transition phase.

The sex recession is part of a broader pathology in our culture, just as the sexual revolution was born out of a broader philosophy. The post-1960s understanding of ourselves—oriented toward autonomy and averse to connection—courses through the veins of our culture. Our hyperindividualism has caused a relationship recession and a Baby Bust, because it has made our culture family unfriendly.

Despite all the signs of loneliness and alienation, we cling as a culture to autonomy and run from connection, in part because we fear that anything else is too controlling—even patriarchal.

CHAPTER 11

We Need a Family-Friendly Feminism

U.S. Birthrates Decline as the Rotten Fruits of Feminism Increase," writes conservative commentator Candace Owens.[1]

Left-wing feminist Jill Filipovic agrees: "Women Are Having Fewer Babies Because They Have More Choices," was the headline on her *New York Times* op-ed ascribing lower birthrates to "feminist cultural shifts, and better access to contraceptives."[2]

Owens, of course, intended this as a critique of feminism. Filipovic meant it as praise. Much of the media analysis of the Baby Bust agrees with the diagnosis.

The *Times* ran a large feature in 2018 headlined "Americans Are Having Fewer Babies. They Told Us Why." Reason No. 1 was female empowerment. "Now we know we have a choice," Jessica, age twenty-six, said. "Like an increasing number of people in her generation, she does not plan to have children," the *Times* explained. The story was illustrated with a photo of Jessica playing with her cat.[3]

If feminism truly deserves the credit (or blame) for the Baby Bust, and if we agree that the Baby Bust will impose real harms on our economy and culture, then we have a real quandary here: a choice between feminism and our demographic well-being.

To reverse our decline, according to this framework, we need less feminism. Faced with this argument, some feminists, like Filipovic, try to argue that there is no harm in our lower birthrates.

Other feminists reject this framework and offer a more nuanced rejoinder: *Yes, the Baby Bust is a problem. Yes, we need to reverse it. But no, the answer isn't less feminism—it's more.* Call it Feminist Fecundity: *More gender equality means higher birthrates.*

"Want more babies?" asked *Times* columnist Michelle Goldberg in 2018. "You need less patriarchy."[4]

"Feminism is the new natalism," British member of Parliament David Willets wrote in a 2004 manifesto that may be the origin of this movement. Willets and his allies base their argument in national-level correlations.

"The birthrate is low in Japan," a *Times* caption declared in 2021, "in part because of cultural factors, like rigid gender roles."[5] "Traditional Catholic societies such as Italy and Spain have fewest babies," wrote British feminist columnist Polly Toynbee. In these unfeminist societies, Toynbee wrote, "women are on strike, neither working nor bearing many children."[6]

And where birthrates are high?

"Countries that have had a feminist revolution have the highest birth rates," Willets wrote. Goldberg put it this way: "Developed countries that prioritize gender equality—including Sweden, Norway and France—have higher fertility rates than those that don't."

"There is nothing mysterious about the approach that is working in both France and Scandinavia," French journalist Anne Chemin explained. "It combines the idea of a modern family based on gender equality and powerful government policies."

Through what mechanism could feminism increase the birthrate? Goldberg explained: "In countries that support working mothers, like

Sweden, Denmark, Norway and France, birthrates are basically fine."[7] A headline in the *Guardian* put it this way: "France's baby boom secret: Get women into work and ditch rigid family norms." Polly Toynbee declared that on birthrates, "Sweden, with its universal childcare, comes [out on] top."

This Feminist Fecundity argument boils down to this: women will be able to achieve their desired family size when they can more easily achieve career goals. Giving women more education, hiring more women, promoting more women, and treating female employees equally to male employees is a start. Completing this revolution, though, involves changing "family norms."

Does Feminist Fecundity make sense? Could it work in the U.S.? The argument rests on a notion that researchers call the "Child Penalty."

The Child Penalty

The Child Penalty is a concept economists use to study the tension between home life and professional life. Women with children do less paid work than women without children, and they earn less, too. These gaps between mothers and non-mothers in (1) hours worked and (2) annual earnings are the two dimensions of the Child Penalty.

Feminist Fecundity argues that shrinking the Child Penalty is the key to reversing our demographic decline. Arrange society so that women don't have to sacrifice as much professionally in order to have a family, and you will get more family. If we can better understand the Child Penalty, economists hope, we will find the best path to Feminist Fecundity, which will make America family friendly.

Danish economist Henrik Kleven delved into "why child penalties are so large even in modern societies." Baby Boomers incurred a smaller Child Penalty than their parents did, but there has been no improvement since the 1990s. Kleven, like a hundred other economists, tried to root out what determines the Child Penalty. His contribution to the research was in exploring the geographical variance. He showed that "child penalties vary enormously over space."[8]

"[T]he earnings penalty ranges from 21% in Vermont to 61% in Utah." That is, in Vermont an average mother makes one-fifth less over the course of an average year than a non-mother of equivalent age and education. In Utah, that gap between the mother and non-mother is three times as big.

If you know anything about Utah and Vermont, you can probably guess what's going on here: the Child Penalty has something to do with the culture of a place. Societies with more "gender progressivity," as Kleven puts it, have lower Child Penalties. This explains why Child Penalties fell through the 1960s, '70s, and '80s—we were all becoming more feminist. It also explains why progressive, secular Vermont has a lower Child Penalty than conservative, religious Utah and culturally similar Idaho.

You could come up with a dozen ways to explain this variation. Maybe conservative, religious places have more sexist bosses, and so women face more discrimination in the workplace. Maybe progressive places are better at educating women and encouraging them to work. Maybe it's just more normal for women to stay at home for longer in some places, and so they earn a lot less in the end. Maybe some places make it easier for mothers to work. Also, in Vermont, being a mom typically means raising one or two kids and thus giving up only a few years of work, while in Utah, being a mom often means raising four or more kids, thus stepping out of full-time work for a decade or more.

Whatever the explanation, we have already hit a snag in the case that "feminism is the new natalism." The premise of Feminist Fecundity is that feminism and natalism go together—that eliminating the Child Penalty would give us more children. Yet Utah has one of the highest birthrates in the U.S., while also having the highest Child Penalty.

If the parts of America with high Child Penalties and low "gender progressivity" have higher birthrates, the Feminist Fecundity crowd has some explaining to do. As it turns out, they do have an explanation. It involves France and northern Europe, and it relies on a U-curve.

An Incomplete Feminist Revolution

Many stories in demographics involve a U-shaped curve. Here's the chart the Feminist Fecundity crowd would draw to explain the relationship between gender equity and birthrates.

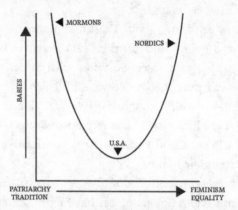

The left side of the chart is a high-patriarchy, high-birthrate culture. Slide to the right and you become more feminist and more equal. In this telling, some religious subcultures—such as the Mormons of Utah—are back in the patriarchal and fertile part of the curve, while most of the U.S. is in that childless valley in the middle.

Put another way, most of the U.S. has begun its feminist revolution, but hasn't completed it.

Fear not! The argument goes. *While increased economic opportunity and bodily autonomy have led women to have far fewer babies (and far fewer than they want), what we need to get back to a fecund society is a more complete feminist revolution!*

As described in the journal *Demographic Research,* "Very low fertility is the result of incoherence in the levels of gender equity in individually oriented social institutions and family-oriented social institutions."[9]

It's a helpful frame. Our workplaces and schools (the individually oriented places) have moved seriously toward gender equity. More women than men have college degrees, and more women than men are finishing high school. Multiple federal laws ban gender discrimination in pay and hiring. Major corporations talk about feminism and equity constantly, and they try their best to bring about equity in the workplace.

Yet despite the equality in inputs—education, company policies, government policies—nobody has achieved equity in outcomes. There is still a wage gap. Women are less likely than men to enter the labor market. The overwhelming majority of executives and partners are still men. The problem has bedeviled not only feminist theorists, but feminist employers, too.

One global consulting firm wanted to go full feminist in the mid-2010s, but they hadn't been able to pull it off. Despite their best egalitarian efforts, the firm found that 90 percent of partners were men.[10] Women who climbed up toward the top of their corporate ladder tended to jump off. The "biggest obstacle to women in joining the highest ranks of the business world is a lack of family-friendly policies," the firm concluded. So the bosses retained a few professors from the Gender Initiative at Harvard Business School to help them retain and promote women.

The Harvard crew began its interviews, but the trail didn't lead where the firm assumed it would. They didn't find that women received less support than their male counterparts. They didn't find that the firm lacked special accommodations for women. They did, however, find inegalitarian attitudes among employees—and not merely among the men. Both men and women at the firm admitted that what they expected from male colleagues differed from what they expected from female colleagues. These different expectations, the firm believed, surely fed into the very unequal balance in the partner ranks.

Here was the surprise: The most important expectations weren't about leadership style, office dynamics, or work product. They weren't about work at all. They were about *home*. While men were expected to lead in the workplace, women were expected to lead in the home. Men at the office late looked like hard workers, while women at the office late looked like shirkers.

"When I look at a female partner" and all of the late hours this entails, one female lawyer told the professors, "it does leak into my thinking: *How do I think she is as a mother, in addition to how do I think she is as a partner?* When I look at men, I don't think about what kind of father they are."

If the consulting firm was to achieve equity, and to revive the feminist revolution, it would have somehow to stamp out these deep-seated prejudices among both men and women, not only in management but also among the rank and file. In other words, this was less a problem of policy and once again, more a problem of *culture*—and not merely workplace culture.

Claudia Goldin, a Nobel laureate for her economic research on feminism, family, and work, has telling research here. The pay gap between women and men, she found, comes down almost entirely to women's greater demand for flexibility, which is rooted in women's greater domestic duties.[11] That is, the feminist revolution hasn't made a complete incursion into the home, leaving us with only partial gender equity— the valley in that U-curve.

This gets employers off the hook. The change we need, to get Feminist Fecundity, is in *the home*. So how can we change the home? Discourses on Feminist Fecundity include nods toward dads pulling their weight at home, but ultimately the goal here is not so much for men to do more, but for women to do *less* unpaid familial labor at home. Using the demographers' frame, if feminism is reaching only the individualistic parts of society, the feminist revolution requires making family life more individualistic. Mothers, the argument goes, need to shift more of their life into the open market, where we all pursue our own interests and exchange our labor for money.

That points us toward a very specific and common arrangement: both parents employed full time, paired with full-time professional childcare.

"What Do Moms Need?"

"Shrinking Families and the State of Motherhood—What Do Moms Need?" The 2022 newspaper column headlined with this question offered a simple answer: "safe, affordable child care."[12]

Making high-quality childcare more available and affordable would be good for many reasons. The biggest one: poor parents often have to rely on low-quality daycare centers that can be unsafe or unhappy for children. Some parents (mostly mothers) who desperately want to return to work feel they cannot because they can't find or afford decent childcare.

One study in Germany found that places with more affordable childcare had slightly higher birthrates.[13] Recall the *Guardian* headline: "France's Baby Boom Secret: Get Women into Work and Ditch Rigid Family Norms." The subheadline claimed, "Gender equality, pro-child policies and generous childcare provision are all bolstering French fertility rates rather than hindering them."[14] A United Nations report later that year concluded, "Of all the policies introduced over the years, provision of childcare services appears to be the most effective in encouraging families to have children and women to remain in the workforce."[15] *New York Times* correspondent Claire Cain Miller wrote a story about how government could boost birthrates and concluded, "Public child care is the only policy that has been shown to increase fertility in a lasting way, research shows, especially if its quality is high, and if it's available for children of all ages and covers a range of work hours."[16]

So here's the centerpiece of the Feminist Fecundity theory: *Become more like France and the Nordics by liberating women from their unfair share of domestic work, thus making it easier for women to enjoy the increased gender equality at the office, and you'll get more babies.*

How does the data bear this out? When British politician David Willets made that argument in 2004, he could point to the Nordic countries as evidence. So could feminist commentator Michelle Goldberg when she wrote on feminism as the new natalism in 2009. But in the following decade as this experiment played out, the numbers became less promising: Sweden, that poster child of Feminist Fecundity, saw its birthrate drop from 1.94 babies per woman in 2009 to 1.7 in 2019—no higher than the U.S. Denmark also dropped to 1.7. Norway plummeted from 1.98 babies per woman to 1.53. Baby-making in those three countries fell by nearly 14 percent, while the rest of Europe fell less than 4 percent. Meanwhile, conservative, traditionalist, Catholic Poland had a slightly higher fertility rate in 2019 than in 2009.[17]

Feminist Fecundity proved more elusive than some commentators and lawmakers assumed.

The False Promises of Universal Daycare

The Nordic Baby Bust in the decade before COVID undermines the Feminist Fecundity argument because promoting professional child-care in pursuit of gender equity doesn't seem to make lasting increases in the birthrate. Digging into the data reveals plenty of reasons why subsidized or "universal" daycare isn't the fix so many commentators and politicians think it is.

The single best study into pro-natal government spending was published in the *European Journal of Population* in 2013. Economist Angela Luci-Greulich and demographer Olivier Thévenon conducted a comprehensive study of data on birthrates, public spending, and demographics from eighteen wealthy countries, and ran regressions to try to isolate which factors actually might cause couples to have more babies.[18] The authors tout childcare subsidies as one of the most effec-tive pro-natal factors, but their numbers don't show that.[19]

According to their data, the three factors that seemed to juice birthrates were, from most to least statistically significant, (1) the gen-erosity of cash benefits to parents (such as a child allowance or child tax credit), (2) the generosity of a one-time Birth Bonus, and (3) the percentage of children under age three who were enrolled in daycare. Every layer you dig deeper, you find more and more problems with the assertion that daycare subsidies can help couples have more kids.

First off, daycare enrollment had *much* less impact than cash to parents did. The effect of straight cash was five times as great as the effect of daycare enrollment.

Second, while daycare *enrollment* was correlated with (small) birth-rate increases, *government spending* on childcare services showed no significant impact. This finding alone is enough to undermine the claim that government support for childcare could help women have more babies. But there's still another layer to dig into.

Some policies help women have babies earlier than they otherwise would, which is great. But that doesn't mean they help women have more babies overall or achieve their desired family size. That is, some policies speed up the *tempo* of births, but don't really increase the ultimate number of births. Luci-Greulich and Thévenon separated out that tempo effect and came up with a number they called "Tempo adjusted TFR," which should predict how many children a woman will end up with. And here's the final nail in the coffin of Feminist Fecundity: neither daycare spending nor daycare enrollment has a statistically significant effect on births, by this measure—and child allowances become even more powerful.

That is, the single most comprehensive study, across eighteen nations, couldn't detect that childcare significantly helped women have as many kids as they wanted. Childcare subsidies may still provide some benefit in some regards, but this study demolishes the claim that more mothers at work and more babies in daycare will yield higher birthrates.

And that UN study of France, reportedly finding that "provision of childcare services appears to be the most effective in encouraging families to have children"? Once again, a closer look at the study shows something else.

The UN authors reported that in France "63 per cent of children [ages 0–2] were cared for mainly by a parent (nearly always the mother)." The rest were mostly cared for by friends or family. Only 10 percent of under-3 French kids were in a daycare center in 2012, according to the UN. This is no surprise, given France's stay-at-home benefit—a significant monthly payment to working parents who opt out of the labor force at any time in their children's first three years. "The stay-at-home allowance," the UN reported, "clearly encourages childcare by mothers, given that 98 per cent of the beneficiaries are women."[20]

What about that *Guardian* article on France that repeatedly stated that cash didn't work as well as "childcare services for toddlers"? The article admitted in passing that of French children, "only 16% have a place in a day nursery." France, which supposedly shows the triumph of daycare subsidies, actually shows something else: when given subsidized high-quality childcare to enable work, and also cash to simply stay at home, French mothers opted to stay at home. French mothers also had more kids than mothers anywhere else in Europe. That tells us something about what sort of government spending actually empowers women.

Again: France pays parents—almost exclusively mothers—to stay at home for years, and France has the highest birthrate in the European Union.

Most important, while we're talking about giving women what they want, the lesson from France applies to the U.S.: only a small minority of women want to put their kids in daycare if they can avoid it. Two-thirds of U.S. mothers in a 2021 poll said that the best arrangement to care for children under five is for parents—with one or both sacrificing work—to be home caring for their kids. Only one in eight said that center-based childcare was optimal.[21]

These survey results cast in a different light the Feminist Fecundity argument that we need to "get women into work" and subsidize putting their kids in daycare. It's an odd sort of progress that pulls mothers away from what they want. It's an odd feminism that tries to tell women that they are choosing wrong for themselves.

With this in mind, let's return to that central foe of Feminist Fecundity, the so-called Child Penalty.

When Is a "Penalty" Not a "Penalty"?

"I had an honest internal struggle," says Ellen, one of three homeschooling moms in Woodside Park in Farmington, Utah. "I can go get my graduate degree. I can see myself being the CEO if I wanted." She looks over at her young children, currently climbing a tree a few yards away with the help of older kids in the same co-op, who are ingeniously using a rope to create a high-tension wire. "But I recognized that would sacrifice this valuable time with my kids."

"I have conscientiously chosen that this is what I want," she tells me, as her youngest helps her pluck seeds from a freshly picked sunflower. Ellen's friend Shea was in the workforce for ten years before becoming a full-time mom a couple of years ago. At first, she second-guessed her choice. But "I let that go. . . . I completely want to help them become healthy adults" by homeschooling and full-time parenting.

Both women are members of the Church of Jesus Christ of Latter-day Saints, which they say made it easier to choose to jump off the career track. "I'm grateful for the values of the church," Ellen explains—specifically, that the church highly values parenthood.

"It's part of our culture," Natalie Gochnour, the demographics expert at the University of Utah, tells me. "It's what we do. Big families are very accepted here."

One state away, Noelle, a recent graduate of BYU–Idaho and now a professor there, hopes to be a stay-at-home mom. She says her husband is ready to serve as a stay-at-home dad. "We just feel that family is really one of the most important things about this life," she tells me. "I think the world shies away from that because it's challenging—it's hard being married, it's hard having children, especially when you're uncertain about the future. And I think this school, this community, encourages families because it can also be one of the biggest blessings of life, and it can be one of the biggest supports in an uncertain world."

These places, where pregnancy seems spread through the air, are where Danish economist Henrik Kleven found a higher Child Penalty—more wages and hours sacrificed by mothers compared to non-mothers. Meanwhile, in places like Vermont and Maryland, the measured Child Penalty was smaller. Some questions are in order. We could start by asking this: If the penalty for children is low in Vermont, why did Vermont have fewer births than deaths even before the pandemic? If the penalty is so high in Utah, why is Utah always in the top five states in birthrate?

Penalties tend to discourage what they are penalizing. But the Child Penalty doesn't seem to discourage having children. This makes the Child Penalty more of a mystery.

What exactly determines the different Child Penalties in different places, and how does this relate to birthrates? Kleven's research has a clue. He looked at what happens to women who move. If a woman is born in Maryland or Vermont, but moves to Idaho or Utah and has a kid, does she experience the small Child Penalty of Vermont or the large Child Penalty of Utah? And what happens if she moves the other way?

The data suggests you can take the girl out of Utah, but very often you can't take the Utah out of the girl. "The child penalty for U.S. movers is strongly related to the child penalty in their state of birth," Kleven wrote. "Parents born in high-penalty states (such as Utah or Idaho) have much larger child penalties than those born in low-penalty states. . . ." Immigrants had the same experience: women from Muslim countries experienced much larger Child Penalties than did women from China or Sweden.

"The findings," Kleven wrote, "suggest that culture and gender norms have strong effects on child penalties." That is, women from Utah experience a large Child Penalty not because of employers in Utah, but because of something about the culture they grew up in. It's not a matter of culture forcing them out of work when they have children, *because they experience that large "penalty" wherever they end up.* The causal factor in the culture of Utah—or Vermont—is something that women have internalized and take with them.

Cultural norms that aren't imposed on us by our current cultural setting but that we carry with us, those have a name: "personal values." So maybe the Child Penalty—lower income as a result of having a child—isn't a *penalty* at all. It's a *choice*, grounded in values. Those values happen to differ from the values of the economists who call it a "penalty."

Who Stopped the Feminist Revolution?

Once we accept that the values of some American mothers differ from the values of most economists and gender scholars, some of the "mysteries" of work and family life cease being mysteries.

"An economic mystery of the last few decades has been why more women aren't working," Claire Cain Miller wrote in a *New York Times* piece. "A new paper offers one answer: Most plan to, but are increasingly caught off guard by the time and effort it takes to raise children."[22]

When this piece ran in the summer of 2018, women made up 49.7 percent of all employees, and that share was creeping toward 50 percent.[23] So why should we expect more women working? It's because of a different data point: the portion of women who are in the labor force. That climbed from the mid-1950s to the mid-1990s,[24] and everyone expected that it would keep climbing until it equalized with men. Yet in the 1990s, the trend stopped. Miller's explanation, that "the time and effort it takes to raise children" was too high, reflects that notion of an incomplete feminist revolution: even if glass ceilings were cracked and women were getting more education, the *home* wasn't egalitarian enough to allow the revolution to complete itself.

"The Mommy Effect" was a 2020 study that aimed to explain and enumerate the arrest of women's workforce participation. Something was happening to make some American women more "anti-work" as adults than they had been as teenagers. The study compiled surveys of women before and after they became mothers. The most interesting strain of findings begins here: "[B]efore motherhood, most women say that work does not inhibit women's ability to be good wives and mothers, but after the birth of their first child they become significantly more negative toward female employment."[25]

But that was just part of a bigger shift. More broadly, the study found that "motherhood is associated with women changing their views in an anti-work direction." The most important questions came from the Longitudinal Study of American Youth. High schoolers in the mid- to late 1980s were asked about "goals you may or may not have for your life," and whether those goals were very important, somewhat important, or not important to them. First on the list was "being successful in your line of work."

Those same Americans were asked years later, as adults, how important career accomplishments were to them. Mothers were far more likely than non-mothers to downgrade career success. Specifically, college-educated women and women whose own moms had worked outside the home were the most likely to shift, upon becoming mothers, and say that career wasn't as important as it had once seemed.

The researchers call this an "anti-work" shift, but you could just as easily call it a "pro-family" shift: millions of American women who had planned to be career women changed their minds after having a baby and dedicated themselves more to raising a family. This isn't a puzzle when you put it that way.

Along the same lines, in 2022 three business school scholars in the U.S. and Italy—Ekaterina Netchaeva, Leah Sheppard, and Tatiana Balushkina—compiled studies on why women don't fill as many leadership roles in work. Their conclusion: men simply "exhibit greater leadership aspirations than women," and this is a central cause of the gender gap in management and leadership positions.[26] Getting more women executives and partners would require forcing women into jobs they don't want—or somehow changing what women want.

Women made great gains in the workforce from the 1950s to the 1990s, as successive generations of women gained more and more autonomy to pursue career goals, less restrained by societal prejudices. The "incomplete feminist revolution" is actually *complete* if the goal was removing barriers to women in the workforce and helping women choose their own path in life. It seems that some feminists, however, are upset that more women, when free to choose, choose family over work.

Feminism or Workism

When they see new mothers learning they love work less and family more, why are economists and commentators surprised? When the best research shows that daycare doesn't boost birthrates, and when polls consistently show that mothers prefer other childcare arrangements, why do so many commentators and politicians continue to tout the daycare-and-work combination as the only option for mothers?

It seems that elite institutions *want* subsidized childcare to be the best way to support families, even though the data doesn't come close to showing it. Why would there be a fierce lobby for more childcare? As with everything touching on public policy, there are competing interests here.

A certain strain of feminism sees universal childcare as good in itself because it holds out the promise of advancing us toward a particular understanding of equality. "Gender symmetry"[27] is a term some scholars use. Gender symmetry requires equal representation of men and women in all parts of society. This sort of feminism also tends to hold *individual autonomy* among the highest goods. France's stay-at-home benefit gets criticized on these scores because it has the effect of temporarily pulling mothers out of the workforce.

But this symmetry-demanding, autonomy-maximizing egalitarian feminism isn't the biggest interest competing with family. The main culprit is something just as individualistic but far more powerful: efficiency-obsessed growth-centered economics.

"As a country," with nearly 30 percent of married mothers at home raising children instead of laboring for pay and spending more, "we are clearly leaving GDP points on the table," Slate's Jordan Weissmann fretted in early 2019.[28] Weissmann, a veteran center-left economics columnist, said that economics demands we shift childcare away from parents. We should be "reserving more child care for professional centers that can do it a bit more efficiently," he wrote. By his calculations, "[e]ven if you factor in rent and other overhead, it's probably more cost-effective for one caretaker to watch over four infants than it is to have every parent looking after their own."

Joe Biden echoed that technocratic idea in the first days of his presidency, laying out his ambitious agenda. Expanding the federal tax credit for daycare "would put 720 million women back in the workforce," he explained. "It would increase the GDP—to sound like a wonk here—by about eight-tenths of 1 percent. It would grow the economy."[29] Aside from the impossibility of 500 percent female labor-force participation, the laser focus on GDP is very typical in the push for daycare subsidies.

Feminism in the twenty-first century, wrote columnist Polly Toynbee, requires we "expand the workforce by getting as many people of all ages into work as possible." Willets, in his feminist manifesto, wrote: "Europe needs more consumption, more spending and more borrowing."[30] Democrats' universal childcare program was touted in part as a way of boosting the "caregiving economy."

That is, if your eyes are trained not on family aspirations but on dollar-denominated outcomes—greater GDP and growth in the childcare industry—then you will see subsidized daycare as the most important policy. Ultimately, subsidizing daycare doesn't really subsidize family. It subsidizes *work*.

Work is good for us, of course. A work subsidy, in some cases, is exactly what a family or a parent needs, but subsidizing paid work is not a good way to make America more family friendly. Here's another problem: subsidizing paid work through childcare is more lucrative for higher earners, who have more to gain from returning to work. "Plowing more public funds into early education isn't about helping poor kids get ahead," as Lyman Stone puts it; "it's about helping the upper-middle-class *stay* ahead."[31]

A certain sort of feminism—the one that seeks to remove women and men equally from the task of raising children—becomes indistinguishable from corporate workism, the line of thinking that prioritizes paid work and professional accomplishment over all else. That is why the Nordic Feminist Fecundity flamed out.

The Sad Fate of Feminist Fecundity

Feminist Fecundity in the Nordic nations was supposed to represent the end stage in the feminist-egalitarian revolution. After passing through the valley of low-birthrate half feminism, we were supposed to come to rest at family-friendly full feminism, in which the workplace and the home were both egalitarian.

Yet from the Great Recession to the eve of COVID, Sweden, Denmark, and Norway saw their birthrates drop three times faster than the rest of Europe.

"This pattern in the Nordic countries is particularly puzzling," demographer Wolfgang Lutz wrote in the 2020 *Vienna Yearbook of Population Research*, "given that these countries used to be seen as the prime examples for the premise that ensuring the compatibility of work and family and having generous child support systems will result in relatively high fertility levels." He concluded glumly, "Demography is still groping in the dark for explanations for these changes."[32]

It turns out that Feminist Fecundity, rather than the destination of the feminist revolution, was a passing phase. The data here tells a slightly twisting tale, so bear with me.

First, it's important to recognize that one major claim of the Feminist Fecundity thesis is correct: in the modern wealthy world, egalitarian societies generally have more babies than less egalitarian societies. But here's a key distinction that the Feminist Fecundity thesis missed: this pattern for *societies* doesn't hold for *individuals*. Demographer Peter McDonald found that, in the developed world, more egalitarian societies have more kids, but women with more egalitarian values do not.[33]

This undermines the second half of the Feminist Fecundity argument—that we need to change the structure of the family at home and "ditch rigid family norms." It seems that on the family level, gender equality doesn't have any positive impact on birthrates. That's why Utah has more babies than Vermont or Maryland.

Here's the second twist: that positive connection between a society's gender equality and its birthrates doesn't hold up in all wealthy countries. Specifically, researchers Laurie DeRose and Lyman Stone found that egalitarian societies had more kids *only* if those societies, when faced with the conflict between work and family, came down hard on the pro-family side. Charting birthrates, workism, and familism, DeRose and Stone took a stab at solving that Nordic puzzle: "Denmark, the only Nordic country with a decrease in work importance, also had the smallest decline in fertility over the period measured. Finland, meanwhile, had the biggest rise in work importance, along with the largest fertility decline."[34]

Among wealthy, egalitarian countries, more workism means fewer babies.

This can explain the reversal in birthrates, for example, in Sweden. From 2000 to 2010, as Sweden rolled out its egalitarian policies to help women work, it also helped women have more babies. Over the next decade, though, Swedish birthrates dropped fast. Why? The pro-work policies that made life easier for the moms of Generation X may have had a different effect on Millennial women: they have inculcated a value system that prioritizes work over family.

When you subsidize a thing, you get more of that thing. Paying people to have kids (child tax credits, family allowances) seems to yield more kids. But indirect subsidies for parents don't have the same effect. Subsidizing daycare, rather than subsidizing families, as stated earlier, actually subsidizes work. More work, in the long run, means fewer babies.

So the Nordic reversal could be explained this way: Government programs that make it easier for mothers to work can in the short run help women have more babies, but such programs also shift a society to value work over family. Within a generation, this reduces birthrates. "[P]olicies that try to help families by routing benefits through employment," DeRose and Stone wrote, "or giving extra benefits to working parents, will sow the seeds of their own failure"[35] because "they strengthen a 'workist' life-script rather than a 'familist' one."

In the end, the Feminist Fecundity becomes a feminist justification of a workist dogma.

And *dogma* is the right word here, because in wealthy societies, strong dedication to work takes on a religious significance.

The Church of Workism

The idea of workism as a religion was first defined in 2019 by writer Derek Thompson.[36] Americans have fled organized religion at a furious pace in the past fifty years, but we haven't quite secularized. Man is a religious animal, created to seek something greater than himself. "The decline of traditional faith in America has coincided with an explosion of new atheisms," Thompson explained. The most powerful atheism, especially for the college-educated class, is workism.

Workism is "the belief that work is not only necessary to economic production, but also the centerpiece of one's identity and life's purpose," as Thompson defines it. Work, for the elite, has transformed from a way to earn money to a source of meaning, "promising identity, transcendence, and community." Northern Europe has seen workism spread, but the U.S. may be the central locus of this religion. College-educated Americans have seen their work hours increase. Higher-income men work longer hours than anyone else. This isn't about need, it's about devotion.

Workism is arguably the official religion of the U.S., and we're passing it down to the younger generation. A Pew poll in 2018 asked teens what was important to them. Almost all of them—95 percent—agreed that "having a job or career I enjoy" was important or very important. Only 39 percent said the same about having children.[37]

Millennials came of age during a massive Great Aworkening. (Sorry.) That generation was raised in workism: bust your butt in high school, get into a good college, sign up for everything, keep your nose down, and do as you're told. The result is that the largest generation, in its prime childbearing years, is the most workist generation.

"Why am I burned out?" liberal Millennial writer Anne Helen Petersen asked in a BuzzFeed article in 2019. "Because I've internalized the idea that I should be working all the time. Why have I internalized that idea? Because everything and everyone in my life has reinforced it—explicitly and implicitly—since I was young."[38] That's how her generation was raised. Burnout, she wrote, is "the Millennial condition."

WeWork runs coworking spaces with Millennials as their target audience. Their office throw pillows say "Do what you love." The implication, given the location, is clear: "what you love" is work. The neon signs in these places say "hustle harder."[39] Hustling harder can pay off, and even build virtues, but the danger of workism is that people fall in love with work and define their self-worth by it. Work is good, but it is not worthy of our full unconditional love. Believing otherwise is selling ourselves short. But that's what so many young people have come to believe—whether out of a misguided feminism, a gullibility to hustle talk, or adherence to the individualistic philosophy of our age.

How convenient it is for corporate America that the virtues preached by this new religion all redound to the owners of capital, and that the lifestyle preached by this brand of feminism leads to a work-first mindset. The feminism-individualism-workism confluence is a powerful force on the American left in the twenty-first century. It's a central tenet of the secular religion of our elites. This was evidenced by a poll of parents in 2021 about their ambitions for their kids.

"If you had to choose one of the following courses for your child's life to take by the time they reach age 40," parents were asked, "which would you prefer: happily married with children but just getting by financially, or financially well-off but single with no children in the household?"[40]

While most American parents put family over career for their own children, Democrats were nearly evenly split on the question.

It all connects to Stephanie Murray's observation about individualism versus familism. When "children are a personal choice and therefore a personal problem," the logic of the market steers people and culture away from family formation. When autonomy is held as the highest virtue, it severs the individual's bonds from any other commitments, and it gives license to the powerful to make absolute claims on the time and attention of every individual. The market, like a hungry predator, loves nothing more than the isolated individual, untethered from other people, institutions, or places. Our hyperindividualistic age has transformed many of us from neighbors, coaches, volunteers, fathers, and mothers into, above all, workers.

"Rather than making room for dependents and the asymmetrical duties of care that inhere in both sex and caregiving," legal scholar Erika Bachiochi wrote, "we have sought to remake women (and men) in the exalted image of the ever-competitive, rights-bearing, unencumbered, pleasure-maximizing, autonomous individual of Thomas Hobbes' imaginings."

Family-Friendly Jobs or Job-Friendly Families

Let's return to that consulting firm that hired the professors from Harvard's Gender Initiative, in the hope that the right family-friendly policies could "decrease the number of women who quit and increase the number who were promoted."

What systemic obstacles were there to women climbing the ladder, becoming partner, staying in the company? The firm, you'll recall, already had plenty of flexible-work policies, and the female employees were already more likely to take advantage of those policies. Charged with rooting out inequalities in the office, the Harvard professors instead found a grim *equality*. "[M]en were at least as likely as women to say the long hours interfered with their family lives," the *New York Times* reported, "and they quit at the same rate." It turns out *nobody* liked the long and lengthening hours at this firm. The firm was typical among white-collar employers: hours for college-educated workers have been rising for a generation, up 5 percent from 1979 to 2013.[41]

"Last year was hard with my 105 flights," one man at the firm said. "I was feeling pretty fried. I've missed too much of my kids' lives." There's no such thing as a family-friendly workload that includes 105 flights per year.

That doesn't mean there wasn't inequality. The attitudes of colleagues, regarding work-family balance, contained unequal expectations. Recall the words of that female associate: "When I look at a female partner, it does leak into my thinking: How do I think she is as a mother in addition to how do I think she is as a partner? When I look at men, I don't think about what kind of father they are."

"It's not really about business," sociologist Mary Blair-Loy said; "it's about fundamental identity and masculinity. Men are required by the culture to be these superheroes, to fulfill this devotion and single-minded commitment to work. Women have an out because they have an external definition of morality or leading the good life, which is being devoted to their children."

At this firm, it seems that men were miserable and climbing the ladder by neglecting their families, while women's careers were lagging because they were openly valuing family. This wasn't the answer the firm wanted from Harvard's Gender Initiative. Here's the climax of the *New York Times* story on the whole effort:

"The researchers said that when they told the consulting firm they had diagnosed a bigger problem than a lack of family-friendly policies for women—that long hours were taking a toll on both men and women—the firm rejected that conclusion. The firm's representatives said the goal was to focus only on policies for women, and that men were largely immune to these issues."

Has a study ever clarified a problem so well? When corporate America talks of gender equality, they mean *we want the women in our firm to become good company men—totally devoted to work and only lightly attached to family.* As liberal author Ruth Whippman mocked it in the *Times,* "Women! Be more like men. Men, as you were."[42]

The "gender revolution at home" is mostly about daycare, because it's mostly about detaching adults from family and attaching them to work. To adapt a phrase from Brookings Institution scholar Richard V. Reeves, what many employers, commentators, and politicians are trying to forge are not family-friendly jobs, but job-friendly families.

Family-Friendly Feminism

Liberal Feminist Fecundity has failed because it rested on women working more and transforming the family to accommodate work. So, are the conservatives correct? Is feminism the enemy if we want a more family-friendly America?

Not necessarily.

A family-friendly feminism is possible, but it cannot be a feminism whose foundations are autonomy, symmetry, and individualism—because that becomes a *workist* feminism. Remember that finding by Stone and DeRose: egalitarianism only yields more babies when paired with familism. This shows us how a real Feminist Fecundity would work.

The feminism that will give women the families they want will be a feminism where the family is not reimagined to serve careers, but where work is adapted to put family first. Women currently bear most of the burden in supporting families, but establishing a healthy egalitarianism and a family-friendly feminism will largely be men's work.

Men can help women here, but not by encouraging their daughters and wives to be brass-tacks, hard-nosed Girl Bosses. We don't need working women to become Company Men. We need Company Men to become Family Guys. Put another way, feminism doesn't help people attain the families they want if feminism means keeping women away from their families. Feminism is helpful if it involves changing men so that they go home to their kids.

Men need to lead the way in changing workplace expectations. The Harvard study of the consulting firm had a telling line: "When a man left at 5 p.m., people at the office assumed he was meeting a client. . . . When a woman left, they assumed she was going home to her children." If, in fact Matthew is leaving for a meeting while Mary is leaving for family time, Mary has chosen the better part. If, instead, Matthew is merely using these assumptions as a cover for going home, he needs to fess up.

A man can help working mothers—and the young women who want to be working mothers—by leaving work at 5 p.m., explicitly to make it home for family dinner, or to coach his daughter's softball game. The workplace "allies" that women need are male bosses and colleagues who say loudly, to workers of both sexes, "Family is the most important thing"—and then act that way. This isn't quite about husbands shouldering more domestic duties to boost their wives' careers. This is mostly about men using their cultural power to set the expectation that family is more important than work. The more dads do this, the less employers can punish the moms for demanding flexibility.

That means that family dinnertime determines what time you leave work, not the other way around. It means a man can't sneak out of the office, riding on the expectation that "he must have a client meeting." Instead, a man must march out proudly saying, "My kids need me at home." And yes, the more time dads spend with their kids, the more kids they will likely have. Research finds that the more the father is committed to helping with the children and at home, the more likely the mother is to want another child.[43]

Dads putting in more hours as dads and husbands should count as feminism—and it's precisely the sort of feminism we need now. Those traditional societies with sagging birthrates? The feminists have a fair critique of them: too many of them excuse fathers from actually being fathers.

It turns out, the tech explosion and the sexual revolution both left us in desperate need of one thing: better men. If we have better men, we'll get more babies.

Remember that 2018 *New York Times* feature "Americans Are Having Fewer Babies. They Told Us Why"? The star of the article, pictured in the lead photo, was twenty-six-year-old Jessica Boer, who, according to the *Times*, had "a long list of things she'd rather spend time doing than raising children," such as "traveling; focusing on her job as a nurse; getting a master's degree; playing with her cats."

Well, she's changed her mind. "I was young and stupid when I agreed to talk to that journalist," Jessica told me in 2022. "I can't wait to be a mom!" What's changed? "My problem was I was paired with the wrong guy at the time. . . . I'm happily married now and hoping to have kids in the next few years."

What Jessica needed in 2018 wasn't the feminism that put cats above kids and choices above all. What she needed was a man who was willing and able to lay down his life for marriage and family. That's what a lot of American women need.

The feminism America needs is not one that erases differences between the genders, but one that makes men be better men—that starts with men taking their dad roles seriously. This will be good for men and women in the workplace, it will be good for marriages, and it will be good for the community.

It will also be good for all adults to be reminded that their value is not primarily in the work they do, but in the love they give and receive.

CHAPTER 12

You Should Quit Your Job

With my brown leather bag slung over my shoulder, maybe loosening my tie knot, I like to embrace the cliché and call out, as I step through the front door, "Hi, Honey, I'm home!"

But many days, instead of children racing into the front hall crying, "Daddy! I missed you!" I have no greeting committee at all. Instead, my kids are scattered throughout the house and the yard, playing with the McGoverns, the Kilners, or the Migginses. Katie might be sitting at the coffee table with Lori or Elena or Nancy. A few times, Lori has apologized as I've entered: "Don't worry, we're leaving, I can't believe it's already five thirty." Half the time, however, we decide it's pizza night and convince her and her kids to stay.

And just as often, this scene unfolded with Katie as the only adult around. On one not-atypical Thursday as I worked on this chapter, Katie's friend Kathleen was at the hospital because her mother needed surgery. Kathleen's husband was out of town on work, so Katie picked up little Levi and Kelly at school along with our Eve and Meg, and then a few hours later got Caroline, May, and Hank at the bus stop along with our Lucy, Charlie, Brendan, and Seán.

When my children look back on their childhoods, I suspect it will be these sprawling, accidental, chaotic playdates they'll recall. I know that when Katie looks back on our kids' younger years, these are the moments that come to mind. And these moments all happened because Katie and a handful of her friends have as their daytime employment *family and home*.

We have been fortunate that we could afford this arrangement in which she can focus full time on managing our household of eight humans and two dogs. The beneficiaries have been our kids, our dogs, me, Katie's sisters, our schools, our parishes, and our neighborhoods. Everyone around us is better off because our household has a stay-at-home mom.

America needs more stay-at-home moms like Katie, and more stay-at-home dads. A married couple in which one parent doesn't work full time for pay is one of the best arrangements for a family.

It's not the *only* good arrangement, of course. And for many couples, it's simply not economically feasible: one income or one and a half incomes may not be enough to cover the rent, the groceries, and the orthodontist bills. For some couples, neither adult is interested in or temperamentally disposed to full-time parenthood and homemaking. Just as not everyone is called to parenthood, not every family has a parent called to stay at home.

But in whatever ways possible, we ought to change our policies, our culture, and our own lives in order to help more parents make parenting their full-time job.

An America with more moms and dads at home throughout the day will be an America with safer neighborhoods, which in turn is an America with freer kids and freer parents. An America with more full-time moms and dads is an America with happier kids, healthier kids, and, in the long run, more kids.

Finally, there's the simple matter that American mothers, on net, want to work for the boss less and spend time with the kids more. If feminism is about liberating women to fulfill their desires, it should actually mean supporting stay-at-home parents.

Even a small bump in the number of stay-at-home parents could make a big difference, because it could create a positive feedback loop: being a stay-at-home mom is less isolating if more of your friends and neighbors are stay-at-home moms; being a stay-at-home dad would be less odd if more neighborhood guys were doing the same thing. (There's a macroeconomic feedback effect here, too: more married couples dialing back to one income will apply an upward pressure to wages, making it easier for more couples to dial back themselves.)

"More stay-at-home parents" isn't a popular argument in media, academia, or political circles. Policymakers, journalists, and economists take it for granted that both parents should be in the workplace, and that getting mothers into full-time paid work is an unmitigated good.

Those who dissent, who say we need more stay-at-home parents, are called sexist and accused of wanting to keep people in poverty. Viva, a young bartender in London, told me she wants six kids and wants to be a stay-at-home mom, but sees that these choices are "very shamed-upon." Shame needs to be removed from this debate on all sides.

Of course no parent should be forced, coerced, or guilted into staying at home. *Of course* it's great that women have more career opportunities than they did in past generations. But we will help American parents live the life they want and have as many children as they want if we can find ways to help more parents stay at home—whether that means exiting the workforce fully, or dialing back so that they can be home when the school bus picks up and drops off.

What Women Want

Most married mothers in the U.S. want to stay at home while their husband works for pay, or vice versa, until their youngest is at least five years old, a 2021 poll found.[1]

This may shock you if you learn about American culture from mainstream media, where the idea of a stay-at-home mom is anathema. But a silent majority of Americans generally think it's good for kids and good for communities if one parent can mostly stay at home.

"Nearly 60 percent of Americans," reported Pew Research in 2016, "and a majority of both registered Republicans and registered Democrats—believe that children are better off with one parent at home than they would be in a day-care arrangement." In every age group Pew analyzed, clear majorities said children are better off with a parent at home.[2]

One in three mothers in a different survey said that the best child-care arrangement was "one parent stays home full time to care for the child," while another third said the best arrangement was "both parents work flexible hours and share child care."[3] Put another way, two-thirds of American moms believe parents should cut back on paid work in order to care for kids.

There's a gender divide. Fathers in this survey were much *less* likely than mothers to support stay-at-home parenting (even part-time stay-at-home parenting) for either parent. Fathers are also more likely to believe that daycare is the best arrangement.

There's a class divide here, too. Working-class parents mostly favor a stay-at-home parent. Couples with two college degrees between them are relatively more favorable to the dual-income-plus-full-time-daycare arrangement[4]—but even among elites, a slim majority favored one parent at home.

But on the whole, American parents—especially women and the working class—believe the ideal work-life balance involves more time with the kids and less time at the office.

So that's what Americans actually want, but we know they aren't living that way. So are parents just mouthing the pro-family stuff they feel they *should* say while living the way they actually want?

Actually, data show a dissatisfaction that seems genuine and pervasive, revealing that a working life *isn't* working for most parents.

Among mothers with children at home, 28 percent are not employed either full time or part time. Among mothers who do work for pay full time, a majority wish they were working part time or not at all. Why do they feel this way? They feel paid work is dragging them away from their more important work. "Full-time working moms are more likely to say being a working parent makes it harder for them to be a good parent," reported Pew Research.[5]

Academia and the media are sometimes blind to this reality. Their constant promotion of universal daycare is particularly out of touch with ordinary parents' concerns.

"Half the country has too few licensed child-care options," reported the liberal Center for American Progress in a 2018 report on "America's Child Care Deserts."[6] If you poked around their map, though, you noticed something: many of these "child care deserts" were neighborhoods where middle-class people are having tons of babies.

Kemp Mill, the fecund Orthodox Jewish neighborhood in Silver Spring, Maryland, was a "child care desert" according to CAP's map. So was Rexburg, Idaho, the population center of Madison County—the county with the most babies per capita. The parents of Kemp Mill and Rexburg are not desperately lacking care for their kids, though. The only thing they're "lacking" is a quantity of licensed daycare providers that one D.C. think tank finds adequate.

If parents of young children had their druthers, most of them woul'druther work less and care for their babies more, rather than putting little Olivia and Darryl in daycare. This is a case of our elites believing that parents—especially mothers—don't know what's good for them.

Who's Afraid of the Stay-at-Home Mom?

"The devaluation of mothers' work permeates virtually every major institution," wrote mother and feminist author Ann Crittenden. "Not only is caregiving not rewarded, it is penalized."[7] It's scorned, too—"shamed-upon," as Viva in London put it. "People should be more open to the idea of a housewife," Viva said. But the idea has become a political battleground.

Part of the case against Republican presidential candidate Mitt Romney in 2012 was that his wife "actually never worked a day in her life," as Democratic operative Hilary Rosen put it.[8] You see, Ann Romney mostly forswore paid jobs in favor of raising her five sons full time.

This disdain toward mothers who don't do full-time paid work is an occasionally recurring feature in our politics. Democratic senator and presidential candidate Chris Dodd once riffed on full-time child-rearing as a "wonderful luxury" for women who "want to go play golf or go to the club and play cards."[9]

Elizabeth Warren, in her days as a scholar, understood the value of one parent staying at home. But as a politician, she spoke as if staying at home was a failure: "I think about how many women of my generation just got knocked off the track and never got back on," she said in a presidential debate; "how many of my daughter's generation get knocked off the track and don't get back on, how many mamas and daddies today are getting knocked off the track and never get back on."[10]

Anything that *hints* at helping more parents stay at home evokes charges of sexism and oppression. "How to spot a sexist leftist" was the headline of an article by leftist feminist Jill Filipovic. She had found a fellow progressive arguing that government should offer parents "a choice between heavily subsidized child care services or a cash benefit to compensate them for care at home."[11] That's sexist because it would amount to "pushing women out of the labor force," Filipovic argued.[12]

When Arizona U.S. Senate candidate Blake Masters in 2022 said it would be great if a family could live on a single income—literally, that's all he said—the local Democratic Party blasted him as a sexist.[13]

When the *Atlantic* ran a piece about mothers whose pandemic experience drove them to scale from full-time work down to part-time work from home, *Washington Post* columnist Helaine Olen groaned, "Give. Me. A. Break." She said these women's stories were perpetuating "a lousy old myth . . . that many of these women are better off for cutting their (paid) work hours and downscaling their professional aspirations in favor of tending to family responsibilities."[14] The logic here is clear: women should never give up paid work in the economy for unpaid work at home.

Claudia Goldin, the Nobel-winning economist who has done some of the most incisive research into women, motherhood, and work, revealed her own opinion in a discussion about the idea of husbands and wives specializing. It makes economic sense, she agreed, for one parent to develop a high-skilled and highly connected paid career that pays a lot while another focuses more on domestic tasks. "It just so happens that in most couples," Goldin said, "if there's a woman and a man, the woman takes the back seat."

It's quite the assumption that feeding the family and raising the kids is the "back seat," while commuting an hour each way, taking orders from bosses and customers, is the "front seat."

Modern feminism is too workist. It misses the mark in its fight for equality because it devalues both family and the other work a stay-at-home parent does.

In late 2022, in an effort to finish this manuscript, I escaped my family and the Beltway in favor of the Berkshires—the lovely hilly region in western Massachusetts. While writing from a local pub, I met a Baby Boom–aged woman named Lynn, who was a professional therapist. We started talking about my book topic, but she quickly turned it into an examination of my marriage, which she saw as emblematic of the inequality in our society. I explained that I am a very involved dad, and I make sure my wife regularly gets breaks from the kids, both at home and away, so no, this trip to the Berkshires didn't make me feel *too* guilty.

This didn't satisfy Lynn. "You give your wife breaks from the kids, but does she get to go away for a week to finish *her book*?" she asked. "She gets to catch up on sleep and showers, and you get to *finish your book*?" The question bugged me—was our relationship really that unequal?

I called Katie first thing in the morning and ran this argument past her. She reminded me of the times she went up to New Jersey for a long weekend to stay up all night feeding her sister's newborn twins. We recalled the times I was home alone with our own kids so that Katie could stay with nieces and nephews to give another sister a chance for a romantic getaway. We remembered the times Katie

dragged a depressed or stressed friend out of her house for a walk or
a drink, and was able to give undivided attention not to a manuscript
but to someone she loved.

I hope someday Katie does write the book she's been thinking of,
but that's not the real parallel to my own professional undertakings. Being an indispensable and ever-available friend, sister, and neighbor—
laying down her life for her friends—is the work she does outside the
home. When friends needed their whole house packed up and moved
while they were three states away dealing with medical emergencies,
Katie was there. When our daughter's classmate ran away from home,
Katie was just about the first person to show up at the parents' home.

This is her "side gig." The pay is mostly in gratitude and apprecia-
tion. "'Acts of service' is my love language," Katie says. She wouldn't
give up this service to her family and friends (and sometimes near-
strangers) for anything. Lynn's mistake was in supposing that only
side gigs that pay in money or fame are truly valuable, forgetting
those that pay in something deeper.

A workist, materialist culture is a family-unfriendly culture because it preaches a message that the work of loving and helping friends
and family—including our offspring—is mere drudgery.

Goldin, Filipovic, and Olen, though, do raise a good question:
When one parent stays at home, why is it typically Mom?

The feminists, it turns out, have the answer: women are different
from men.

Women Are Different

It was the year 2000 when I first encountered someone who simply
didn't believe single-earner married couples existed. Ironically, the
woman's argument helped explain why stay-at-home moms are more
common than stay-at-home dads.

Reporting on a UN resolution about the family, I was interviewing
a feminist activist who was lobbying for aggressive language on gen-

der equity. "Do you think that still exists?" the lobbyist said, laughing at me, in a shocked tone. "I don't know a single family today that operates under that old model."

Encountering a stay-at-home denier was good preparation for reading the op-ed pages of the 2010s and 2020s. But the woman said something else that permanently shaped my thinking.

Speaking about how hopelessly male-centric the UN was, the lobbyist pointed to the building's bathrooms as a quotidian but illustrative case of unthinking sexism. The men's room and the ladies' room just off the General Assembly were laid out symmetrically and equally, she said. The two bathrooms are the same exact size and shape. This was thoughtless and dumb.

Men's rooms include urinals, which take up less space than toilet stalls. That means men can fit more bathroom "customers" per square foot. Women also take longer in the bathroom than men, she said, and so *equity* demands that women have significantly more square footage than men when it comes to public restrooms.

I was sold, and since then I've called myself a Bathroom Feminist. Women are often excluded from planning and decision-making, and men end up building and planning things with only men in mind. Women suffer as a result, because women have different needs, tendencies, and abilities. That is, men too often fail to realize that men and women are fundamentally different.

The UN lobbyist who made me a Bathroom Feminist added a final reason why women should have larger public restrooms: "Women are still the ones more likely to be caring for children." Thus, in the same conversation where she laid out the key insight that our economy and public spaces don't take account of women's differences, she grudgingly acknowledged a difference she thought should be eradicated.

Ironically, the preferred way of eradicating women's disproportionate share of child-rearing seems to be turning working mothers into company men, and abolishing the whole idea of a stay-at-home parent.

Any talk of "stay-at-home parents," objects Filipovic, "gives the impression that we're talking about parents generally. But we aren't. Overwhelmingly, we're talking about mothers." The Filipovic Feminist conclusion: it's sexist to support parents staying at home.

As an alternative, let me offer the Bathroom Feminist conclusion: let's make our world more accommodating of stay-at-home parents (which mostly means moms, but also means dads).

Filipovic is correct that only about one in six stay-at-home parents is a dad.[15] While the gap is smaller than it was a generation ago, it's still significant. While we cannot rule out "gender norms" and societal expectations as causes, at some point we need to admit that human nature is the main reason men are more likely to work outside the home and women are more likely to take up child-rearing full time.

This runs directly contrary to the received wisdom of America's elites. Under the official dogma of twenty-first-century America, the only reason we have more stay-at-home moms than dads is cultural conditioning—centuries of discrimination that have created systems of oppression. "The belief that men and women are psychologically indistinguishable became sacred" at some point in the last two generations, writes psychologist Steven Pinker.[16] It's heresy to suggest otherwise. But it's simply true that in general, on average, women are more fit than are men for rearing young children, especially babies. This isn't true in every case. This doesn't imply that exceptions to this rule are weird in any way. It does, however, explain why mothers are more likely than fathers to stay at home.

Oxytocin is "the love hormone" that "can help us bond with loved ones," as *Harvard Women's Health Watch* puts it.[17] Women's bodies have more receptors for oxytocin, and this is especially true during pregnancy and breastfeeding. Nature has shaped women to feel more emotionally attached to their children.

The old cliché that "becoming a parent changes you" is upheld by physiology. The emotional changes of becoming a mom can be charted in women's brains. "Women experience a flood of hormones during pregnancy, childbirth, and breast-feeding that primes the brain for dramatic change in regions thought to make up the maternal circuit," explained mother and health care columnist Chelsea Conaboy in the *Boston Globe*.[18]

She continued:

> Affected brain regions include those that enable a mother to multitask to meet baby's needs, help her to empathize with her infant's pain and emotions, and regulate how she responds to positive stimuli (such as baby's coo) or to perceived threats. In the newborn months, a mother's interaction with her infant serves as further stimulus to link her brain quite tangibly to her baby's.

A gender-neutral policy, such as France's stay-at-home benefit, or a cultural shift toward stay-at-home parents in general *will* mostly move women out of the workforce. But that's a good thing, because American mothers, on net, *want* to work less than they do, and because the broader result of more stay-at-home parents would bring about so many good effects that it would offset any harms caused by reducing women's time in the office.

And what about the old story that stay-at-home moms are simply miserable? Historically, there was a bit of truth to this. When almost all married women were staying at home because they felt they had no other choice, a sizable portion were unhappy. Sure enough, in the 1970s, stay-at-home mothers were less satisfied with their work (raising kids and keeping house) than were employed mothers. By the 2010s, when stay-at-home mothers were more likely to be at home *by choice*, the happiness gap for stay-at-home mothers versus other mothers had disappeared.[19]

"Are you very happy?" the General Social Survey asks. Stay-at-home mothers are just about as likely as working mothers (roughly 40 percent) to say yes. (In fact, since 2002, stay-at-home mothers were more likely to call themselves "very happy.")[20] Likewise, most mothers believe that being a homemaker is just as fulfilling as being employed.[21]

It's Good for Both Parents

One parent staying home is good for everyone in the family, because having two parents with varying schedules helps avoid burnout, increases mutual support, and encourages the sort of habits that make life better for the whole family, like cooking at home.

If you've regularly scrapped your plan to cook a family dinner on a Wednesday night after work, you can imagine how being a full-time homemaker could make this easier. Even sneaking in twenty minutes at two thirty to do some prep work can make a dinner happen that wouldn't otherwise.

Kids and adults who eat more home-cooked meals do better in life, multiple studies have shown. "Eating out very frequently is significantly associated with an increased risk of all-cause death," one 2021 study found.[22] In another study, Japanese researchers found that regularly eating out was associated with "inadequacy of dietary fiber, vitamin C and mineral intake."[23]

More home-cooked meals are just one small but material way in which parents do better when one of them is mostly at home, not doing paid work.

Adam Smith spent about a thousand pages explaining the virtues of specialization (most of it had to do with nail makers), and those insights apply in marriage, too. My wife and I are both better at our jobs because of the support we get from the other, and because of our specialization. On top of my column writing and blogging, I could not write books and give speeches were I also 50 percent responsible for cooking, picking up kids from school, cracking the whip on homework, and keeping the house in order.

I believe I am more productive with my current family arrangement—six kids and a stay-at-home wife—than I would be were I a childless bachelor. That's because I benefit from our family's full-time manager, my wife. Katie is naturally more gifted than I at management, scheduling, and multitasking, plus she now has nearly twenty years of experience running our family.

The benefit of specialization does not accrue only to me. Because I am out of the house most days, dealing with adults, when I get home, I am happy to take over with all our children, of whom my wife may be tiring by 6 p.m.

Finally, separating out tasks is good for marital peace and happiness, as there are fewer fights over who should do what and how. Again, this is all basic economics.

While "Adam Smith and Elizabeth Warren" may not be a standard pairing, Warren joins Smith as having made one of the best cases for the single-earner couple. In 2004, Warren coauthored, with her daughter, *The Two-Income Trap*. In it, she explained how middle-class Americans were in a more financially precarious position in the twenty-first century than in the decades before, and argued that the norm of the two-income family was a root cause. "As millions of mothers poured into the workplace," Warren wrote, "it became increasingly difficult to put together a middle-class life on a single income."

By bidding down the price of labor and increasing the consumption norms of middle-class families, this shift left families more precarious. For one thing, losing a stay-at-home mom meant losing a player who could sub into the workforce in a pinch. "If her husband was laid off, fired, or otherwise left without a paycheck," Warren wrote, "the stay-at-home mother didn't simply stand helplessly on the sidelines as her family toppled off an economic cliff; she looked for a job to make up some of that lost income."

Thus, "A stay-at-home mother served as the family's ultimate insurance against unemployment or disability—insurance that had a very real economic value even when it wasn't drawn on."

Warren's book calls for reshaping our economy into one in which a single income is sufficient to raise a family. On a personal level, it serves as a warning that getting accustomed to two incomes is living on the edge. Shifting to one income is thus a way to structure one's life in a less precarious way.

Ellen, Stephanie, and Shea, the homeschooling moms I met in a park in Farmington, Utah, explained that being free of a paid job, they had the time to better budget and plan and find savings. Saving a few hundred bucks a month is equivalent to earning a few hundred (untaxed) bucks a month.

It's Good for Kids

To say "children do best when one parent stays at home" is fraught.

Countless working mothers have heard that as an indictment or a guilt trip, because they couldn't pull it off financially or temperamentally, or simply felt called to full-time paid work. Workplace discrimination against women was often rooted in the dogma that a stay-at-home mom was universally the best model.

The emotional and professional harms from these practices ought to remind us not to guilt or pressure women into staying home. But that's not an argument for ignoring the benefits to kids of having parents in the office less and with the kids more.

"When parents spend high-quality time with their children, their children are more likely to succeed." That's the basic thrust of the research on parenting, according to Ariel Kalil, codirector of the University of Chicago's "Parenting Lab."[24]

While American parents generally need to back off and helicopter less, Mom and Dad simply *being around* has high value for kids. As with all things, virtue is in the mean. Little Tyler doesn't need you playing Legos with him for hours, but Kalil has found that reading to your child seems to increase your child's reading ability.[25] Countless studies have found that eating family dinner together is associated with good outcomes for kids. These high-quality interactions are much easier in a family where one parent is home during the day.

When the child is very young, direct attention from a parent is important. "Children do tend to do worse if their mothers work full-time in their first year of life," found Columbia University's Jane Waldfogel. There are "negative effects found on health, cognitive development, and externalizing behavior problems."[26] Again, this isn't reason to guilt a mother who has to work, or who isn't temperamentally disposed to taking care of a baby. It is reason to stop denigrating and discouraging stay-at-home moms.

American media and academia, however, like to argue that it's *bad* for daughters if Mom stays home, and they claim they have the research to prove it. Many studies purportedly find the children of working moms do better than the children of stay-at-home moms. The fine print in the findings, though, consistently undermine the whole argument.

Consider the 2015 declaration from Harvard Business School: "Kids Benefit from Having a Working Mom."[27]

"Women whose moms worked outside the home are more likely to have jobs themselves," the business school states. Women did better professionally if their mothers worked outside the home, the researchers reported. But there was an exception: this rule didn't apply to "women who reported conservative attitudes toward gender equality."

Why would having a nonworking mom seem to affect conservative women differently from other women? The answer is obvious with a little bit of digging. Start with this observation from the same paper: "Parents transmit gender attitudes to their children."

Then consider what attitudes the authors considered "conservative." If you agreed that "being a housewife is just as fulfilling as working for pay" or agreed with most of Americans that ideally the mother stays home until the kids are school age, you were a "conservative." A better label may be "family-centered."

Such family-centered women, as the authors stated, likely grew up in conservative, family-centered households. The authors acknowledged that the supposed harms of Mom staying at home didn't apply in these conservative family-centered households.

Put another way, the paper asserted that Mom harms her daughters by staying home, but admitted that this conclusion doesn't apply if Mom is staying home *because she values staying at home*. The girls who suffered were those whose moms stayed home while *not* valuing staying at home. Who would stay at home if she didn't value staying at home? It's women who are out of the labor force against their wishes: disabled women, chronically ill women, women in abusive relationships, or single mothers on welfare. The real takeaway is that girls do better professionally if their mothers are living the lives they want to live, whether that be working outside the home *or* working in the home. No mother should feel pressure to work outside the home to be a role model for her kids—if she's happy staying at home, there will be the same positive effect in the kids' future earnings.

One 2012 meta-study compiled the results of sixty-nine different studies on the same question about the benefits of having an employed mother. Studies that sampled mostly single parents found that children of working moms did better, but that's because they were contrasted with single unemployed parents. Sure enough, studies that sampled mostly married parents found the opposite, because there was still an employed parent in that picture.[28]

In other words, these studies don't show that stay-at-home moms harmed their daughters. They show that growing up on welfare without a dad is suboptimal. Kids need the stability and example of a working parent. This is a warning against some pro-natal government spending such as in France, but it certainly doesn't make a case against a married mom or dad staying at home, as long as the other is working.

It's Good for Community

The benefits of stay-at-home parents also spill over into the community.

Travis is a father of three who works for the Calvert County Sheriff's Department in Maryland. He and I ended up on the same trivia team at the Ruddy Duck Tavern. Travis grew up in Calvert County and says the area is "a good place to raise kids."

"You don't have to be a helicopter parent here," he says. A big reason: you get support from the community in this endeavor. This was true when Travis grew up there, too, but Travis uses an interesting formulation to describe the help his parents got. "We got ass-whoopins," Travis explains. "Our neighbors would beat my ass when I was a kid here in Calvert." That is, if Travis did something stupid, dangerous, or disrespectful somewhere across town from his parents, other adults in the neighborhood knew they were deputized to provide discipline. Attitudes on disciplining kids—especially other people's kids—have certainly changed since Travis was young. But setting the "whoopins" aside, we should recognize the value of that kind of universal parental presence.

Bob Driscoll, as a high school senior in Boston's suburbs in the 1980s, was allowed off campus during lunch break or a free period. "My group would often go to [a] close-by Stop & Shop for a donut or soda," Bob explains. And most of the time, he was seen: "My mom would mention someone saw me there, and who I was with, and at what hour." That'll keep a kid honest. Notably, that requires moms or dads in the neighborhood at lunchtime.

Again and again, when I speak with adults born in the 1970s or earlier, I hear stories like this. One man recalled getting in trouble for chucking gravel at a dog, an act spotted by someone else's mom on a front porch. One woman told me that her own mother had learned of her good deed—helping a boy who had wiped out on a bicycle— because a neighborhood mother had witnessed the act through a kitchen window.

"It gave us security," Mark tells me on Pearl Place, the street in Falls Church, Virginia, where he grew up. Pearl Place is exceptional because there are still a handful of stay-at-home moms there today. When Mark grew up on Pearl, the background presence of moms wasn't odd at all.

"There were always eyes on the street," Mark says, looking around as if he can see his old pals and their moms on the front stoops. He stresses how middle-class the neighborhood was back then. He points to one house: "Policeman." Then another: "A barber there. A butcher next to our house. A shoe salesman in the big house up there. Up on the corner was a mechanic. That house was a milkman."

Want to know how life got harder for parents? Consider how rare such a block is today. Letting your children run around unsupervised is easier when they're not really unsupervised. One reason it's harder to be a free-range parent nowadays is that there are fewer parents with eyes on the street, because there are fewer stay-at-home parents.

This unofficial surveillance state of friends and neighbors is of no small value—and it should appeal across ideological lines. Want to fight delinquency and petty crime without ramping up police presence? Then you want moms pushing strollers down the sidewalk at 10 a.m. and more dads shooting on the local hoops at 3 p.m.

Just as crucial is stay-at-home parents' availability as volunteers. At our old elementary school, lunch hour was mostly staffed by parent volunteers. Some had full-time jobs that allowed them to work from home, and others ran their own small businesses out of their garages, but most were stay-at-home moms and dads. The field trip chaperones were also mostly stay-at-home parents.

Katie, who has stayed at home since our first was born, regularly gets calls from other moms who find themselves stuck late at work or in traffic—*Can you please pick up little Benjy?* Our four-year-old niece has 1 p.m. Friday ballet lessons, and if her baby sister is sick, Katie does ballet duty. When someone delivers a baby, loses a parent, or has a bad accident, in our social circles, the people organizing the Meal Train and baking the casseroles tend to be the stay-at-home moms. As I write these words, early on an October afternoon, Katie is volunteering in our kindergartner's classroom reading a book to the class.

This is a story older than America, historian Anne Firor Scott explained. Women during the American Revolution "banded together to raise money, provide amenities to the soldiers, and support the movement for independence."[29] Yet from 1965 to 1993, the number of women doing volunteer work every week fell by almost half. "In the years since women's liberation, this kind of civic engagement has dropped precipitously," wrote journalist Emma Green. "The most vulnerable members of society have lost their best allies—women—partly because those women are too busy working."[30]

The collapse of civil society is the most important story of the past two generations in America. The loss of the stay-at-home mom is a contributing factor in this dark story. This is yet another reason to stop trying to universalize the daycare-and-full-time-job model: using public policy this way erodes the infrastructure of support that stay-at-home mothers and fathers need, resulting in fewer parents at home with their kids and making their communities healthier.

Government policies can meaningfully boost the birthrate only if they change the culture. The most meaningful cultural change that we can affect with public policy would be to smooth the way for the return of stay-at-home parents. Those parents who stay at home, and their neighbors who both go off to work, will all find the world more family friendly when Mom or Dad is around during the day.

How to Get More Stay-at-Home Parents

So how do we do this? How do we get more moms and dads staying home during the day, either working part time or not earning a paycheck at all?

Deregulation will be part of the answer. For instance, labor laws that make part-time work a legal minefield for employers also make family-friendly jobs scarcer. California, for instance, has an overbearing law called AB-5 that largely outlaws contractor arrangements. Labor unions want to limit who can work as an outside contractor, citing abuse of the rules by employers. These abuses definitely happen, but every "protection" for a low-wage worker guaranteeing full benefits and overtime pay also threatens to eliminate a flexible ad hoc job.

Barriers to entrepreneurship also make it harder to be a stay-at-home parent. I know stay-at-home moms who baked fudge and sold it from their kitchens—something that's illegal in many states, thanks to poorly written food safety regulations. Occupational licensing laws that add fees and hundreds of hours of required training make it tough to turn a profit running a part-time business. Reforming these regulations would open the door for stay-at-home moms and dads to work at their own pace and start to lay the foundation for a full-time return to the workforce down the line.

The federal unemployment program could be reformed to be more generous to single-income families, giving bigger benefits to sole breadwinners who are temporarily out of work.

Here we need to talk again about the various subsidies that exist for parents in the U.S., in some of our states, and in Europe. The U.S. has a Child and Dependent Care Tax Credit that is explicitly not available to stay-at-home parents. If you pay a nanny in order to earn money, you can claim this tax credit. But if you pay a nanny in order to homeschool your older children, chaperone a field trip, make a Home Depot run, go to CrossFit, or just get in a nap, you're out of luck. My former home county provides subsidies for hiring childcare, but likewise, the subsidies are only available while you're working, not if you need to take your oldest kid to the orthodontist during the baby's naptime.

These benefits are poorly targeted social engineering. They declare that paid-childcare-plus-paid-work is the best course for everyone. Most policymakers don't even think about how unfair this is for stay-at-home parents or those who want to prioritize unpaid family and community work.

Another perverse aspect of daycare-and-work subsidies is that they are available only for *taking time away from children.* What if you want to spend time *with* your children, and it's the *other things* that get in the way?

This is my story constantly. On perfect fall Saturdays, when I could be playing football with my kids or taking them for a hike, I have instead spent the entire day pulling down vines or restaining a deck. Back before my sons were old enough to mow, I would spend half a day mowing.

Then, one year, I hired a high school kid to mow, which made me feel like a shirker. When I said that out loud, my wife set me straight with some questions: "Do you remember what you were doing three weeks ago when Henry showed up?"

"Taking the kids to the zoo."

"And two weeks ago?"

"I was at the pool with them."

"And last week?"

"We were in the woods."

That is, I had literally bought time with my wife and kids. If governments are going to give money to families, why is it always to take parents away from their kids, rather than to occasionally help parents spend time *with* their kids?

One college classmate of mine lives in Belgium and uses a wheelchair. She told me the government provides her with low-cost housework, which frees her up to be a parent. She gets to do the work *she* wants to do, visiting parks and museums with her children, because she is able to offload the domestic tasks she doesn't want to do.

I don't think a weekly lawn-mower benefit for parents would be good public policy. Rather than stacking up competing subsidies, federal and local governments should fold them all into something much simpler that is proven to boost family formation: a straight cash benefit or tax credit for parents. Congress should end the federal child and dependent care tax credit and roll that money into a larger child tax credit. If Montgomery County can afford a few million to subsidize daycare, it can afford to just hand that same few million to parents and say "spend this on daycare if you want, or use it as a cushion so you can switch to part-time work—or heck, hire the neighbor's kid to mow your lawn so you can take your kids to the zoo."

Another vital need is tackling parents' loneliness. Parents at home with their kids during the day need community, and they need somewhere to go. Like most things pro-family, parents being out and about the neighborhood during the day is contagious.

Neighborhoods with lots of stay-at-home parents will have more businesses serving those parents: a family-friendly coffee shop or lunch place, a Little Gym with midday open play, a community ice rink with discounted off-hour skating sessions, and playgrounds that get more TLC. I complain a lot about Montgomery County, Maryland, but it is excellent at providing daytime activities for tots and their parents at libraries and community centers. "Mommy and Me Yoga" may not turn Mommy or Baby into gymnasts, but it gives stay-at-home parents opportunities for community and connection.

The opposite is also true. Shawn is a dad I met in Winchester, Virginia. When he and his wife had kids, she stayed home with the baby—something they both wanted. But "she got to the point where she got kind of cabin fever, and it was 'I can't stay home anymore.' I tried to push her to get out," either by herself on nights or weekends, or with the kids, "but she always felt guilty because it cost money." She took a job making less money than she was paying in childcare just to get out of the house. There wasn't free stuff or affordable family stuff in the Winchester area.

This becomes a mental health story, too. Staying at home with young children, more than most vocations, demands company, because it can be soul-crushing. "The loneliness is the thing," Bethany, a mom of six, told me with a wince, recalling her earliest days staying at home. But "lonely" isn't quite right. If you have a newborn and a three-year-old, you might never actually be alone, but you can certainly be isolated. Your children don't yet provide intelligent conversation, and half of the culture dismisses or diminishes the work you do or pretends you don't actually exist.

Some mothers who spend all their time with their kids don't have these feelings—they rarely feel sad or isolated or alone. But my wife is not one of those lucky moms. Katie loves her work as full-time homemaker, and her devotion to her family is unmatched. At the same time, she's naturally an introvert who has struggled since childhood with anxiety, depression, and an audio processing disorder. The "beautiful chaos" that so many large Catholic families celebrate is often *maddening chaos* for her.

Although she's never thought "I wish I were back in the office right now," on some days, after a couple of hours of giving the kids after-school snacks, listening to the sagas of their school days, cracking the whip on homework, and telling them to play outside, she takes time to simply *hide* from the children. Part of my job is to help her escape, taking over homework when I get home, running family outings on the weekends, and even dragging all six kids on vacations solo.

Indispensable, though, to Katie's sanity have been those nearby friends and sisters engaged in the same sort of full-time-parenting work. These women support her, understand her daily struggles, and simply provide company, even when these friends arrive for coffee with their own mobs of rowdy kids. Sometimes the kids play together perfectly, and so ten kids in the house is actually easier than six. Other times, they cling to Mom's legs. Regardless, spending time with other adult humans is an emotional salve.

Shea, Stephanie, and Ellen in Farmington, Utah, homeschool as a co-op for a reason. The moms-of-five in Kemp Mill make sure to get together regularly. But many moms do not have such ready groups of moms available in their communities.

Churches and other local groups should fill these gaps. Silver Spring Christian Reformed Church, in my old neighborhood, hosts a weekly "coffee break" on Wednesdays. It's an informal women's Bible study, which is great, but here's the key detail: the church operates a simultaneous Bible Story Hour for kids aged two to five, and a nursery for those younger.

Every religious congregation and community center should have a moms' group that meets during weekdays and organizes email lists, group chats, and message boards. Again, what stay-at-home moms need most is relief from isolation.

For stay-at-home dads, the loneliness takes on another form. Hanging out with a bunch of moms day after day is likely to fall somewhere between lame and inappropriate for a married man. Male-only or at least male-heavy groups of stay-at-home parents would make more stay-at-home dads. Any progressive city governments out there that want to promote gender equity should run daddy-and-me woodworking classes on Tuesday mornings.

Employers, again, can help by guiding soon-to-be-parents toward new-parent jobs that are stay-at-home friendly. Transition your beat reporter into a features editor. Transition your front-desk receptionist into a spreadsheet-diving numbers cruncher. Ask yourself which tasks can be done on a time lag and done remotely, and package those tasks into part-time, stay-at-home jobs for new parents.

Schools should prepare workers for these jobs, too.

Most large public school systems would never consider this, because it is anathema to workism and gender symmetry. But private schools, especially religious schools, should lay out all the information for the kids (and yes, this will mostly be girls) who would like to eventually stay home with children if life gives them a family of their own.

Master English grammar and style, and if you ever have children, you can go home and work as many hours as you want as a freelancer. Editing other people's writing allows you to scale your workload up and down around the births of your children. The same is true for computer programming.

Goldin, the economist, crunched all the numbers on the pay gap between women and men, and found that it's basically all attributable to mothers seeking greater flexibility. Fields that provide that flexibility have almost no gender pay gap. This knowledge can be incredibly powerful for would-be parents.

Alternatively, get trained in nursing. While working from home won't be possible, you will have a hundred different ways to make a living, with a hundred different work arrangements, and bottomless demand. This will put you in the driver's seat, even after taking a few years off.

In contrast, if you become a lawyer, you may have to choose between long hours at the office or zero income.

Moms and dads who stay at home mostly tell me that the change they want is more respect from the culture toward those who choose parenting as their full-time job. This means fewer Hilary Rosens on CNN saying stay-at-home moms don't work, and fewer Chris Dodds suggesting stay-at-home parents lounge at the country club all day.

It also means fewer breadwinners thinking their income is *theirs*. I explain to my children that just as every belonging Katie and I own is jointly owned, every penny "I earn" is really earned by both of us.

Here's an analogy: Apple has stores that bring in revenue. It also has product designers, who don't directly bring in revenue. Nobody would argue that the Apple Store is more important and deserves more respect than the designers. Likewise, our marriage and family are a jointly held enterprise in which both adults' contributions are of equal value, even if only one of us is a revenue center.

Independence

This brings us to the greatest worry many women have when they think of staying at home, and this goes beyond economics—it goes to the very center of how we understand ourselves, find meaning, and derive our purpose. I've been discussing policy and employer-level fixes, but we need to go deeper.

"I believe I could find child-rearing incredibly meaningful and rewarding, but leaving the workforce would make me vulnerable," one college woman told me in 2022. She worried that her skills and connections would wither if she took even a few months off. "Then if my marriage failed, I would have only the protections afforded me by divorce law in whatever state I happened to live."

This fear comes up every time I discuss stay-at-home parenting. It's not unfounded. Adults who step out of the workforce for years—whether due to disability, chronic unemployment, or raising children—really do suffer career-wise.

Young women are barraged with this message. "Consider this a warning to new mothers," the headline at Salon.com read: "Fourteen years ago, I 'opted out' to focus on my family. Now I'm broke."[31]

"My biggest handicap may be my history of spending daylight hours in the company of my own kids," the author wrote, in a story picked up by National Public Radio.[32] "Just having them is bad enough."

These articles come at young women like commuter trains on a brutally regular schedule. Listen more closely to these warnings, and you hear the notes of sadness. It's a sad way to go into marriage—structuring your life around the assumption it could end at any point. It's also sad to give up something so meaningful and irreplaceable—thousands of hours of your sons' and daughters' childhoods—for what amounts to a financial insurance product.

This posture of fear and this demand for independence aren't just about finances. They are part of the prevailing philosophy of twenty-first-century America and Western Europe. Autonomy is the one good in our culture that must not be compromised.

Autonomy precludes being dependent on anyone. You are vulnerable if you rely on someone else. Trusting another person with your fate, leaning on someone, is weakness—it's a betrayal of your own self-determination. Independence and connection are often inversely related. Belonging is usually purchased at the price of your autonomy.

In the feminism of the 1990s and 2000s, writes author Christine Emba, "Dependency was pathologized as weakness, and connection was seen as a risk."[33]

Commerce and interchange with others is inevitable, but it can be made clean—you can remain *independent*—if it stays strictly transactional, if every interaction is 100 percent consensual and never comes with any ongoing commitment. Keep it all at arm's length, and you keep things sterile and fully chosen. To borrow a term from cryptocurrency and cybersecurity, in the modern world, you can build a zero-trust life. Our culture will sell you this zero-trust life as the only way to maintain your optionality and economic bargaining power.

The constant op-eds celebrating divorce lean on this language of autonomy and independence. "Everything is my choice and I am in charge" is how one divorced mom endorses her regained singlehood.[34]

Another *Times* writer explained how much better her life is now that she's escaped marriage. "Every divorced woman I know is happier post-marriage."[35]

What was wrong with marriage?

She was philosophically opposed, it turned out. "I realized that my soul was no longer aligned with my husband's, much less the whole project of straight monogamous marriage." *One must never let tradition, norms, or commitment to another person interfere with that cosmic mandate of being true to thine own self.*

But also, it was about socks.

Now that she's divorced, "My home is tidy," she writes. In fact, she recommends that even married couples adopt a divorced-like legal arrangement. As she explains, her relationship with her ex-husband and children is also tidier: "[T]here is a lot of very tidy and business-like communication," she writes. Things are now pleasantly "transactional." And she can finally "self-actualize" and "stop spending her weekends picking a grown man's socks off the floor."

Maybe we shouldn't read too much into a fear of socks. Sometimes kaltsaphobia is just kaltsaphobia. But sometimes it's something more. Marriage, even marriage to the most diligent sock-putter-awayer, will always be messy. Parenthood, even if you have a nanny, a house-keeper, and 1.7 perfectly trained children, is always messy.

Yet if we place independence as the highest good ("everything is my choice"), we cannot tolerate other people's messes, because messes intrude on our autonomy. If we are supposed to be the authors of our own lives, then only the one-man or one-woman show will meet our standards.

The only other path is a messy road strewn with socks and reliance—in other words, a family.

Surrender

Surrender is the word my mother-in-law uses to describe family life. This isn't some patriarchal *Handmaid's Tale* stuff: she preached surrender to me to help me understand my role as husband and father. Neither was this some cynical bitterness: surrender isn't an act of sadness; it's an act of love. More important is the converse: love is an act of surrender.

It's anathema (or patriarchy!) in this day and age to expect someone to surrender, but the road of surrender and love is and always has been the only path to happiness.

One of my last moments as a bachelor comes to mind here. My brother had recently moved out of the row house we had shared for years. My lonely bachelor pad, which would become our marital home in a few weeks, began to fill up with boxes of wedding gifts for me and Katie. One day, I started opening them, to put the kitchen wares away in my cupboards. In the first Crate & Barrel box sat the drinking glasses we had chosen for our wedding registry.

"We" is a fiction here. I had no role in selecting most of the products for our registry, and most of them came as surprises. Usually I love surprises. But as I pulled the glasses out of their wrapping and beheld their nonstandard shape, I whined loudly in my tiny, empty row house, "I don't want to drink from square glasses!"

Soon I realized that this was what marriage was.

I cannot count on all our children's toes and fingers even a small fraction of the times my wife, similarly, has surrendered her preferences to mine. My "Bailey's Irish Cream" mirror with all the counties and villages of Ireland was never her choice of wall hangings, yet it has hung on our walls for most of our marriage.

Make surrender a habit, and soon you've surrendered part of your autonomy. You've certainly surrendered your independence. And now, enmeshed in a web of reliance, you can specialize, trusting that your partner will do his or her part. Just as an internal organ cannot survive on its own, someone who has fully surrendered his autonomy and adopted a role in a family has become dependent on the other organs.

Is this terrifying? Yes. Does it ever go wrong? Often. That's why divorce law, alimony, and child support law need to be strict. More important, social stigma needs to be greater for men who leave their wives or who are unwilling to marry the mother of their children if she so desires.

Modernity focuses on the risks of interdependence and tries to construct a culture and an ethics that eliminates those risks—a zero-trust culture. Many writers and philosophers have crafted moral systems based on autonomy.

All such systems become incoherent once you introduce a baby.

A baby demolishes the coherence of an autonomy philosophy, because of what young children so clearly *lack* and what they so clearly *have*. Young children clearly lack the rationality that is the foundation of all philosophies of autonomy. And they so clearly have a claim on us—on our time, on our resources, on our bodies, and on our love.

Children not only are dependent on us; they also strip us of our own independence. To have children is to surrender autonomy—and that's why they are an invaluable blessing.

"What I didn't understand—couldn't have, at the time—was that deserting yourself for another person really *is* a relief," journalist and mother Elizabeth Bruenig writes about her pre-child life. "For this member of a generation famously beset by anxiety, it was a welcome liberation."

Independence can never be an end in itself, and holding it as an ultimate good is a formula for unhappiness. Only through vulnerability and surrender do we ever find meaning in life. And for most people, the most natural way to find something worthy of our surrender, sacrifice, and vulnerability is to start and raise a family.

CHAPTER 13

A Culture of Sterility

The idea that every woman should have as many
babies as she wants is to me exactly the same
kind of idea as everybody ought to be permitted
to throw as much of their garbage into their
neighbor's backyard as they want.
—*Paul Ehrlich, author of* The Population Bomb

It was "one stinking hot night in Delhi" when Paul Ehrlich first
felt the threat of overpopulation. In a taxicab with his wife and
daughter, Ehrlich was appalled that Delhi's "streets seemed alive with
people. People eating, people washing, people sleeping. People visiting, arguing, and screaming. People thrusting their hands through the
taxi window, begging. People defecating and urinating. People cling-
ing to buses. People herding animals. People, people, people, people."[1]

The Population Bomb, Ehrlich's bestselling 1968 tome about overpopulation, cast this landscape of "People, people, people, people" as a
vision of hell. Streets "alive with people" were a horror.

The modern mindset that demands independence above all else also demands control and thus abhors whatever seems to have a life of its own. The *inert* is much more manageable, more fit for rational arrangement, for planning. This is increasingly the worldview of the wealthy West, and this philosophical shift makes our culture discordant with the realities of human life. To speak Greek for a moment, it's an *anti-biotic* mindset.

Human life has always been "stinking hot." It is inevitably chaotic. We adults can engineer for ourselves some modicum of control, some illusion of cleanliness, sterility, and predictability, but once a baby enters the picture the illusion ends. With a baby comes all that dreaded *eating, washing, sleeping, defecating, urinating*. What's more, because it takes a village to raise a child, your baby makes you dependent on other adults, which means *visiting, arguing, screaming*.

People, people, people, people.

Human life has a life of its own, and thus human life is a mess. Yet the modern mind believes life can and should be ordered and made safe. This requires life be made a little less lifelike—made sterile. Wealthy Western countries have succeeded in eliminating many risks and uncertainties from life—infant mortality is way down from historic norms; life spans are much longer.

Yet in a hundred other ways, life in the West has become more precarious. For the middle class and the working class in the U.S., the old forces of stability—community, faith, tradition, extended family—are all eroded.

Robust institutions of civil society are stabilizing forces. They serve as human-level safety nets and provide mentorship, belonging, and purpose. Such institutions are prevalent today mostly in religious communities—like Mormon Utah or Jewish Kemp Mill—and in upper-middle-class, college-educated zip codes. But even in those privileged pockets, the places Charles Murray dubbed the "SuperZIPs," parents always feel that their children are one misstep away from falling off the narrow elite ledge and into the underclass.

When life seems at once controllable yet precarious, the least tolerable thing is unneeded risk. We have become convinced that safety and certainty are attainable, and so we tolerate nothing less.

Thus the ethical codes for Millennials and Generation Z have been built upon a new set of *thou shalt nots*. Thou shalt not commit too early, thou shalt not get pregnant too young, thou shalt not make yourself dependent or expect loyalty.

Inviting the unplanned or uncontrollable into your life is unthinkable because one unwanted nudge could send you off the rails. But "rails" may be the wrong metaphor here. The modern view of control is not really a detailed life plan leading to a particular destination—which is its own sort of folly. Instead, young adults maintain control by *not* committing, by always keeping options open. Optionality has become a good in itself, which is why marriage, children, or other commitments are seen as unneeded risks.

An anti-biotic mindset gives us more sterile lives. Which gives us less love, less marriage, and far less baby-making.

Every pro-family change we need—from individuals or from the culture—requires making things messier, giving up control.

Having lower ambitions for your kids really means loosening your grip—believing that your children will turn out okay even if you don't spend every minute and every dime to give them the best athletic training, best academic tutoring, best professional connections. It means having faith that an *expansive* childhood—with all the unknowns that entails—will be the most fruitful.

Losing your children more means exposing them to more: more germs, more risk, more opinions, more challenges.

Leaning on community—on "the village"—means more "people, people, people, people" and all their noise and mess. It means being dependent on—and dependable to—others.

And of course, a pro-family feminism is one that knocks autonomy off its pedestal.

What a scientist like Ehrlich hates, what all the tastemakers who embrace population control hate, is *dependence*. These *stinking, hot, poor* Indians, dependent on their neighbors and on the foreign passersby—like the unlucky man whom the Good Samaritan found on the road from

Jerusalem to Jericho—represent to people like Ehrlich the failure of humanity, because people like Ehrlich see man's end as one of *independence*.

But Ehrlich is wrong and always has been wrong. The visibly needy, in their neediness, more accurately represent mankind. They make manifest the often-hidden essence of humanity: dependence.

"Dependence is our default state," as writer and mother Leah Libresco Sargeant puts it. Meditating on the chubby helpless fingers of her newborn, or the kicks of her unborn child, or the needs of the elderly, she notes that "self-sufficiency" is "the aberration."[2]

Giving up on the individualistic, self-determined, autonomy-centered religion of independence (whether feminist, workist, or capitalist) also means embracing a more *fertile* life—and thus a life less predictable, less sanitary, and less sterile.

Every Child Is Unplanned

"Do you have a birthing plan?" a friend asked Katie the day before our first baby was born. *Sure*, Katie replied, *but we don't actually expect to stick to it*. I piped in and quoted contemporary philosopher Mike Tyson: "Everyone has a plan till they get punched in the mouth."

Iron Mike's philosophy, channeling Socrates' definition of wisdom and David Hume's notion of epistemic humility, has been indispensable in our two decades as parents. Understanding all your plans as tentative is the necessary foundation of having children at all.

But modern parenthood—especially among elites—increasingly insists on planning. This is part of why parenthood seems to impose a greater cost than it used to.

"[F]or many parents today from the middle class and above, caring for children is not an obligation or a necessity, but a long-anticipated life decision," Emily Brooks, author of *Small Animals*, wrote; "we take on parenthood after a level of deliberation and preparation that would have been foreign to our grandparents or even our parents."

Even the word *parenting* makes it sound like some sort of profession, as other commentators have noted, rather than simply part of ordinary daily life. When people *just have kids*, it's natural. It doesn't even deserve its own verb.

"But when *being a parent* is . . . a thing *you* in particular have chosen," Brooks writes, "a special duty and responsibility that only some accept, the stakes rise. If parenthood is no longer just a relationship or part of 'ordinary life' but instead a new kind of secular religion," then it becomes much more of a burden, filled with a million choices that all carry unimaginable weight.[3]

Some celebrate exactly this shift. We have moved beyond the bad old days when "parenting was simply an assumed part of adult life," writes liberal feminist Jill Filipovic in the *New York Times*. "Thanks to feminist cultural shifts, and better access to contraceptives, more women now approach childbearing the same way we approach other major life decisions: as a choice weighed against other desires, assessed in context."[4]

All this choosing and planning, though, is rooted in an illusion, and not a salutary one. "I remained fixated on making the right choice for my children," Brooks writes. "It was only much later that I began to see how profoundly the choosing itself—the false sense of control and entitlement that choosing entails—had affected my experience as a mother. It created an extra layer of anxiety."[5]

Recall the wisdom of free-range guru Lenore Skenazy: the first error of all-controlling, all-planning parents is the belief that we *can* control and plan a child's life.

"No child is truly planned," wrote Charles Fain Lehman in an essay on loneliness in America, "because all children bring unexpected and enormous changes."[6]

I have been constantly surprised by my children. One of the biggest surprises was how different all my children were from me and Katie and from one another. The physical differences were apparent right away. The personality differences were apparent within the first two years. Somehow, I had believed that if my wife and I raised the kids basically the same, then the kids would end up basically the same. This was a stupid conclusion from an impossible premise.

Embracing the unplanned is central to parenthood. And *embracing* doesn't mean merely *tolerating*. It's *loving* the unplanned.

"Going for a walk with a two-year-old is like going for a walk with William Blake," as mother, philosophy scholar, and psychologist Alison Gopnik puts it.[7] Walk to the corner store as an adult, and you almost don't experience anything. The adult brain, Gopnik explains, rationally has stopped absorbing new data because it doesn't have use for it. "But if you do the same walk with a two-year-old," Gopnik observes, "you realize, wait a minute: This, three blocks, it's just amazing. It's so rich. There's dogs and there's gates and there's pizza flyers and there's plants and trees and there's airplanes."

I never noticed airplanes overhead or silly decorations in windows until I took walks with my children. I never paid attention to the dozen different shapes of leaves on our block until my three-year-old began asking why the leaves on our sidewalk all looked different from one another. My kids made our street more *alive*.

Kids fertilize our world. Childhood is expansive, and not just for the children.

Human wisdom, as Socrates and Tyson explained, is knowing the limits of your own knowledge and your own planning. Human happiness, likewise, is grounded in the unexpected and unplanned. Again, one reason we loved college, and one reason people love living in walkable, park-filled, neighborly places is the constant appearance of the unplanned. It's the serendipitous encounters that make our lives rich. This is antithetical to the scientistic, hyperrational, planner mindset characteristic of modernity, but it's reaffirmed by experience every day.

Filling our life with serendipity and the unplanned gives us an expansive view of life. Aware that infinite variety and possibility lie beyond what we can see or predict, we are cured of the false belief that the world is a fixed pie, over which we all have to fight. A fertile, unplanned life full of the unexpected is a life filled with more hope.

Nothing provides more serendipity, more unexpected friendly encounters than adding roommates to your life who will stick around for eighteen or more years.

And these roommates are essentially unchosen. Sure, you may have *planned* a child, but you didn't get to choose *this* child. A kid isn't like a soul mate you chose or a best friend you elected to move in with. You don't assemble your family the way LeBron James, Chris Bosh, and Dwyane Wade assembled the 2010 Miami Heat. Your kid is more like the way we got a freshman roommate in my day: randomly assigned to you by some higher-up.

One of our weirdest experiences as parents was our very first moment as parents. I had been prepared for Katie's pain in labor and delivery. I had been prepared for the unreal quantity of blood involved in this ordeal. But I wasn't prepared for the first time seeing my daughter's face, and neither was Katie.

"Tim!?" Katie shouted, in disbelief, when the doctor handed her Lucy. *"Tim! Tim?!" What is going on?* was the tone in her voice as her eyes became huge, almost in panic. *What do we do now?* I was having the same exact feelings.

We had named Lucy seven months earlier, the moment we found out she was a girl. Lucy is my mother's name, and my mother's mother's name, and her mother's name before that. I had planned since childhood to keep this tradition alive.

Katie and I had sung lullabies and Irish rebel songs to Lucy in utero, we had set up her nursery, and we had already found her some friends, because Katie's sisters and childhood pals were pregnant at the same time. But after all these months of preparing for her, Lucy entered that labor and delivery room, and I had the strangest reaction:

Who is this person? I have never seen her before. This girl was supposed to be part of our family, but she was a total stranger.

Seven hours later, when I mistook her for another baby in the nursery, it was understandable. We'd only met once before.

We had acquired a roommate for two decades and a friend for life whom neither of us knew. That's not the sort of thing a smart planner does.

"A Very Nice Nursing Home"

"Oh my God, that sounds terrible," Amanda gasps when I tell her I have six children. Thanks to a serendipitously placed open stool at the bar, Amanda has ended up on our trivia team of random strangers at the Ruddy Duck Tavern in southern Maryland. She's thirty-two, and grew up as an only child. She has a good job selling medical equipment. She's happily married, but doesn't want kids.

Why?

She points to uncertainty. "Civil unrest, the international scariness . . . inflation . . . We're going to eventually crash and burn like a 747. So I'm scared for that reason."

Amanda's job has shaped her view of life.

"In the medical field, I've seen a lot of cerebral palsy, Down syndrome, and autism," she explains. "Not only does your life change when you have kids, but your life *really* fucking changes when you have a sick kid. And you have to quit your job, and you have to dedicate your life to that. And I barely, *barely*, maybe like *this much* want kids," she says, holding her fingers half a centimeter apart, "and if I had a kid that had a medical problem like that, I don't know if I'd be able to live with myself. And then I would hate myself because I'd feel like I should love my kid. But my life would change so drastically."

She's right that having kids changes your life. She's right that a child with a serious health problem could change your life "so drastically." And she's articulating the modern ethos in her refusal to risk such disruption to her life.

She sips her vodka and diet ginger ale, and then continues. "I hate the argument, 'Who's going to take care of you when you get old?'" Nobody at the bar has made this argument; Amanda is responding to her own fears. "Not my kid who's addicted to drugs, I can tell you that. Not my cerebral palsy kid who can't take care of anything."

Relying on others is dangerous, especially if those *others* are unknown to you, as all future children are. Amanda has a cleaner plan: "If I *don't* have children, the amount of money I'll be able to save in place of having a child, I'll easily be able to pay for a very nice nursing home, thank you very much."

Safe. Rational. Antiseptic.

Cleanliness is a theme in her comments. Amanda, like Ehrlich, and like so many of the child-free adults I've encountered, keeps mentioning *litter* in her case against children. She mentions a friend whose eight-year-old still wets his bed. The thought of people evokes the thought of filth.

Then again, this was 2021, and so sanitation may have been at the forefront of everyone's mind.

Germination

The first time a stranger told me on Twitter that I didn't deserve to be a parent, it was because I was insufficiently terrified of germs.

"I feel America has forgotten we're still in the middle of a pandemic," wrote liberal commentator Wajahat Ali. "I see packed restaurants and people inside stores and malls and their kids aren't wearing masks. I feel I'm in a horror movie."[8]

That "horror movie" talk was typical of the time. Commentators like Ali spent much of the pandemic sounding like Paul Ehrlich. Human faces, specifically *children's* faces, were the stuff of nightmares. These nightmares, being nightmares, were divorced from the reality of the virus.

Ali wrote of this "horror movie" from Washington, D.C., in late June 2021, when less than one percent of all COVID tests in D.C. were coming back positive. Over the previous two weeks, the District—population 692,000—had suffered a total of four deaths with coronavirus. COVID hospitalization had fallen by nearly 30 percent; cases had fallen by more than 30 percent and were now averaging fewer than ten per day.[9]

Even the overly cautious governments of D.C., Fairfax County, Virginia, and Montgomery County, Maryland, had lifted their mask mandates in most public places. And an overwhelming majority of adults, along with many children, had been vaccinated.

If full restaurants or children's faces, amid near-zero prevalence, looked like a "horror movie," that said something, I speculated, about one's experience with film. "We watch different horror movies," I joked on Twitter.[10]

"You don't deserve those kids you have," replied a man named Rene in San Francisco.[11] It was a common argument at the time: good parents are constantly horrified by the coronavirus. On one level, this was just a new variation on the inescapable theme that if you are not constantly in terror, you are a bad parent. Remember, *don't touch dirt or have a sip of wine while pregnant, don't let your kids walk home from school, don't leave your child unattended in public for one minute.*

But with COVID, this overvigilant, utterly risk-averse talk took on a new character and connotation. When I wrote an article in the *New York Times* calling for more aggressive school reopenings[12] (this was in 2021, after nearly a year of closures, distancing, and masking), the readership response was almost entirely negative. "Until there is a vaccine that protects children, teachers, and staff, there is no justification for herding them together in potentially dangerous classrooms and school corridors," one commenter wrote.

That language of "herds" of children was standard, as was the description of all gatherings as "dangerous." The commenter summed up his view of school: "kids spread germs." The people who closed the schools across two school years had a habit of calling their students "little vectors"[13] or "germ bombs."[14]

Of course, none of this started with coronavirus. This level of fear couldn't have come out of nowhere. When you think back on March and April 2020, and how insanely locked down and isolated so many Americans' lives were in those weeks, it's easy to say, "Oh, there was so much we didn't know then." But you also have to ask how in the world so many of us so quickly accepted the notion that we needed to stay away from everyone.

Our churches and schools and coffee shops all closed. We stopped visiting neighbors, parents, grandkids. We tried to never touch any surfaces outside our homes. We sprayed everything with Lysol for weeks. Some of my friends started washing their groceries because they may have been touched or breathed upon at some point by a farmer, a grocer, or a delivery boy.

Don't go near people. People are dangerous. People are bad.

It was a shocking view of the world, yet it instantly sank in every-where. Right away, Americans adopted social distancing, and many were unwilling to give it up even years later. How could this have become our way of life so quickly? Maybe because it was already in the back of our minds. Many of us already suspected that other people were dangerous and bad. We were already primed to see other people as vectors—or even pathogens themselves.

"We are the virus" was a ridiculous and ridiculed online message in 2020, but it was also the subtext of a massive genre of serious mainstream media content: terror-posting pictures of large outdoor places—beaches, parks, shopping centers—with hundreds of people walking or hang-ing out. Any place that looked "alive with people," to borrow Ehrlich's phrase, was a horror show. The message was clear: *people are threats*.

For many in government and the major media, no amount of pre-caution was too much.

Two years into the pandemic, school superintendents refused to drop their COVID precautions—such as mandating masks on students and barring parents from the building—until the virus was eradicated. "The only off-ramp I want is the one where COVID no longer exists," said Monica Goldson, head of the 110,000-student Prince George's County, Maryland, public school system. "I don't think that that off-ramp will exist. I think this is how our life will be."[15]

When people in China—at the *end* of 2022—started to protest two full years of lockdowns, *Washington Post* reporter Taylor Lorenz as-sailed the protesters. Her own newspaper had tweeted about a "critical flaw in Beijing's 'zero covid' strategy": its perennially locked-down population hadn't gained any level of immunity to the virus. Lorenz rose to defend China's policies and rejected the idea of acquiring im-munity to a virus. "Choosing not to kill off millions of vulnerable people (as the US is doing) isn't a 'critical flaw.'"[16]

Anti-germ maximalism appeared everywhere.

"You may think you're totally safe because you wear a mask and gloves during the pandemic," began an op-ed in the *Washington Post*. "But do you put alcohol up your nose and antiseptic on your eyelids when you come home?"[17] In addition to wearing goggles, a mask, and a face shield, the writer explained, she used tons of chemicals. "I sanitize the car's indoor and outdoor door handles, steering wheel, gear shift and radio buttons." She washed her nostrils throughout the day, reasoning that "a little bit of soap and alcohol probably can't hurt. I also dab my eyelids with Ocusoft Lid Scrub in the hopes that any virus on my eyelids won't go any further."

"When I come in contact with a person, I hold my breath and turn my face away, regardless of whether they wear a mask."

Biology is risk. *Chemistry* is safety.

"There's no such thing as a good cold," Vox explained in a 2022 piece warning people away from the notion that getting sick by living life can be mostly harmless—or can even build up natural immunity. "When it comes to respiratory viruses, you never know what you're breathing in: a mild virus that will cause a few days of snot, or something more deadly."[18]

Rather than risking infection and depending on acquired immunity to prevent really bad conditions, Vox's health reporter wrote, "a safer bet—for immune systems young, old, and everywhere in between—is not getting sick to begin with. Wearing masks, maximizing our indoor air's ventilation and filtration, and other pandemic-era strategies prevent more than just Covid-19."

If *breathing* is a threat, then it's no wonder we want fewer people. Birthrates collapsed in 2020 and 2021. In some places they never recovered. Polls on *attitudes* toward marriage and family formation in 2020 were pretty consistent: on net, the pandemic reduced Americans' desire to get married or have children.[19] And there was a political valence to this shift: a paper in *Scientific American* reported that states with harsher lockdowns and more social distancing protocols had more of a COVID Baby Bust.[20] Longer closures, more mask mandates, and more "stay six feet apart" orders meant fewer children. Again, this is a story about our psychology of sterility and fertility.

Tellingly, children were the main target of pandemic closures and mandates. Many city and state governments lifted their mask mandates for all public places except schools and daycares in 2022. Quarantine rules for exposure were stricter for children than for adults. Bars, concert venues, and tattoo parlors were all opening in fall 2020 while local health officials were barring schoolhouse doors.

Science couldn't explain the stricter lockdowns and mandates on children, because science showed that children were extraordinarily safe from the virus. The cause of this disparate treatment was deeper in our cultural psyche. It was a fear of the *alive*, and nothing teems with life more than children.

Which brings us back to the question: What had primed the adults of 2020 to irrationally fear the alive and find safety in sterility?

Bitter Pill

"The semipermanent hormone disruption of the female sex is a high price for women to have to pay for entry into the professional or sexual worlds."

Christine Emba, the author of these words, is a fairly progressive college-educated Millennial writer at the *Washington Post*. Around age thirty, Emba began to second-guess the dominant sexual ethic of her peer group, and of elite culture. That women *should* want and pursue commitment-free sex, just like men, was pounded into the heads of her generation. But living that way didn't bring the happiness or liberation she was promised, she noted in her 2022 book, *Rethinking Sex*.

A related dogma that went unquestioned in Emba's circles was that girls should get on hormonal birth control in their teens and stay on it permanently, until one day, with career, housing, and partner in order, they may choose to let their natural fertility return.

Who would question these doctors' orders? What were the alternatives? More teen pregnancy? Puritanical sexual repression? Women giving up on their careers?

For two generations, continuous chemical suppression of female biology has been declared the very foundation of prosperity, equality, and independence. In order to self-actualize, women are told, they must pharmaceutically make their body a little more *anti-biotic*.

The chemical and hormonal effects of birth control are profound, and not yet fully understood. The cultural effects are even larger. The birth control pill sterilizes the individual by tricking the ovaries into thinking they have already ovulated. The Pill sterilizes our *society* in three ways: it preserves optionality, it erases difference, and it reduces uncertainty.

Optionality: The Pill is an *optionality* drug. Having children is a commitment. Delaying children keeps you free to choose whom you marry, if you want to marry, whether to settle down, where to move, what job to take.

The Pill also increases your sexual optionality. Margaret Sanger pursued the development of the pill as "something magical that would permit a woman to have sex as often as she liked without becoming pregnant," as friendly biographer Jonathan Eig put it.[21] You could call it a tool for "making your body ready for unprotected sex at any moment," as feminist writer Katherine Dee put it.[22]

Difference-Eraser: The Pill is a difference-eraser as well. Men have always had access to seemingly consequence-free sex. The Pill promised to give that supposed superpower to women. Sterility provided uniformity.

A Certainty Pill: The Pill is supposed to be an inoculation against uncertainty. Life will happen on *your* timeline. Once again, the predictability of chemistry conquers the chaos of biology.

Sterility became a central organizing principle of modern adulthood. The next phase in this sterility culture, following chemistry and optionality, is surgery and permanence—sterilization for men and women.

In the stories of those who increasingly choose this route, the sterility sought was something broader than reproductive infertility; it was the safety that comes from conquering biology. "The procedure was a total relief, almost like the covid shot," college administrator Andy Gress told a *Washington Post* reporter, "like I'm safe now."[23]

The echoes of COVID or infectious disease are everywhere in discussions of sterilization. "One man asked for a sort of 'vasectomy passport,'" like a vaccine passport, the reporter explained, "a letter from [the surgeon] to show his wife that sex would now be free of worry." The virus against which they sought inoculation, in this case, was a child—or perhaps just fertility.

Pregnancy-as-disease is now a mainstream concept. The 2010 Affordable Care Act included a provision requiring health insurance plans to cover 100 percent of the cost of all "preventive care" for women. "We also need to make sure preventive care—so important to women—things such as mammograms are covered in our health care plan," ACA supporter Amy Klobuchar said on the Senate floor at the time.[24]

"Preventive care," as commonly understood, keeps us from getting sick—it's about the prevention of *disease*.

The U.S. Department of Health and Human Services, however, used the "preventive care" provision to require employers to cover all forms of contraception plus sterilization. We now believe, as a society, that we have a right be inoculated against risk—sterilized against uncertainty or change.

This might be the Pill's greatest impact: it has created a widespread demand for and belief in inoculation. The Pill's primary impact certainly hasn't been the prevention of unwanted or unmarried pregnancy: In 1968, 1 in 14 parents was unmarried; fifty years later, the number was 1 in 4.[25] One in three children in 2019 was living with a solo mom, solo dad, or unmarried parents.

When the Pill hit American society full force in 1970, the U.S. had 26 births per 1,000 unmarried women of childbearing age.[26] By 2016, after two generations of the Pill, the number rose to 42 births per 1,000 unmarried women.[27] "Meanwhile," Pew research noted, "birthrates for married women have declined, from 121 births per 1,000 down to about 90."

How the Pill Works

How could the birth control pill cause an increase in unwed motherhood but a decrease in married childbearing? The short answer is that the Pill fueled the sexual revolution by divorcing sex from marriage and family formation. (This, in turn, divorced sex from love.)

Here's a better answer, though: the Pill transformed how the public thinks about pregnancy and parenthood in a family-unfriendly way. Reproduction, as Kim Brooks and Stephanie Murray explained, has shifted from being a natural occurrence to being an individual choice.

This changed how our culture sees "other people's kids," and how men see their own biological children. Janet Yellen, a few decades before Barack Obama appointed her to head the Federal Reserve and before Joe Biden named her Treasury secretary, explained how contraception, abortion, and unmarried births could all go up together. In an essay coauthored with her husband, George Akerlof, also an economist, Yellen wrote:

> Before the sexual revolution, women had less freedom, but men were expected to assume responsibility for their welfare. Today women are more free to choose, but men have afforded themselves the comparable option. "If she is not willing to have an abortion or use contraception," the man can reason, "why should I sacrifice myself to get married?" By making the birth of the child the physical choice of the mother, the sexual revolution has made marriage and child support a social choice of the father.[28]

This is how the Pill changed America—not primarily through changing women's biology, but through changing our culture's sense of commitment.

The data about the sexual revolution don't really make sense if you are asking questions strictly about medical technology or law or economics. This is a story about the whole culture. Changing our views on marriage, love, sex, and pregnancies resulted in more single motherhood, but on net the Pill's cultural changes drove *down* birthrates— not just through the chemical effect on women's bodies, but through the cultural effect on society.

The Pill made our culture less child friendly because making children into a "choice" has relieved society from its duty to care for children.

Again, the incisive words of writer Stephanie Murray: "Children are a personal choice and therefore a personal problem, many people seem to believe. Have as many as you want—just make sure they don't bother the rest of us."

This is how we get a culture in which parents who dare to bring their baby onto an airplane feel they are a burden to all their fellow passengers. It's how we get a society that sees career maximalism as the default and children as a hindrance. This is how people like Republican senator Ron Johnson can argue against a child tax credit by saying, "People decide to have families and become parents. That's something they need to consider when they make that choice. I've never really felt it was society's responsibility to take care of other people's children."[29]

The sexual revolution, and especially the Pill, entrenched the view that a child is a consumption item or a lifestyle choice—like buying a boat—that comes with predictable costs. This has undoubtedly made America a worse place to raise children, because it has wiped out the view that children have a claim on society.

Perhaps the most pernicious idea in the history of birth control was the notion that there is a whole portion of humanity that is better off never being born.

The Perfection of the Race

"More children from the fit, less from the unfit—that is the chief issue in birth control."

Thus proclaimed the editorial in the May issue of the *Birth Control Review* in 1919. The editorial lamented that uncontrolled birth was "cluttering the highway of progress with cripples, imbeciles and mendicants"—or as Amanda at the Ruddy Duck would put it a hundred years later, "kids who are addicted to drugs" or "cerebral palsy kids who can't take care of anything."

This was a special issue of the *Birth Control Review*, a journal that existed to stand athwart willy-nilly reproduction crying *Halt!* The ed-itorial about progress versus "cripples" was reprinted from the journal *American Medicine*, along with an op-ed by Margaret Sanger, one of the mothers of the Pill—and a eugenicist.

The same issue included a list of recommended "Books on Birth Control and Kindred Subjects," including *Uncontrolled Breeding* by Adelyne More (a pseudonym for Charles K. Ogden), the alternative ti-tles of which were *Fecundity Against Civilization* and *Parenthood and Race Culture*. The book was dedicated to "Francis Galton, the August Master of All Eugenicists."

Uncontrolled Breeding mocked the sentimental notion "that the ne-gro is mentally and morally the equal of the Caucasian," and painted the average woman without birth control as the "unfit breeder of the unfit." The result of uncontrolled breeding is "the rapid increase of the feebleminded."

Birth control, of course, is the norm now in the wealthy world. Most women use birth control pills or devices at some point in their lives, and the evangelization for birth control—by governments, non-profits, or public health officials—rarely has even a hint of eugenics these days. But the eugenic ideas of the early twentieth century are not as dead as one might assume.

The eugenicists' greatest enemy was Christian anthropology. The Christian believes that man is good but fallen, and that we are not perfectible. What's more, the Christian believes that human nature is fixed. The eugenicist believes that humans are like a variety of flower (but a particularly gnarly flower) that can be improved with some se-lective breeding.

"Race improvement" was one of the ways eugenicists described their project. It sounds creepy to the modern ear because it is creepy. The birth control movement a hundred years ago saw as its aim the improvement of the human race. That notion—that the human race can be and must be improved—is still popular today. One premise of today's race-improvers is that human existence can be cleansed of evil and scrubbed of risk, not through selective breeding but through enough government action. This goal is behind some arguments against having children.

The belief that life can and must be made risk-free is tied to a deeper, unstated premise here: that we can and must make humans much better than we are. The error is not merely in believing that human nature is changeable. The error is also in believing that we are, at present, not good.

CHAPTER 14

Civilizational Sadness

Birth rates and a welcoming attitude reveal how
much happiness is present in society. A happy
community naturally develops the desire to
generate and welcome others, while an unhappy
society is reduced to a group of individuals
defending what they have at all costs.
—*Pope Francis*

Every hour in Germany, an average of 84 babies are born, and
about 122 Germans die.[1] This birth deficit has persisted since 1980
and is getting worse every year.

Germany, home to Europe's largest economy, has had a birthrate
lower than France, the United Kingdom, the United States, and the
overall European average consistently since 1960. It dropped below 1.5
babies per woman in the mid-1970s and didn't return above that level
for forty years. In 1994, Germany's birthrate hit a shockingly low 1.24.[2]

While the U.S. was experiencing its twenty-first-century mini Baby
Boom before the Great Recession, German demographers reported that

"no other OECD country worldwide has fewer births per 1,000 inhabitants than Germany."[3]

In 2015, the BBC reported, "Germany passes Japan to have world's lowest birth rate." Italy's birthrate was right behind Germany's and Japan's.[4]

One couldn't help but notice that the countries least interested in reproducing were the countries that had been on the wrong side of a world war or two in the previous century.

Germany's infecundity seems germane. The German birthrate plummeted during World War I, along with birthrates in the rest of Europe. After the Armistice, France rebounded to a birthrate above its prewar trend, making up for some of the babies forgone during the war; Germany simply returned to its prewar downward trend.

As the Nazis took power, preaching race improvement, they tried to implement the old eugenic game plan: "more children from the fit, less from the unfit." But the Nazis undermined their own plans for more Aryan babies by starting yet another war. Waging war, for many reasons, is rarely a pro-family policy. After World War II, Germany—both East and West—had a small Baby Boom, a little bit later than the U.S. and a lot smaller.

Then, in the 1960s, about the time that the German people belatedly began reckoning with the unspeakable evil their country had committed, a two-generation-long German Baby Bust began. This wasn't a question of couples having smaller families because of birth control. Childlessness quadrupled over the course of a generation, with nearly one-third of West German women childless by the time they aged out of their fertile years.[5]

Economics cannot explain Germans' extraordinary aversion to reproducing themselves. When Germany lagged economically behind the United States, United Kingdom, and France, Germany lagged in birthrates. When Germany's economy was growing faster than those others, Germany still lagged in birthrates. And it's not geography: Germany had a lower birthrate than every large or medium-sized country it borders almost every year from the mid-1950s until 2000.

One of the factors driving Germany's extraordinary Baby Bust, no doubt, was the belief that they, as Germans, were not good.

Adolf Hitler was not some outside conqueror imposed upon the Germans—Germans had chosen him. The Holocaust was not carried out only by evil generals but was also perpetrated by a significant slice of the German population. The war—the invasions, the mass slaughter, the senseless death—was a war of aggression waged by Germany as a whole. Once Germans started to confront this past, they lost their appetite for making more Germans.

So here's the question for our times: How much is the German postwar experience echoed in America's Baby Bust today? How much of our resistance to family formation is rooted in the belief, stated or unstated, that *we simply aren't good*?

No sane person would assign to twenty-first-century Americans the guilt of mid-twentieth-century Germans—or anything close. But on a smaller scale, something similar is happening in the American psyche.

For a contrast, consider America in the 1950s and '60s. The Baby Boom wasn't merely a return to the prewar norm as Germany had in the 1920s. Americans weren't just making up for lost baby-making time during the war. This was an unprecedented, generation-long climb in birthrates—one that demographers had thought impossible. And no other country had a Baby Boom even close to the size of America's.

The Baby Boom had a hundred causes (just like our current Baby Bust). But one cause was the national mood. Our young men got off a boat, having just saved the world by defeating two evil empires—some of the worst evil mankind had ever seen—and they were greeted by young women who had kept the economy going for five years.

Never before that moment or since have Americans been as certain that we were good. Our young men and women were the heroes of the planet. So these hero men and hero women high-fived one another, smooched on the pier, got married, went back to their new homes, and started making babies.

While this was an extraordinary moment in modern history, and there were many pro-family dynamics at play, there's also a universal rule at play here. A crucial and underappreciated factor in the desire of a people to reproduce itself is how the people answer this question: *Are we good?*

The *we* in this question is as subjective as the *good*. Maybe the *we* you think of is Americans, maybe it's Mormons, maybe it's working-class Hispanics, maybe it's San Francisco hipsters.

And maybe your definition of *good* is based on whether we harm or help the planet. Maybe it's based on whether God loves us.

Germans in 1970 couldn't say "We Germans are good." Can today's upper-middle-class liberals say "We are good"? Can those who believe we face a climate apocalypse of our own making believe that we are good? Can those who think that America is essentially and irreparably racist believe that we are good? Can you scroll social media all day long and think we are good? Can modern men and women who increasingly reject the idea of a loving God look beyond their own failings and see an ultimately good soul?

Or are we all overcome by a mixture of guilt, despair, and grief—a civilizational sadness?

Civilizational sadness is not unique to our time and place. It's not the only cause of our Baby Bust. But it's clearly a major cause, and it underlies many of the others.

It's especially pernicious because, unlike Malthus's model of birthrates, in which Baby Booms and Busts are self-correcting, sadness is self-reinforcing. Malthus thought fewer babies led to prosperity and thus hope. The twenty-first century shows us the opposite: a sadder society has fewer children, and in turn a more childless society has less joy and less hope, causing more sadness.

One main source of our sadness is the steady diet of fear fed us by the news media, which often ties this fear directly to family formation. Under the headline "To Breed or Not to Breed," a *New York Times* obituary reporter recited a litany of terrors: "A rise in political extremism, at home and abroad. A pandemic that has killed more than five million. Thousand-year floods that wiped out Western Europe towns. West Coast wildfires that grow more unimaginable in scale each summer."[6]

The message has sunk in. Pew Research asks Americans, "Looking ahead to the next 10 years, do you think your life overall will be better?" A clear majority (62 percent) said yes in 2014. By 2022, it was a minority (46 percent).[7]

If the world really were doomed, maybe it would be cruel to have children. But this laundry list of potential catastrophes is an incomplete account of our pessimism. There is something going on here under the surface that is worse, and hard to see clearly.

Our cultural "duty to fear" is often a culture-wide cover for unresolvable *guilt*.

A Cover for Guilt

"Your Kids Are Not Doomed" was the startling headline above a 2022 *New York Times* story by liberal writer Ezra Klein. He felt he had to say it, because the most frequent question he gets at speeches, during dinner parties, and from podcast listeners is *Should I have kids, given this climate crisis?*[8]

If you wanted evidence of sadness, start with that grim detail: lots of Americans apparently turn to their favorite policy wonk at the *New York Times* for advice on how to live their lives. But Klein had a good answer. He would observe a telling fact: Climate scientists and climate activists keep having kids. Why?

"I unequivocally reject, scientifically and personally, the notion that children are somehow doomed to an unhappy life," climate scientist Kate Marvel of Columbia University told him.

"What looks like apocalypse in prospect," commented *Uninhabitable Earth* author David Wallace-Wells, who has two children, "often feels more like grim normality when it arrives in the present."

Klein got more precise: the people (like Miley Cyrus) saying they couldn't bear handing a burning, flooded, poisoned world to their kids are disproportionately rich people in the world's richest country. These are precisely the people least harmed by climate change and most capable of adaptation. "Wealthy Californians breathing in wildfire smoke are not facing the suffering of poor Bangladeshis whose homes lie in the path of cyclones."

What's more, even if climate change makes human life worse than it would have been, it's madness to conclude that human life over the next century will be worse than it has been in past centuries. Plagues, pestilence, war, crime, and violence have all been far worse through most of human history than they are now. Even the dourest climate alarmists paint a picture of human life in 2100 that is far healthier and far happier than much of the past ten thousand years.

The other totems of dread similarly don't hold up as rational arguments against continuing the species. Racism is inextricable from any culture, and America has a particularly evil history on this front. But the increased racial pessimism, blame, and guilt in recent years makes no sense if you consider how much greater equality is, and how much less present racism is in the 2020s compared to most of American history—or if you consider how much more equal twenty-first-century America is compared to most civilizations in history.

So why do wealthy Western liberals spend so much time expressing these fears, particularly as arguments against procreating? Is it simply an excuse by people who feel inadequate, despair of their marriage prospects, or are too lazy to give up a life of video games?

We shouldn't be that uncharitable, but we should question how real the expressed fear is. Part of it is the precarity-amid-stability we spoke of last chapter. Extreme weather is psychologically more disconcerting to modern wealthy man, who has convinced himself that he can make life predictable.

Klein has an additional explanation that is at once skeptical but generous: "The fear about the future our children will face, when voiced by well-off residents of wealthy countries, sometimes strikes me as a transference of guilt into terror."

The guilt here is guilt that we—in this case, "we" means "the well-off residents of wealthy countries"—through our consumption and lifestyle have poisoned the planet in a way that will make life miserable for others.

Climate change, like litter, comes up again and again in discussions of family. These are both best understood as totems—symbols that represent something much larger and much harder to express.

Climate change is a totem of dread. Dread is a cover story for guilt. The people asking Ezra Klein if it's okay for them to have kids are people who worry, *We make the world worse; we are not good.*

"We Are the Source of Our Harm"

"In general, do I think people are good?" child-free Amanda at the Ruddy Duck asked rhetorically. "No, I don't. I think we're the cancer of the Earth."

Principal William A. Burley would be proud.

"Virtually all degradation of the environment, all exhaustion of natural resources and substantial human suffering can be attributed to the crushing effect of a population that is too numerous for our planet," wrote Burley in 1990, head of the now-shuttered John Petti-bone School.[9]

"All people shoulder some blame," he asserted in his *New York Times* op-ed. Children must be brought "to see that the earth cannot withstand mistreatment by hordes of people. And [we must] show them how the American life style is particularly damaging to the environment."

The op-ed, recall, was illustrated with cartoon drawing of an endless swarm of cute bunny rabbits devouring the Earth in the form of a head of cabbage. Principal Burley's lesson to the little children was clear: *You are the harm.* This lesson has rained down on young Americans for more than thirty years.

We are the virus, and conscientious people do not spread a virus.

"Children, in a kind of cold way of looking at it, are an externality," explains Travis Rieder, a professor at Johns Hopkins University. "We as parents, we as family members, we get the good. And the world, the community, pays the cost."

Rieder lectures college students the way Burley lectured his students, using "the prospect of climate catastrophe" in order "to convince them not to have children," as NPR put it.[10]

"Should We Be Having Kids in the Age of Climate Change?" was NPR's headline. Rieder's wife, Sadiye, who came from a big extended Turkish family, "enjoyed having people around all the time" and wanted a big family. But she found "it's not easy to convince a philosopher," and so they have one daughter and will have no more: "One and done," Sadiye says.

"Every new human comes with a carbon footprint," the *New York Times* warns would-be parents. This constant drumbeat is sinking into young Americans' minds. Climate change, say 13 percent of childless American Millennials, is a major reason they don't have children. Another 21 percent say it is a minor reason. That means one in three childless Millennials cite climate change as a cause of their childlessness.

The "movement to not have children owing to fears over climate change is growing and impacting fertility rates quicker than any preceding trend in the field of fertility decline," Morgan Stanley wrote to investors in the summer of 2021.[11]

Climate guilt and fear are central to the story of why Millennials and Gen Z seem so averse to family. But climate isn't the only source of guilt. From every direction comes the message: *We cause harm. We are not good.*

We are told America is a force for evil in the world, a colonialist power exploiting poor countries through rapacious capitalism and greedy wars. America is irreparably racist. White Americans are by nature racist, and black Americans will always be despised by their country. We are vectors of disease, sources of litter, the scourge of animal and plant life.

The creed of doom keeps going. As *trauma* becomes a major source of identity for many young people, a sort of neo-Freudianism implants the belief that the parent-child relationship is inherently harmful. "My generation is very aware of the ways that our parents traumatized us," said Millennial Darlene Nickell, in explaining why she had herself sterilized.[12]

Parents are de facto sources of trauma—that was the message of Sigmund Freud, and it's a central message on TikTok and Instagram. If this were true, it would be ludicrous, even monstrous, to become a parent.

"Would Human Extinction Be a Tragedy?" asked a *New York Times* headline around Christmas 2018.[13] "Our species possesses inherent value," the subhead granted, "but we are devastating the earth and causing unimaginable animal suffering." Philosophy professors place such pieces in major publications on a regular schedule.

"There's this view," psychologist Clay Routledge explained to me, "that humans have been bad for the world. It's actually moral to select ourselves out."

More concisely, many young Americans believe "humans were a mistake."[14]

This belief has consequences.

What Civilizational Sadness Does

Overdose deaths hit an all-time high in 2020.[15] Suicides hit an all-time high in 2018.[16] From 2010 to 2019, alcohol-related deaths increased by nearly 40 percent. "Deaths of despair," as they are known, are startlingly on the rise in the U.S. And this is just the surface of our sadness, what we can measure.

We trust one another far less than we used to. "In the 1970s," pollster Ryan Burge noted, "about 40% of 18–35 [year] olds said that people could generally be trusted. By the 2010s, that had nearly dropped in half to 22%."[17]

We are lonely. Most men are unhappy with the number of friends they have, while 15 percent report having no close friends at all—that latter number was 3 percent as recently as 1990.[18]

Loneliness has been on the rise for years, and the pandemic and its lockdowns made things far worse.[19] Americans spent nine more hours alone each week in 2021 than they did in 2013, and that came at the expense of time spent with friends and companions.[20]

Loneliness is tied up with not only personal sadness but a broader sadness that becomes a negativity about humanity. "Unchecked, loneliness can also lead to misanthropy," as writer Cathy Reisenwitz put it. "If the problem isn't me, it must be them. Or maybe it's both of us."[21]

Loneliness, friendlessness, mistrust, and deaths of despair are symptoms of civilizational sadness.

The causes for our Baby Bust, we noted in the previous chapter, are tied up with disordered demand for sterility and a disdain for all things messy, noisy, unpredictable, and otherwise life-affirming. Likewise, all the problems we laid out throughout this book—starting with travel sports—are made worse by sadness. The changes we need in order to make our culture family friendly, and to emerge from this demographic valley, are all about overcoming sadness and embracing humans' inherent value.

Overly ambitious parents raising overextended children are both a cause and an effect of sadness. When parents organize their lives and their kids' lives around the relentless pursuit of perfection, they can convey the notion that their child's worth is tied up with worldly success. At best, this is an accidental implication. At worst, it is the parents' or the kids' actual belief. This view, that humans are good only if they succeed, is a sad—and incorrect—view of mankind. It's not accidental that this belief rises as family size shrinks. "Quality over quantity" parenting is really "anxiety over charity" parenting. Yes, Katie and I can tell you that raising six kids can be harrying and exhausting, but it's a picnic compared to trying to raise one kid to perfection.

Fear, too, is sadness. It reflects the misanthropic view that every stranger is a threat. Love's opposite is not hate so much as fear, and so a life full of fear is a life lacking in love.

Accepting and seeking the help of our neighbors—and offering our own help in return—is also an antidote to sadness, as the data on our loneliness epidemic shows. Loneliness and isolation cause sadness, but at the same time it goes the other way: sadness causes loneliness and isolation. We have ceased to believe our neighbors are good—or we no longer believe we are worthy of their help.

Is there anything that has so obviously spread unhappiness and embedded sadness in our culture as addictive smartphones and social media? These enemies of friendship, dating, love, and reproduction are devices that mass-produce loathing and sadness.

A family-friendly feminism involves accepting our natural differences, counting on the goodwill of others, elevating human relationships over material acquisition, and finding our meaning outside worldly success. Workism is a religion of sadness, and its antidote—a family-friendly feminism—is an embrace of embodied humanity.

Finally, the demand for sterility is fundamentally an atomistic, antibiotic, fearful view that sees our fellow humans as threats, but also throws doubt on the value of our own lives.

Until we reject these destructive trends and attitudes, and embrace the full, messy, unpredictable *fertility* of life, we will be a sad civilization. And while civilizational sadness pervades all ages and demographics, it resides most heavily in the hearts of those who could—who should—be forming families right now.

We Need to Talk About the Millennials

How sure am I that this sadness drives our demographics? I can't prove it, but the circumstantial evidence is pretty strong.

Wherever civilizational sadness shows up, the Baby Bust shows up. Demographically, ideologically, and geographically, sadness and infecundity go together.

Michigan State University psychologist Jennifer Neal sought out personality differences between (a) adults with children and (b) their peers who had chosen to be "child-free." (This second category does not include the involuntarily childless.) She couldn't find any personality differences between parents and the child-free, but she did find *ideological* differences. "We did find that childfree individuals were significantly more liberal than parents, even after controlling for demographic characteristics."[22]

Child-free Democrats were twice as likely to cite climate change as a reason for their infecundity than were child-free Republicans; independents were in the middle.[23] The *Times* reported in 2021 that "the people who cited climate change as a reason to have fewer children were significantly more likely to be college-educated and Democrats, and slightly more likely to be white, nonreligious and high earners."[24] This lines up with the demographics of civilizational sadness.

Pew asked Americans their views on the U.S. compared to other countries. Does the U.S. stand above all countries, is it one of the greatest countries, or neither—is it worse than other countries? Only 23 percent of Americans said that the U.S. is worse than other countries (equal to the percentage that said the U.S. is the greatest). But a clear majority of Democrats under age thirty said other countries are better than the U.S., while only 5 percent said the U.S. is the greatest. This survey was in July 2021, so this wasn't just hatred of Donald Trump speaking. Millennial and Gen Z liberals do not think America is good.

Our epidemic of unhappiness, anxiety, and loneliness is concentrated among Millennials and Gen Z. Anxiety rates are much higher among Millennials and Gen Z than they were among previous generations.[25] Only 55 percent of Millennials believe that humanity is basically good, one 2019 poll found.[26]

This sadness is personal, too. "Liberals, especially liberal women, are significantly less likely to be happy with their lives," reported Brad Wilcox, citing YouGov's 2022 American Family Survey. Conservative women were twice as likely as liberal women to say they were "completely satisfied with life."[27] Eight in ten Millennials believed themselves to be "not good enough" in general.[28]

Every disproportionately sad demographic in America today is also a more childless demographic.

Democratic counties are also the counties with lowest birthrates—and the difference isn't small. Demographer Lyman Stone found "the most pro-Biden counties having total fertility rates almost 25% lower than the most pro-Trump counties." This wasn't just because Republican counties tend to have more space and lower housing costs—even controlling for population density, having more Republicans predicted having more babies. What's more, counties that have drifted rightward over the past few decades have become more fecund as they drifted.[29]

Individual surveys show this correlation, too. Liberal women ages 30 to 44 average about 1.5 babies. Conservative women in that age range average about 2.4. "Conservatives generally have more kids, and have them earlier," Stone summarized.

The childbearing gap between conservatives and liberals has been pretty steady since the early 1980s. (There's some evidence it has widened since around 2015.) This hints toward a politically controversial but mathematically straightforward explanation for our falling fecundity: liberal women have long had fewer babies and have had them later; the change over the last twenty years has been that more and more young women are liberal. In the twenty-first century, increasingly, being a young liberal woman means being sad and afraid.

There are a hundred reasons Millennial and Gen Z women might be more liberal than their predecessors. That's a topic for another book. But why are they more fearful, more eager for sterility and certainty? Perhaps it was 9/11. For those of us who were adults in 2001, warnings of the "existential threat" of Islamic terrorism sounded like overheated political rhetoric, and the TSA pat-downs and security state seemed like an annoying intrusion. For those who were children at the time and unable to discern the validity or reasonability of these responses, the security measures were declarations about the nature of the world: *We are under serious threat at all times.*

Or maybe it was the financial crisis. For Generation X and older, the crisis of 2008 was upending, impoverishing, and rattling. This once-in-a-lifetime event destroyed savings, ruined careers. For the kids just coming out of college, though, it was much more. It seemed to set an expectation that everything can turn upside down at any moment.

In his 2023 film *Birthgap*, statistician Stephen Shaw pinpointed the start of some countries' Baby Busts at the 1974 oil crisis, and others' at the 2008 financial crisis. Long after the economy recovered from these shocks, young adults were left with a lasting sense of precarity.

However, the most persuasive clues come from examining who isn't sad, and what makes them unique. If Millennial liberal women are most susceptible to sadness, who is most immune? You'll find them in Rexburg and Kemp Mill.

The mobs of kids on Purim at Kemp Mill Synagogue dressed as LeBron James or Batman testify to this truth. So does the baby boutique on College Avenue, just off the campus of BYU–Idaho. So do the dads pushing strollers through Jerusalem's Old City.

So, too, does my own life.

On a given Saturday, you will find me at a picnic or a backyard barbecue where the child-to-adult ratio is about 3-to-1. As I've described earlier, our large family lives in an ecosystem of other large families. Our kids have forty cousins, and many of their friends have more. Here's another way to measure it: Katie and I have seven joint godchildren, the children of family and close friends; those godchildren average five siblings each.

Many of our friends and family go to Mass seven days a week. Our children's schools make Mass and Confession available every day. We have three priests in our extended family, and other priest friends who are part of our lives. Our faith is the tree planted in the center of our lives, and one of the fruits of that tree is a home, and a community, teeming with life. *People, people, people, people.*

We have planted ourselves, like the Jews of Kemp Mill and the Mormons of Rexburg, in family-friendly subcultures in the midst of a family-unfriendly culture. Why are the religious so fecund? We could answer, along with Oren, the shopkeeper in Jerusalem, *"Mitzvah!"* It was God's first commandment. But that isn't quite adequate. Again, religion is the first seed that helps create an environment that welcomes big families. But the environmental explanation needs to be expanded a bit.

Religion is an inoculation against civilizational sadness.

Religiosity breeds happiness—the social science confirms it, even if Hollywood scripts say otherwise. Specifically, being religiously active—belonging to a religious community and attending services at the church, synagogue, or mosque—predicts happiness. In the U.S., the religiously active are 50 percent more likely to say they are very happy than are the unaffiliated or the inactive.[30] That's a massive gap, and the numbers are similar in nearly every country.

Notably, Utah and North Dakota rank near the top of most happiness measures, and they rank at the top of birthrates.

This dividing line on happiness is also the dividing line on baby-making. Americans who go to church, synagogue, or mosque at least weekly reproduce at or above the replacement rate, while others are well below replacement.

Weekly attendees had 2.2 children each before the pandemic. The nonreligious have consistently lagged the religious by about three-fourths of a baby, and they dropped to 1.4 babies just before the pandemic. Those who attend church but do so less than weekly consistently fall in the middle.

Our birthrate is falling because we're becoming less religious. The fastest-growing "religious" group in the U.S. is the "nones." These aren't all devout atheists, but they are people who simply don't belong to a religion.

As a result, the actively religious population is shrinking, especially among Protestants, who made up a majority of the U.S. population in 2007; they had dropped to 40 percent in 2021. While the percentage of Catholics is holding steady at about one in four or one in five Americans, most of those Catholics are not in the pews on a given Sunday. Although Sunday Mass is an obligation in Catholic teaching, only 26 percent of self-identified Catholics say they go to church weekly.[31]

Young Americans are leading this march toward secularization. A full 40 percent of Millennials identified as religiously unaffiliated in a 2019 poll.[32]

Pop culture and media portrayals of organized religion paint a picture of dark, brooding, guilt-ridden worlds of fire, brimstone, and fear. A de-Christianizing America was supposed to be a happier, more liberated, brighter one. Instead it's an America that traded out hope and love of mankind for self-loathing and a constant terror of the coming inferno.

We have exited the garden that made family easier and more natural, and found ourselves toiling in an infertile landscape. The dread, guilt, and sadness taking over our society are the evils that rush into the vacuum created by a culture that tried to discard God and all other traditional sources of meaning.

UP, UP, DOWN, DOWN

Food and shelter are not sufficient for human life. It turns out that parties, sex, video games, Netflix, and margaritas in Paris are also ultimately unsatisfying.

Something is missing in modern wealthy lives.

Americans are blessed. Most of us have a roof over our head. We're not afraid of losing a limb to gangrene. We have endless entertainment and delicious, filling food. All of these are good things.

But along with our individual-level comfort and health, we suffer from a lack of meaning, and this is at the heart of our civilizational sadness. We have less interpersonal connection. We have less sense of purpose. When we try to find purpose and connection elsewhere, such as work or politics, we come away empty.

Some people succeed in building lives full of connection and purpose through volunteering, joining, and loving our friends and neighbors with sacrificial love. While doable in today's world, it is difficult— which brings us to one final argument for becoming a parent, and even a parent of a big family.

Much of this book has discussed choices we can make and the changes our culture should make in order to ease the burden of being a parent.

Quitting your job, pulling your kid from travel lacrosse, moving next door to a playground, moving across the street from your sister, and losing your kids from time to time are all ways parents can make their lives easier. Neighborhoods built for people rather than cars, child tax credits, and free babysitting through your church are all ways that people with power can make parents' lives easier. This is among the most important functions of community and civil society: lightening the burdens and increasing the enjoyability of parenthood. Governments, communities, friends, neighbors, and parents themselves should see making parenting easier as one of their central responsibilities.

But let's be honest: parenting will never be easy, or even close to easy.

If you undertake it, raising children will be the hardest job of your life. No matter how easy you make it for yourself, it is still a decades-long, around-the-clock commitment with high stakes.

It couldn't be any other way. Nothing you do in your life will carry the weight of forming a human soul, teaching her the meaning of love, convincing him he has infinite value, and at the same time imbuing a love of sacrifice and a sense of duty. Beyond these lofty character-istics is the bare bones of it: parenting is physically and mentally ex-hausting. As Katie puts it, raising babies is "needing to be everything to irrational humans." It involves screaming, whining, and watching *Teletubbies* while cleaning vomit. As Paul Ehrlich puts it, people "beg-ging . . . defecating and urinating." And there are few thank-yous for the first two decades.

We could implement every policy change suggested herein, trans-form our culture, and individually reset our expectations and habits, and parenting would still be the single hardest job in the world.

I have more fun as a parent than I ever did beforehand, but also more pain. Choosing to go down this road is choosing a life of toil, anguish, and difficulty. It's a hard road, but if your life is one aimed at a worthy destination, it is also the easiest road available.

If you aspire to anything beyond a life of self-satisfaction, if your guiding star is a higher one than hedonism—that is, if you aspire to a good life, and to become a man or woman of virtue—then there is no easier road than the road of parenthood.

To borrow video game terminology, parenthood is a "cheat code" for virtue. Men and some women of a certain age will recall "UP, UP, DOWN, DOWN, LEFT, RIGHT, LEFT, RIGHT, B, A, START." This is not some variation of the Electric Slide, but the "Konami Code." While loading the game *Contra* on your Nintendo, if you hit the control pad and buttons in that order, the game gave you thirty free lives. It was the most famous early cheat code in gaming.

The way I look at it, parenthood is a cheat code for sainthood.

Those web videos—*gain success with this one easy trick!*—that's parenthood, as long as you have an appropriately lofty understanding of "success." I'm not saying parenthood is the only road to virtue, or to salvation. Again, it's the easiest one.

When St. Paul wrote to the Corinthians, he suggested that maybe the single, celibate life was a higher calling. "I wish that all were as I myself am," he wrote, but he acknowledged that not everyone could hack that. St. Paul focused in his letter on the difficulty of celibacy, but he could have made a broader point, and it's one Yair Treister made to me on Purim in Kemp Mill: The package of marriage and parenthood "forces adults to be less selfish."

I think the first selfless things I ever did were for my wife after we got married. Now that we are raising children, we have people for whom to lay down our lives, and do so happily. I have known extraordinary people of astounding selflessness who, by their nature, would give their lunch to the homeless or take in the destitute. You may be blessed with such people in your life. My nature is uglier. That's why I need the cheat code.

The Bible tells us to feed the hungry and clothe the naked. As a parent, all I have to do is wake up and—voilà! There are hungry, naked people already in my house. *They're right there!*

Parenthood is mercy and self-giving made easy—or if not always easy, at least simple.

What We Bring

Civilizational sadness and the road to sainthood might seem very distant from where we started—on a couple of tee-ball fields in the suburbs.

But actually, this story has brought us back to St. Andrew Apostle, the place we called home for a decade before moving to Virginia in 2022. St. Andrew's was where our kids went to school, where they received Baptism, First Communion, and Confirmation, and where we went to Mass every Sunday. The kids played basketball and baseball and tee-ball for St. Andrew's. Funerals, weddings, Christmas concerts, Easter plays, and fall festivals all happened there. I learned much of my own faith there, after I got recruited as a Sunday School teacher to second graders.

Our lives were built around parish life. Katie and I started the tee-ball-and-cookout tradition on Fridays in the spring. St. A was also the source of service opportunities—for us and our kids, within St. A and in the broader community.

Before we moved across the river in 2022, my last service for St. A was moderating a small group discussion as part of the global synod Pope Francis had called. I sat at a table for a couple of hours with co-parishioners, mostly older ladies I knew a little but not a lot. The topic was communal connection within the parish. At one point, one church lady, addressing me, referred to "what you bring to the parish." I assumed she was talking about tee-ball, or Sunday school, or some other volunteering Katie or I had done at St. A. But this wasn't what she meant at all.

"What you bring to the parish—your children in the school, your sons serving at Mass, your daughter reading, and taking six kids to Mass every Sunday . . ." That is, we brought *bodies*. We brought *souls*. We put eight butts in the pews on Sunday, brought eight customers to each fish fry, and generally filled the halls and fields of St. Andrew's with human beings. If the Carneys showed up, it was an instant quorum.

On the final week of school one year, Mrs. Anastasi emailed parents informing us she would miss the last day. Mrs. Anastasi is an amazing preschool teacher, and a big reason we made St. Andrew's our home for a decade. We first came to St. A's in order to put Charlie in her class. The next year, she taught Brendan. A couple of years later, on the first day of school she greeted our Meg, "I've been waiting to teach you since you were a baby strapped to Dad's chest!" Then she taught Seán and finally Eve, our sixth and youngest child. We owed Mrs. Anastasi the grandest of all last-day-of-school teacher presents, but with her early start to summer vacation, we didn't have time to get anything. And so, on the next morning, her last day teaching a Carney kid, I brought her the only thing I could. I brought my kids.

Mrs. Anastasi opened the door at 7:35 to the gift of Eve, Seán, Meg, Brendan, and Charlie, all beaming. She cried and hugged my crew— her crew.

It's common to mock parents for believing their child is "God's gift to the world." But very literally, children are God's gifts to us. My children are gifts to others not because my children are special, but because my children are children.

Humans are good. That truth is obscured at times by our own self-absorption or by others' imperfections, but children, in their innocence, reflect mankind's innate goodness back to us.

In one of Charles Dickens's stories about human wretchedness, the protagonist is a kind and generous child named Nell. The narrator— an old man who wanders London alone—runs into Nell when she is lost and in need of help.

This guileless cherub gives him her trust and friendship, and so instantly cheers and inspires the old man in a way almost any reader would instantly understand. "I love these little people," the narrator says; "and it is not a slight thing when they, who are so fresh from God, love us. As I had felt pleased at first by her confidence I determined to deserve it."

I still get that feeling, even after seventeen years, and even when, again and again, I fail to deserve it.

The first night Katie and I came home with Lucy, as they rested, I went to vigil Mass alone. I can recollect the beginning of that Mass with unusual detail.

It was in our parish's small old church building, which was extra dark for this evening Mass. We sang "O Come, O Come Emanuel" in the simple pre–Civil War church, which was decked in purple, the liturgical color of penance and somberness in the Catholic Church.

Advent, as a season, is a bit confounding in today's culture. Popular culture kicks off Christmas right after Thanksgiving, while the Catholic Church's Christmas season doesn't begin until Christmas Eve. In the four weeks leading up to Christmas, when the rest of the world is playing Christmas carols and decking the halls in red and green, the Church is singing songs of longing and is decked in penitential purple.

Advent is also a season of joy. How do joy and penance go together? This can sound contradictory to the modern ear, where Catholic guilt seems like the opposite of Christmas joy. But it doesn't take a theologian to see how they go together: Dickens's narrator stated it plainly, and any new parent can explain it.

If you have ever held your newborn baby in your hands and stared into her eyes, you have felt that blend of penance and joy. Because the magnitude of this love is so grand, the charge of parenthood is thus so daunting, and it makes you want to be a better man or woman.

So it's not quite a *blend* of penance of joy, because that implies mixing two diverse ingredients—what your chemistry teacher would call a *mixture*. The sensation caused by your own baby's face is no mere mixture. It is a *solution of joy and penance*. The two elements have become inseparable.

When you look into your child's eyes, you see yourself, but it's a vision of you unstained. Every regret is blotted out for a moment. At the same time, your shortcomings weigh even more heavily, because you see clearly what you squandered when you frittered away your own innocence.

In confession, during the Act of Contrition, we Catholics resolve to "sin no more." We know it's impossible, but we speak those words as an act of hope. Neither the contrition nor the hope has ever felt as honest and real to me in the confessional as they did in the labor and delivery room.

Our culture tells us that our failings make us unworthy and that mankind's sins show that humans were a mistake. In a cruel irony, our civilization's sadness makes us afraid to bring babies into this world. It's precisely when we doubt our value that we need the unconditional, all-needing love of a little child to remind us, with a smile or even simply a gaze, that we are good.

Acknowledgments

It takes a village to write a book about family.

This book was the second one inspired by Eric Nelson, my Harper editor and literary instigator. Another godfather of this book was Yuval Levin, an intellectual role model who steadily pushes me to do good and meaningful work.

The American Enterprise Institute was the most important institution in backing this book in every way imaginable. Nicole Penn and Robert Doar in particular have my gratitude. The entire Social, Cultural, and Constitutional Studies division provided great feedback on early drafts.

The people at the *Washington Examiner*, especially my editors Hugo Gurdon and Conn Carroll, were wonderfully supportive, as well.

Much of this book was written on what I call "writing retreats," one hosted generously by the American Institute of Economic Research, another by Charlie and Maricel Heeter, and another by Mark and Amy Alznauer.

Emily MacLean, my dream editor, mercilessly slaughtered tens of thousands of words, and deftly refined every chapter. Hannah Long and James Neidhardt at Harper dramatically improved the copy.

Three research assistants at AEI made this book happen. Ella Reider Fortgang greeted the idea of this book with an uplifting enthusiasm and provided the early research that convinced me it was a good idea. Luis Paralles was my tireless sidekick whose research, feedback, and encouragement was invaluable throughout many months of writing. Max Markon expertly brought the manuscript home.

Jacob Sundel helped unlock the story of Israel for me, and the Catholic Foundation brought me to that fruitful garden for a pilgrimage and reporting, too. Seth Kaplan and Bethany and Seth Mandel opened doors in Kemp Mill for me.

Lyman Stone not only did much of the research I relied on, he repeatedly took my calls as I wrote. As the reader likely noticed, the work of Melissa Kearney, Brad Wilcox, Stephanie Murray, and Kim Brooks was invaluable in my own work. Dan Hess gratuitously supported me with research, as well.

Many friends spoke with me for hours on this topic, including but not limited to Peter Suderman, Matt Mehan, Mike Connolly, and my brothers, John, Brian, and Mike.

My parents, John and Lucy Carney, were necessary for this book. Not only did they help me during the writing process (edits, and a quiet apartment in which to finish two of the drafts), they created me, raised me, gave me a model of sacrificial love, and gave me a great life—especially giving me my three older brothers.

I could write this book only because I *am* a father, which means my bride, Katie, made this book possible. Katie inspired and encouraged me to write this book, helped refine it at every juncture, and indulged my time away from the family to write this book about the importance of family. Also, Katie's parents and brothers and sisters (and all of the brothers- and sisters-in-law) have not only been a model of a large and joyful Catholic family, but they also are the foundation of the "village" Katie and I have relied on in raising our children.

And our children—Lucy, Charlie, Brendan, Meg, Seán, and Eve— tolerated my extra work and rooted for me throughout the process. More importantly, they provided much of the fodder for these chapters. These wonderful kids are what make me Dad, which is just about the greatest thing I could ever aspire to be.

Notes

Preface: Friday Night Lights

1. American Academy of Pediatrics. AAP-AACAP-CHA declaration of a national emergency in child and adolescent mental health. 2021. Accessed August 15, 2022. https://www.aap.org/en/advocacy/child-and- adolescent-healthy-mental -development/aap-aacap-cha-declaration-of-a- national-emergency-in-child-and -adolescent-mental-health/.
2. Peter Gray et al., "Decline in Independent Activity as a Cause of Decline in Children's Mental Well-being: Summary of the Evidence," *Journal of Pediatrics*, October 2023.
3. Mozhgan Hashemzadeh et al., "Fertility Intentions and Effective Factors at a Glance: A Systematic Review," citing Arnstein Aassve et al., "It Takes Two to Tango: Couples' Happiness and Childbearing," *European Journal of Population* 32, no. 3 (2016): 339–54, 341–43, https://europepmc.org/article/med/30976218.
4. Kim Parker, Rich Morin, and Julia Menasce Horowitz, "Looking to the Future, Public Sees an America in Decline on Many Fronts: 1. America in 2050," Pew Research Center, March 21, 2019, https://www.pewresearch.org/social -trends/2019/03/21/america-in-2050/.
5. Alex Williams, "To Breed or Not to Breed?" *New York Times*, November 20, 2021, https://www.nytimes.com/2021/11/20/style/breed-children-climate-change .html.

Chapter 1: Have Lower Ambitions for Your Kids

1. Kevin DeYoung, "The Case for Kids," First Things, November 2022, https:// www.firstthings.com/article/2022/11/the-case-for-kids.
2. Bryan Caplan, *Selfish Reasons to Have More Kids: Why Being a Great Parent Is Less Work and More Fun Than You Think* (New York: Basic Books, 2012), 4.
3. Claire Cain Miller, "Americans Are Having Fewer Babies. They Told Us Why," *New York Times*, July 5, 2018, https://www.nytimes.com/2018/07/05/upshot /americans-are-having-fewer-babies-they-told-us-why.html.
4. Kelley, a woman in her early thirties from Georgia, participated in a 2022 focus group of childless adults.
5. Gerald F. Seib, "Low Birthrates Beckon New Debate: Whether to Encourage Having Children," *Wall Street Journal*, June 7, 2021, https://www.wsj.com/articles /low-birthrates-beckon-new-debate-whether-to-encourage-having-children -11623069236.
6. Kate Dilworth, "Would You Let Your Child Quit a Sport Mid-Season?," *NAYS Blog*, February 11, 2015, https://www.nays.org/blog/would-you-let-your-child -quit-a-sport-mid-season/.

7.   Baxter Holmes, "'These Kids Are Ticking Time Bombs': The Threat of Youth
     Basketball," ESPN, July 11, 2019, https://www.espn.com/nba/story/_/id
     /27125793/these-kids-ticking-bombs-threat-youth-basketball.
8.   Nicolas E. Giusti, Seth L. Carder, Lisa Vopat, Jordan Baker, Armin Tarakemeh,
     Bryan Vopat, and Mary K. Mulcahey, "Comparing Burnout in Sport-Specializing
     Versus Sport-Sampling Adolescent Athletes: A Systematic Review and Meta-
     analysis," *Orthopaedic Journal of Sports Medicine* 8, no. 3 (2020), https://journals
     .sagepub.com/doi/10.1177/2325967120907579.
9.   John W. Miller, "How America Sold Out Little League Baseball," America,
     May 19, 2022, https://www.americamagazine.org/politics-society/2022/05/19
     /catholic-youth-sports-little-league-club-baseball-243016.
10. Peter Gray, "The Value of Age-Mixed Play," *EdWeek*, April 15, 2008, https://
     www.edweek.org/leadership/opinion-the-value-of-age-mixed-play/2008/04.
11. Suniya S. Luthar and Karen D'Avanzo, "Contextual Factors in Substance Use:
     A Study of Suburban and Inner-City Adolescents," *Development and Psycho-
     pathology* 11, no. 4 (1999): 845–67, https://www.ncbi.nlm.nih.gov/pmc/articles
     /PMC3535189/.
12. Suniya S. Luthar and Shawn J. Latendresse, "Children of the Affluent: Chal-
     lenges to Well-Being," *Current Directions in Psychological Science* 14, no. 1 (2005):
     49–53, https://journals.sagepub.com/doi/10.1111/j.0963-7214.2005.00333.x.
13. Leonard Sax, "When Is the 'Best' School Not the Best?" *Epoch Times*, August 21,
     2021, https://www.theepochtimes.com/when-is-the-best-school-not-the-best
     _3955522.html.
14. Amanda L. Gordon and Janet Lorin, "New York's 4-Year-Olds Are Mastering
     Zoom to Get into Elite Kindergartens," Bloomberg, November 17, 2020, https://
     www.bloomberg.com/news/articles/2020-11-17/new-york-s-4-year-olds-are
     -mastering-zoom-to-get-into-elite-kindergartens.
15. Elena Kilner, *Letters to John Paul: A Mother Discovers God's Love in Her Suffering
     Child* (Falls Church, VA: Moorings Press, 2014), 31.
16. Kilner, 105.
17. Paula Fass, *The End of American Childhood* (Princeton, NJ: Princeton University
     Press, 2017), 221.

Chapter 2: "Hey, Parents, Leave Your Kids Alone"

1.   Laura Vanderkam, "What Everyone Can Learn from Parents of Big Families,"
     New York Times, April 16, 2020, https://www.nytimes.com/2020/04/16/parenting
     /big-families.html.
2.   Suzanne M. Bianchi et al., *Changing Rhythms of American Family Life* (New
     York: Russell Sage Foundation, 2007), 64.
3.   U.S. Bureau of Labor Statistics, "Average hours per day parents spent caring
     for and helping household children as their main activity, 2019 annual aver-
     ages," https://www.bls.gov/charts/american-time-use/activity-by-parent.htm.
4.   Bianchi et al., *Changing Rhythms of American Family Life*, 64.
5.   U.S. Bureau of Labor Statistics, "Average hours per day."
6.   Caplan, *Selfish Reasons to Have More Kids*, 3.
7.   Malcolm Harris, *Kids These Days: Human Capital and the Making of Millennials*
     (New York: Little, Brown, 2017), 24.
8.   Caplan, *Selfish Reasons to Have More Kids*, 34.
9.   American Society for the Positive Care of Children, "National Child Maltreat-
     ment Statistics," 2020, https://americanspcc.org/child-abuse-statistics/.

10. Patrick Ishizuka, "Social Class, Gender, and Contemporary Parenting Standards in the United States: Evidence from a National Survey Experiment," *Social Forces* 98, no. 1 (2019), https://academic.oup.com/sf/article-abstract/98/1/31/5257458.

11. Peter Gray et al., "Decline in Independent Activity as a Cause of Decline in Children's Mental Wellbeing: Summary of the Evidence," https://www.peter gray.org/_files/ugd/b4b4f9_0a7c4a1f099b4cadb05aa17210b8524c.pdf.

12. Nicholas W. Affrunti and Golda S. Ginsburg, "Maternal Overcontrol and Child Anxiety: The Mediating Role of Perceived Competence," *Child Psychiatry & Human Development* 43, no. 1 (2012), https://www.ncbi.nlm.nih.gov/pmc/articles /PMC3358037/.

13. Holy H. Schiffrin et al., "Helping or Hovering? The Effects of Helicopter Parenting on College Students' Well-Being," *Journal of Child and Family Studies* 23 (2014), https://link.springer.com/article/10.1007/s10826-013-9716-3.

14. Terri LeMoyne and Tom Buchanan, "Does 'Hovering' Matter? Helicopter Parenting and Its Effect on Well-Being," *Sociological Spectrum* 31, no. 4 (2011), https://doi.org/10.1080/02732173.2011.574038.

15. Elliot Haspel, "How to Quit Intensive Parenting," *Atlantic*, May 10, 2022, https://www.theatlantic.com/family/archive/2022/05/intensive-helicopter -parent-anxiety/629813/.

16. March of Dimes, "Alcohol During Pregnancy," 2016, https://www.marchofdimes .org/pregnancy/alcohol-during-pregnancy.aspx.

17. Ashley Ziegler and Mackenzie Sylvester, "Are Movie Theaters Too Loud for Pregnant People? OB-GYNs Explain," Romper, May 6, 2022, https://www.romper .com/p/are-movie-theaters-too-loud-for-pregnant-women-youre-listening-for -2-21793846.

18. Jeremy Shere, "Pregnant Women Should Avoid Spending Time Near Traffic," Indiana Public Media, June 29, 2011, https://indianapublicmedia.org/amomentof science/pregnant-women-avoid-spending-time-traffic.php.

19. This warning was on a page at the March of Dimes website titled "Caring for Pets When You're Pregnant." You can access the old page via the WayBack Machine, https://web.archive.org/web/20221007052304/https://www.marchofdimes .org/pregnancy/pets-and-other-animals-during-pregnancy.aspx.

20. Christopher Snowdon, Twitter, June 16, 2021, https://twitter.com/cjsnowdon /status/1405103426338537477.

21. Kim Brooks, *Small Animals: Parenthood in the Age of Fear* (New York: Flatiron Books, 2018), 40.

22. Emily Oster, *Expecting Better: Why the Conventional Pregnancy Wisdom Is Wrong—and What You Really Need to Know* (New York: Penguin, 2014), xxvi.

23. Oster, 39.

24. Sabrina Tavernise et al., "Why American Women Everywhere Are Delaying Motherhood," *New York Times*, June 16, 2021, https://www.nytimes.com /2021/06/16/us/declining-birthrate-motherhood.html.

25. Pew Research Center, "Parenting in America," December 17, 2015, https://www .pewresearch.org/social-trends/wp-content/uploads/sites/3/2015/12/2015 -12-17_parenting-in-america_FINAL.pdf.

26. Brooks, *Small Animals*, 105.

27. Brooks, 105–6.

28. Lenore Skenazy, "Why I Let My 9-Year-Old Ride the Subway Alone," Free-Range Kids, April 6, 2008, http://www.freerangekids.com/why-i-let-my-9-year -old-ride-the-subway-alone/.

29. Lenore Skenazy, "I let my 9-year-old ride the subway alone. I got labeled the 'world's worst mom,'" *Washington Post*, January 16, 2015, https://www .washingtonpost.com/posteverything/wp/2015/01/16/i-let-my-9-year-old-ride -the-subway-alone-i-got-labeled-the-worlds-worst-mom/.

30. Kate Julian, "What Happened to American Childhood?" *Atlantic*, May 2020, https://www.theatlantic.com/magazine/archive/2020/05/childhood-in-an -anxious-age/609079/.

31. Hanna Rosin, "The Overprotected Kid," *Atlantic*, April 2014, https://www.the atlantic.com/magazine/archive/2014/04/hey-parents-leave-those-kids-alone /358631/.

32. Peter Gray, "How Magazines' Advice to Parents Has Changed Over a Century," *Psychology Today*, March 17, 2022, https://www.psychologytoday.com/us /blog/freedom-learn/202203/how-magazines-advice-parents-has-changed-over -century.

33. Lenore Skenazy, "School Calls Child Services on Mom Who Was 7 Minutes Late to Pick Up Her 10-Year-Old Son," *Reason*, March 24, 2021, https://reason .com/2021/03/24/janay-dodson-chicago-schools-late-braylin-harvey-child-services -neglect/.

34. Janis Wolak et al., "Child Victims of Stereotypical Kidnappings Known to Law Enforcement in 2011," U.S. Department of Justice, June 2016, https://ojjdp.ojp .gov/sites/g/files/xyckuh176/files/pubs/249249.pdf.

35. Lucy McBride, "Fear of COVID-19 in Kids Is Getting Ahead of the Data," *Atlantic*, August 13, 2021, https://www.theatlantic.com/ideas/archive/2021/08 /children-delta-covid-19-risk-adults-overreact/619728/.

36. McBride, "Fear of COVID-19 in Kids Is Getting Ahead of the Data."

Chapter 3: Want Fecundity in the Sheets? Give Us Walkability in the Streets

1. Erika C., "A Special Family of Fans Brings a Youthful Love of the Nats," TalkNats .com, https://www.talknats.com/2018/06/05/special-family-fans-brings-youthful -love-nats/.

2. Jordan Nickerson and David H. Solomon, "Car Seats as Contraception," https:// papers.ssrn.com/sol3/papers.cfm?abstract_id=3665046.

3. Daniel A. Cox and Ryan Streeter, "The Importance of Place: Neighborhood Amenities as a Source of Social Connection and Trust," American Enterprise Institute, May 2019, https://www.aei.org/research-products/report/the-importance-of -place-neighborhood-amenities-as-a-source-of-social-connection-and-trust/.

4. Ryan Streeter, "Wanted: Better Neighborhoods," *City Journal*, February 6, 2020, https://www.aei.org/articles/wanted-better-neighborhoods/.

5. Noreen C. McDonald, "Active Transportation to School: Trends Among U.S. Schoolchildren, 1969–2001," *American Journal of Preventive Medicine* 32, no. 6 (2017), https://doi.org/10.1016/j.amepre.2007.02.022.

6. Federal Highway Administration, "Children's Travel to School: 2017 National Household Travel Survey," FHWA NHTS Brief, March 2019, https://nhts.ornl .gov/assets/FHWA_NHTS_%20Brief_Traveltoschool_032519.pdf.

7. Scott A. Conger et al., "Time Trends in Physical Activity Using Wearable Devices: A Systematic Review and Meta-analysis of Studies from 1995 to 2017," *Medicine & Science in Sports & Exercise* 54, no. 2 (2022), https://pubmed.ncbi .nlm.nih.gov/34559725/.

8. Dan Reed, "A Plan to Make This Montgomery County Neighborhood Less Boring," Greater Greater Washington, May 22, 2023, https://ggwash.org/view /89588/a-plan-to-make-this-montgomery-county-neighborhood-less-boring.

9. David Roberts, "How Our Housing Choices Make Adult Friendships More Difficult," Vox, December 27, 2018, https://www.vox.com/2015/10/28/9622920 /housing-adult-friendship.

10. Sujata Gupta, "Military Towns Are the Most Racially Integrated Places in the U.S. Here's Why," *Science News*, February 8, 2022. https://www.sciencenews.org /article/military-towns-integration-segregation-united-states.

11. George Foster, "Placemaking at US Military Installations: Human-Scale Walkability," Schreifer Group blog, January 6, 2022, https://www.web.theschreifergroup .com/post/placemaking-at-us-military-installations-human-scale-walkability.

12. Patrick T. Brown, "Is the Future of the Suburbs in Utah's Daybreak?" *Deseret News*, August 22, 2022, https://www.deseret.com/2022/8/22/23313688/future -of-the-suburbs-daybreak-utah-families-neighborhoods-15-minute-city.

13. Fleur Thomese and Aart C. Liefbroer, "Child Care and Child Births: The Role of Grandparents in the Netherlands," *Journal of Marriage and Family Life* 75, no. 2 (April 2013), https://doi.org/10.1111/jomf.12005.

14. Fergus Cumming and Lisa Dettling, "Monetary Policy and Birth Rates: The Effect of Mortgage Rate Pass-Through on Fertility," Bank of England Staff Working Paper No. 835, December 2019, https://www.bankofengland.co.uk /-/media/boe/files/working-paper/2019/monetary-policy-and-birth-rates-the -effect-of-mortgage-rate-pass-through-on-fertility.pdf.

15. Lisa Dettling and Melissa Kearney, "House Prices and Birth Rates: The Impact of the Real Estate Market on the Decision to Have a Baby," *Journal of Public Economics* 110 (2014): 82–100.

16. Joint Economic Committee Republicans, "The HOUSES Act: Addressing the National Housing Shortage by Building on Federal Land," August 2022, https://www.jec.senate.gov/public/_cache/files/efdd0c37-af95-40cd-9125 -e80f8a11504b/the-houses-act-addressing-the-national-housing-shortage-by -building-on-federal-land.pdf.

17. Emily Badger, "Whatever Happened to the Starter Home?" *New York Times*, September 25, 2022, https://www.nytimes.com/2022/09/25/upshot/starter-home -prices.html.

18. Salim Furth, "The Price of New Urbanism: A Hypothesis," *American Conservative*, December 3, 2020, https://www.theamericanconservative.com/the -price-of-new-urbanism-a-hypothesis/.

19. Frank Zimmerman, "Breaking Up with the Double Loaded Corridor," April 2, 2020, https://frankzimmerman.com/Breaking-Up-with-the-Double-Loaded -Corridor.

20. Lyman Stone, "How Many Kids Do Women Want?" Institute for Family Studies, June 1, 2018, https://ifstudies.org/blog/how-many-kids-do-women-want.

21. Susan Adams, "The More Time Dads Spend with Their Kids, the Happier They Are at Work," *Forbes*, January 12, 2015.

22. Martha J. Bailey et al., "The Longterm Effects of California's 2004 Paid Family Leave Act on Women's Careers: Evidence from U.S. Tax Data," National Bureau of Economic Research Working Paper, October 2019, https://www.nber. org/system/files/working_papers/w26416/w26416.pdf.

23. Meg Meeker has collected this data in chapter 1 of *Strong Fathers, Strong Daughters* (Washington, DC: Regnery, 2015).

24. Michael Seifert, LinkedIn, August 2022, https://www.linkedin.com/posts /michael-seifert-b70b6017b_today-yelp-announced-that-they-would-be-activity -6968354278079954945-8uVn?utm_source=share&utm_medium=member _desktop.

Chapter 4: It Takes a Village

1. Richard Weissbourd, et al. "Loneliness in America: How the Pandemic Has Deepened an Epidemic of Loneliness and What We Can Do About It," Harvard Graduate School of Education, Making Caring Common Project.

2. Judith Shulevitz, "Does Co-Housing Provide a Path to Happiness for Modern Parents," *New York Times*, October 22, 2021.

3. Alan Ehrenhalt, *The Lost City: The Forgotten Virtues of Community in America* (New York: Basic Books, 1996), 29.

4. Angela Rachidi, "The Evidence on Family Affordability," American Enterprise Institute, April 2023, https://www.aei.org/wp-content/uploads/2023/04/The -Evidence-on-Family-Affordability.pdf?x91208.

5. Stephanie Murray, "The Parenting Problem the Government Can't Fix," *The Week*, October 25, 2021, https://theweek.com/life/parenting/1005725/the-parenting -problem-the-government-cant-fix.

6. David Brooks, "The Nuclear Family Was a Mistake," *Atlantic*, March 2020, https://www.theatlantic.com/magazine/archive/2020/03/the-nuclear-family -was-a-mistake/605536/.

7. Samuel J. Abrams, Karlyn Bowman, Eleanor O'Neil, and Ryan Streeter, "AEI Survey on Community and Society: Social Capital, Civic Health, and Quality of Life in the United States," American Enterprise Institute, February 2019, https:// www.aei.org/wp-content/uploads/2019/02/AEI-Survey-on-Community -and-Society-Social-Capital-Civic-Health-and-Quality-of-Life-in-the-United-States .pdf?x91208.

8. Brooks, "The Nuclear Family Was a Mistake."

9. *Planned Parenthood of Southeastern Pa. v. Casey,* 505 U. S. 833 (1992).

10. Hannah Dailey, "Taylor Swift's NYU Commencement Speech: Read the Full Transcript," *Billboard*, May 18, 2022, https://www.billboard.com/music/music -news/taylor-swift-nyu-commencement-speech-full-transcript-1235072824/.

11. Bastian Mönkediek, "Patterns of Spatial Proximity and the Timing and Spacing of Bearing Children," *Demographic Research*, no. 42 (January–June 2020), https://www.jstor.org/stable/10.2307/26936796.

12. Fleur Thomese and Aart C. Liefbroer, "Child Care and Child Births: The Role of Grandparents in the Netherlands," *Journal of Marriage and Family* 75 (April 2013), https://doi.org/10.1111/jomf.12005.

13. Francesca Fiori, "Do Childcare Arrangements Make the Difference? A Multilevel Approach to the Intention of Having a Second Child in Italy," *Population, Space, and Place* 17 (2011), https://doi.org/10.1002/psp.567.

14. Margaret Mead, *Blackberry Winter: My Earlier Years* (New York: William Morrow, 1972), 282.

15. Teresa Ghilarducci, "Think Twice, Grandma, Before You Become the Nanny," Bloomberg, July 21, 2021, https://www.bloomberg.com/opinion/articles/2021 -07-21/personal-finance-do-you-really-want-to-watch-grandchildren-full-time #xj4y7vzkg.

Chapter 5: What Killed the Second Baby Boom?

1. Associated Press, "U.S. Experiences a Baby Boomlet," *Los Angeles Times*, January 16, 2008, https://www.latimes.com/archives/la-xpm-2008-jan-16-na -babies16-story.html.

2. Associated Press, "U.S. Experiences a Baby Boomlet."

3. Erik Eckholm, "'07 U.S. Births Break Baby Boom Record," *New York Times*, March 18, 2009, https://www.nytimes.com/2009/03/19/health/19birth.html.

4. Molly Lambert, "Miley Cyrus Has Finally Found Herself," *Elle*, July 11, 2019, https://www.elle.com/culture/music/a28280119/miley-cyrus-elle-interview/.

5. William A. Burley, "Is Overpopulation Too Grim a Tale?" *New York Times*, April 29, 1990, https://timesmachine.nytimes.com/timesmachine/1990/04/29/099690.html?pageNumber=157.

6. Robert Miller, "New Milford Hospital Birthing Center to Close," *NewsTimes*, March 22, 2012, https://www.newstimes.com/news/article/New-Milford-Hospital-birthing-center-to-close-3427928.php

7. National Center for Educational Statistics, U.S. Department of Education, via School Digger.

8. U.S. Census Bureau, "2010 Census Shows Nation's Population Is Aging," https://www.census.gov/newsroom/releases/archives/2010_census/cb11-cn147.html.

9. U.S. Census Bureau, "Annual Estimates of the Resident Population by Single Year of Age and Sex for the United States: April 1, 2020 to July 1, 2022," https://www2.census.gov/programs-surveys/popest/datasets/2020-2022/national/asrh/nc-est2022-agesex-res.csv.

10. U.S. Census Bureau, "How Has Our Nation's Population Changed?" May 25, 2023, https://www.census.gov/library/visualizations/interactive/how-has-our-nations-population-changed.html.

11. Connecticut State Department of Public Health, "Vital Statistics Registration Reports," https://portal.ct.gov/DPH/Health-Information-Systems—Reporting/Hisrhome/Vital-Statistics-Registration-Reports.

12. West Virginia Department of Health and Human Services, "2019 West Virginia Vital Statistics," September 2022, http://www.wvdhhr.org/bph/hsc/pubs/vital/2019/Vital2019.pdf.

13. The World Bank defines the TFR this way: "the number of children that would be born to a woman if she were to live to the end of her childbearing years and bear children in accordance with age-specific fertility rates of the specified year," https://databank.worldbank.org/metadataglossary/millennium-development-goals/series/SP.DYN.TFRT.IN.

14. Congressional Budget Office, "The Demographic Outlook: 2022 to 2052," July 2022, https://www.cbo.gov/publication/58347.

15. Damien Cave, Emma Bubola, and Choe Sang-Hun, "Long Slide Looms for World Population, with Sweeping Ramifications," *New York Times*, May 22, 2022, https://www.nytimes.com/2021/05/22/world/global-population-shrinking.html.

16. Alexandra Stevenson and Zixu Wang, "China's Population Falls, Heralding a Demographic Crisis," *New York Times*, January 16, 2023, https://www.nytimes.com/2023/01/16/business/china-birth-rate.html.

17. Rhythma Kaul and Anonna Dutt, "India's Fertility Rate Drops Below 2.1, Contraceptive Prevalence Up: NFHS," *Hindustan Times*, November 25, 2021, https://www.hindustantimes.com/india-news/indias-fertility-rate-drops-below-2-1-population-stabilising-nfhs-data-101637751803433.html.

18. Lyman Stone, Twitter, December 2, 2022, https://twitter.com/lymanstoneky/status/1466444290331132037.

19. World Bank, "Fertility Rate, Total (Births per Woman)," https://data.worldbank.org/indicator/SP.DYN.TFRT.IN.

20. Anthony Cilluffo and Neil G. Ruiz, "World's Population Is Projected to Nearly Stop Growing by the End of the Century," Pew Research Center, June 17, 2019, https://www.pewresearch.org/fact-tank/2019/06/17/worlds-population-is-projected-to-nearly-stop-growing-by-the-end-of-the-century/.

21. Erin Duffin, "Birth Rate in the United States from 2005 to 2019, by Poverty Status," Statista, September 30, 2022, https://www.statista.com/statistics/562541/birth-rate-by-poverty-status-in-the-us/.

22. Yun Li, "The stock market's gain in the last 10 years is one of its best runs since the 1800s," CNBC, March 15, 2019, https://www.cnbc.com/2019/03/15/the-stock-markets-gain-in-the-last-10-years-is-one-of-its-best-runs-since-the-1800s.html.

23. U.S. Bureau of Labor Statistics, "Civilian Unemployment Rate," https://www.bls.gov/charts/employment-situation/civilian-unemployment-rate.htm.

24. Jeremy Horpedahl, "Who Is the Wealthiest Generation?," Economist Writing Every Day (blog), September 1, 2021, https://economistwritingeveryday.com/2021/09/01/who-is-the-wealthiest-generation/.

25. Suzanne M. Bianchi et al, Changing Rhythms of American Family Life (New York: Russell Sage Foundation, 2007), 64.

26. Sabrina Tavernise, Claire Cain Miller, Quoctrung Bui, and Robert Gebeloff, "Why American Women Everywhere Are Delaying Motherhood," New York Times, June 16, 2021, https://www.nytimes.com/2021/06/16/us/declining-birthrate-motherhood.html.

27. Lydia DePillis, Twitter, September 28, 2021, https://twitter.com/lydiadepillis/status/1442794705717243904.

28. Petula Dvorak, "The Child-Free Life: Why So Many American Women Are Deciding Not to Have Kids," Washington Post, May 31, 2018, https://www.washingtonpost.com/local/the-child-free-life-why-so-many-american-women-are-deciding-not-to-have-kids/2018/05/31/89793784-64de-11e8-a768-ed043e33f1dc_story.html.

29. Jill Filipovic, "Having Kids Is Bad for the Planet," Substack, June 14, 2022, https://jill.substack.com/p/having-kids-is-bad-for-the-planet.

30. Kristen Pyszczyk, "It Shouldn't Be Taboo to Criticize Parents for Having Too Many Kids," CBC News, January 13, 2018, https://www.cbc.ca/amp/1.4481165.

31. Travis Rieder, "Science proves kids are bad for Earth. Morality suggests we stop having them," NBC News, November 15, 2017, https://www.nbcnews.com/think/opinion/science-proves-kids-are-bad-earth-morality-suggests-we-stop-ncna820781.

32. Lydia DePillis, Twitter, June 26, 2021, https://twitter.com/lydiadepillis/status/1408914961498267649.

33. John Tammy, "Baby Bust Is Nothing New; U.S. Is Growing," letter to the editor, Wall Street Journal, May 14, 2021, https://www.wsj.com/articles/baby-bust-is-nothing-new-u-s-is-growing-11621031757.

34. Paul Krugman, Twitter, July 25, 2021, https://twitter.com/paulkrugman/status/1419376063227088898.

Chapter 6: We Can't Afford a Baby Bust

1. Data from the UN Food and Agriculture Organization, https://ourworldindata.org/explorers/global-food?tab=chart&facet=none&country=~OWID_WRL&hideControls=true&Food=Total&Metric=Food+available+for+consumption&Per+Capita=false&Unit=Kilocalories+per+day.

2. Hannah Ritchie, "After Millennia of Agricultural Expansion, the World Has Passed 'Peak Agricultural Land,'" Our World in Data, May 30, 2022. https://ourworldindata.org/peak-agriculture-land.

3. Institute for Health Metrics and Evaluation, "Significant Changes Ahead in

World Population," https://www.healthdata.org/research-analysis/library /significant-changes-ahead-world-population.

4. Organisation for Economic Co-operation and Development, "Working Age Population: Aged 15–64: All Persons for the United States," Federal Reserve Bank of St. Louis, https://fred.stlouisfed.org/series/LFWA64TTUSM647S.

5. U.S. Census Bureau, "An Aging World: 2020," https://mtgis-portal.geo.census .gov/arcgis/apps/MapSeries/index.html?appid=3d832796999042daae7982 ff36835e2e.

6. Gayle L. Reznik, Dave Shoffner, and David A. Weaver, "Coping with the Demographic Challenge: Fewer Children and Living Longer," *Social Security Bulletin* 66, no. 4 (2005–2006), https://www.ssa.gov/policy/docs/ssb/v66n4v66n4p37.html.

7. Kate Ryan, "The Struggle to Fill Police, 911 Call-Taker Positions in Montgomery County," WTOP, February 12, 2023, https://wtop.com/montgomery-county /2023/02/the-struggle-to-fill-police-911-call-taker-positions-in-montgomery -county/.

8. Alan Cole, "Planning on Retiring? Thank a Parent," Full Stack Economics, March 28, 2022, https://www.fullstackeconomics.com/p/planning-on-retiring -thank-a-parent.

9. Charles Goodhart and Manoj Pradhan, "The Great Demographic Reversal and What It Means for the Economy," *LSE Blogs*, London School of Economics and Political Science, September 18, 2020, https://blogs.lse.ac.uk/businessreview /2020/09/18/the-great-demographic-reversal-and-what-it-means-for-the -economy/.

10. Isabel Sawhill, "Let's Have More Immigrants, Not More Babies," Brookings Institution, February 20, 2013, https://www.brookings.edu/articles/lets-have -more-immigrants-not-more-babies/.

11. "Largest U.S. Immigrant Groups over Time, 1960–Present," Migration Policy Institute, https://www.migrationpolicy.org/programs/data-hub/us-immigration -trends?gclid=Cj0KCQjwz8emBhDrARIsANNJjS6gpf-krE-lMMzvtA_Eiwu srq0zpDnW7TOuunWGH2S56F1GNmce1B4aAsB0EALw_wcB#source.

12. Lyman Stone, "The Rise of Childless America" Institute for Family Studies, June 4, 2020, https://ifstudies.org/blog/the-rise-of-childless-america.

13. U.S. Census Bureau, "Total Families with Children Under 18 Years Old," retrieved from Federal Reserve Bank of St. Louis, January 31, 2023, https://fred .stlouisfed.org/series/TTLFMCU.

14. Anna Brown, "Growing Share of Childless Adults in U.S. Don't Expect to Ever Have Children," Pew Research Center, November 19, 2021, https://www.pew research.org/fact-tank/2021/11/19/growing-share-of-childless-adults-in-u-s-dont -expect-to-ever-have-children/.

15. Michelle J. K. Osterman et al., "Births: Final Data, 2021," U.S. Department of Health and Human Services, National Vital Statistics Reports, January 31, 2023.

16. Tavernise et al., "Delaying Motherhood."

17. Two U.S. Census Bureau tables show this. "Black Alone by Age and Sex: 2010" and "Population by Sex and Age, for Black Alone and White Alone, Not Hispanic: 2019."

18. Katherine Kortsmit et al., "Abortion Surveillance—United States, 2020," Centers for Disease Control and Prevention, *Surveillance Summaries* 10, no. 21 (2022), http://dx.doi.org/10.15585/mmwr.ss7110a1.

19. Mei You, Lindsey Myers, and Glenn Radford, "Induced Abortions in Michigan: January 1 through December 31, 2020," Michigan Department of Health &

Human Services, June 2021, https://www.mdch.state.mi.us/osr/annuals/Abortion %202020.pdf.

20. Obama used this phrase in a town hall in Johnstown, Pennsylvania, on March 29, 2008. CNN has a transcript at https://transcripts.cnn.com/show/bb /date/2008-03-29/segment/01.

21. Jeff Grabmeier, "Falling Birth Rate Not Due to Less Desire to Have Children," Ohio State News, January 12, 2023, https://news.osu.edu/falling-birth-rate-not -due-to-less-desire-to-have-children/.

22. Lyman Stone, "How Many Kids Do Women Want?" Institute for Family Studies, June 1, 2018, https://ifstudies.org/blog/how-many-kids-do-women-want. Also, see Megan Brenan, "Americans' Preference for Larger Families Highest Since 1971," Gallup News, September 25, 2023, https://news.gallup.com/poll/511238 /americans-preference-larger-families-highest-1971.aspx.

23. Janet Adamy, "Why Americans Are Having Fewer Babies," *Wall Street Journal*, May 26, 2023.

24. Petra Buhr and Johannes Huinink, "Why Childless Men and Women Give Up on Having Children," *European Journal of Population* 33, no. 4 (2017): 585–606, https://www.ncbi.nlm.nih.gov/pmc/articles/PMC6241073/.

25. Petula Dvorak, "The Child-Free Life: Why So Many American Women Are Deciding Not to Have Kids," *Washington Post*, May 31, 2018, https://www.washingtonpost .com/local/the-child-free-life-why-so-many-american-women-are-deciding-not -to-have-kids/2018/05/31/89793784-64de-11e8-a768-ed043e33f1dc_story.html.

26. Jennifer Glass, Robin W. Simon, and Matthew A. Andersson, "Parenthood and Happiness: Effects of Work-Family Reconciliation Policies in 22 OECD Countries," *American Journal of Sociology* 112, no. 3 (2016), https://pubmed.ncbi.nlm .nih.gov/28082749/.

27. Jennifer Senior, "All Joy and No Fun," *New York*, July 2, 2010, https://nymag .com/news/features/67024/.

28. Daniel Kahneman, Alan B. Krueger, David A. Schkade, Norbert Schwarz, and Arthur A. Stone, "A Survey Method for Characterizing Daily Life Experience: The Day Reconstruction Method," *Science*, 306, no. 5702 (2004): 1776–80, https://www.science.org/doi/10.1126/science.1103572.

29. Bryan Caplan, *Selfish Reasons to Have More Kids: Why Being a Great Parent Is Less Work and More Fun Than You Think* (New York: Basic Books, 2012), 18.

30. Chris M. Herbst and John Ifcher, "The Increasing Happiness of US Parents," *Review of Economics of the Household* 14 (2016): 529–51, https://doi.org/10.1007 /s11150-015-9302-0.

31. Brad Wilcox and Wendy Wang, "Perspective: The Group That's Happiest in the Pandemic May Surprise You," *Deseret News*, September 28, 2021, https:// www.deseret.com/opinion/2021/9/28/22684641/the-group-thats-happiest-in -the-pandemic-may-surprise-you-parents-happiness-covid-19.

32. Herbst and Ifcher, "The Increasing Happiness of US Parents."

33. Will Austin, "Where Have Boston's Children Gone?" *Boston Globe*, June 10, 2022, https://www.bostonglobe.com/2022/06/09/opinion/where-have-bostons -children-gone/.

34. Bjørn Grinde and Kristian Tambs, "Effect of Household Size on Mental Problems in Children: Results from the Norwegian Mother and Child Cohort Study," *BMC Psychology* 4, no. 31 (2016), https://www.ncbi.nlm.nih.gov/pmc /articles/PMC4890284/.

35. A. W. Geiger and Leslie Davis, "A Growing Number of American Teenagers— Particularly Girls—Are Facing Depression," Pew Research Center, July 19,

2019, https://www.pewresearch.org/fact-tank/2019/07/12/a-growing-number
-of-american-teenagers-particularly-girls-are-facing-depression/.

36. Daniel A. Cox, "Emerging Trends and Enduring Patterns in American Family Life," Survey Center on American Life, February 9, 2022, https://www
.americansurveycenter.org/research/emerging-trends-and-enduring-patterns
-in-american-family-life/.

37. Daniel A. Cox, "The Childhood Loneliness of Generation Z," Survey Center on American Life, April 4, 2022, https://www.americansurveycenter.org/the
-lonely-childhood-of-generation-z/.

38. Maxim Massenkoff and Evan K. Rose, "Family Formation and Crime," NBER Working Paper Series, August 2022, https://www.nber.org/papers/w30385.

39. Lukas J. Wolf et al., "The Salience of Children Increases Adult Prosocial Values," *Social Psychological and Personality Science* 13, no. 21 (2022): 160–69, https://
journals.sagepub.com/doi/pdf/10.1177/19485506211007605.

Chapter 7: Should Uncle Sam Subsidize Mom and Dad?

1. Monica Hesse, "The Unreasonable Expectations of American Motherhood," *Washington Post*, June 15, 2021, https://www.washingtonpost.com/lifestyle
/style/birth-rate-american-mothers/2021/06/14/045c4684-c950-11eb-81b1
-34796c7393af_story.html.

2. "Modern State of Fertility 2020: Career & Money," SoFi, accessed February 24, 2023, https://modernfertility.com/modern-state-fertility-2020-sofi-career-money.

3. Jeremy Horpedahl, "The Cost of Raising a Child," *Economist Writing Every Day*, September 7, 2022, https://economistwritingeveryday.com/2022/09/07
/the-cost-of-raising-a-child/.

4. Dan Currell, "The Truth about College Costs," *National Affairs*, Summer 2023.

5. Michele Boldrin et al., "Fertility and Social Security," *Journal of Demographic Economics* 81, no. 3 (September 2015), https://www.cambridge.org/core/journals
/journal-of-demographic-economics/article/fertility-and-social-security
/4FA674742794BC43650452A21CBD1C0D.

6. Robert Bellafiore, "New Report Shows the Burdens of Payroll and Income Taxes," Tax Foundation, March 26, 2019, https://taxfoundation.org/payroll-income
-tax-burden/.

7. Elias Ilin, Laurence J. Kotlikoff, and Melinda Pitts, "Is Our Fiscal System Discouraging Marriage? A New Look at the Marriage Tax," NBER Working Paper Series, June 2022, https://www.nber.org/papers/w30159.

8. Laurence M. Vance, "Four Libertarian Principles to Guide Childcare Policy," *Future of Freedom Foundation*, June 25, 2021, https://www.fff.org/explore
-freedom/article/four-libertarian-principles-to-guide-childcare-policy/.

9. Adam O'Neal, "What Will Tax Reform Do for Puppies?," *Wall Street Journal*, November 19, 2017, https://www.wsj.com/articles/what-will-tax-reform-do
-for-puppies-1511071482.

10. Monica Hesse, "All I Want for Mother's Day Is a Vaccine for My Kid," *Washington Post*, May 5, 2022, https://www.washingtonpost.com/lifestyle/2022/05/05
/mothers-day-covid-vaccine/.

11. "China Fertility Rate 1950–2023," Macrotrends, https://www.macrotrends.net
/countries/CHN/china/fertility-rate.

12. Simon Worrall, "How China's One-Child Policy Backfired Disastrously," *National Geographic*, October 30, 2015, https://web.archive.org/web/20151031140836
/http://news.nationalgeographic.com/2015/10/151030-china-one-child-policy
-mei-fong/.

13. Zhuang Pinghui, "China Offers Baby Bonuses, with Births on Track for New Low in 2021," *South China Morning Post*, July 21, 2021, https://www.scmp.com /news/china/politics/article/3141978/china-offers-baby-bonuses-births-track -new-low-2021.

14. Kevin Andrews, "Population Interruptus," *Spectator Australia,* October 1, 2022, https://www.spectator.com.au/2022/10/population-interruptus.

15. Data from Patrick T. Brown on Twitter: https://twitter.com/PTBwrites/status /1713184683029082142.

16. Jessie Yeung, "China's population is shrinking. The impact will be felt around the world," CNN, January 19, 2023, https://www.cnn.com/2023/01/18/china /china-population-drop-explainer-intl-hnk/index.html.

17. World Bank, "Fertility Rate, Total (Births per Woman)—Singapore," https://data .worldbank.org/indicator/SP.DYN.TFRT.IN?locations=SG.

18. European birthrate data is from the World Bank's data catalog, https://datacatalog .worldbank.org/dataset/world-development-indicators/.

19. Lyman Stone, "Hungary's Demographic Failure," *National Review*, March 17, 2022, https://www.nationalreview.com/magazine/2022/04/04/hungarys -demographic-failure/.

20. Sabrina Volant, Gilles Pison, and François Héran, "French Fertility Is the Highest in Europe. Because of Its Immigrants?," Institut national d'études démographiques, July 8, 2019, https://www.ined.fr/en/news/press/french- fertility-is-the-highest-in-europe-because-of-its-immigrants/.

21. Lyman Stone, "Pro-Natal Policies Work, but They Come with a Hefty Price Tag," Institute for Family Studies, March 5, 2020, https://ifstudies.org/blog/ pro-natal-policies-work-but-they-come-with-a-hefty-price-tag.

22. Libertad González and Sofia Karina Trommlerová, "Cash Transfers and Fertility," *Journal of Human Resources*, May 2023, https://jhr.uwpress.org/content /58/3/783.full.

23. Sarah K. Cowan and Kiara Wyndham Douds, "Examining the Effects of a Universal Cash Transfer on Fertility," *Social Forces* 101, no. 2 (December 2022), https://doi.org/10.1093/sf/soac013.

24. Scott Winship, "Reforming Tax Credits to Promote Child Opportunity and Aid Working Families," American Enterprise Institute, July 2021, https://www .aei.org/wp-content/uploads/2021/07/Reforming-tax-credits-to-promote -child-opportunity-and-aid-working-families.pdf?x91208.

25. Cowan and Douds, "Examining the Effects of a Universal Cash Transfer on Fertility."

26. Stone, "Pro-Natal Policies Work, but They Come with a Hefty Price Tag."

27. Erin Duffin, "Birth Rate in the United States in 2017, by Household Income," Statista, https://www.statista.com/statistics/241530/birth-rate-by-family-income -in-the-us/.

28. "Modern State of Fertility 2020: Career & Money," SoFi, accessed February 24, 2023, https://modernfertility.com/modern-state-fertility-2020-sofi-career -money.

29. Jan Van Bavel, "Subreplacement Fertility in the West Before the Baby Boom (1900– 1940): Current and Contemporary Perspectives," September 1, 2008, https:// paa2009.princeton.edu/papers/90233.

30. Melissa Kearney et al., "The Puzzle of Falling US Birth Rates since the Great Recession," *Journal of Economic Perspectives* 36, no. 1 (Winter 2022), https:// pubs.aeaweb.org/doi/pdfplus/10.1257/jep.36.1.151.

Chapter 8: Israel: The Fruitful Garden of the Wealthy World

1. OECD Data, "Social Spending," https://data.oecd.org/socialexp/social-spending.htm.
2. OECD Data, "Family Benefits Public Spending," https://data.oecd.org/socialexp/family-benefits-public-spending.htm.
3. OECD Indicators, "Education at a Glance 2022: Israel," https://gpseducation.oecd.org/Content/EAGCountryNotes/EAG2022_Israel.pdf.
4. Data from the census population change table. Data considered births reported during July 1, 2019 to July 1, 2020 contained in the table "Estimates of the Components of Resident Population Change."
5. March of Dimes, "March of Dimes Peristats," accessed February 28, 2023, https://www.marchofdimes.org/peristats/.
6. U.S. Census Bureau, "Median Age at First Marriage: 1890 to Present," in Decennial Censuses, 1890 to 1940, and Current Population Survey, Annual Social and Economic Supplements, 1947 to 2022.
7. "Kingdoms of Glory," Church of Jesus Christ of Latter-day Saints, https://www.churchofjesuschrist.org/study/manual/gospel-topics/kingdoms-of-glory?lang=eng.
8. Sarah R. Hayford and S. Philip Morgan, "Religiosity and Fertility in the United States: The Role of Fertility Intentions," *Social Forces* 86, no. 3 (2008), https://www.ncbi.nlm.nih.gov/pmc/articles/PMC2723861/.
9. Lyman Stone, "America's Growing Religious-Secular Fertility Divide," Institute for Family Studies, August 8, 2022, https://ifstudies.org/blog/americas-growing-religious-secular-fertility-divide.
10. Hayford and Morgan, "Religiosity and Fertility in the United States."
11. Ginna Roe, "Dream Come True for Students: Homework Banned at Some Utah Schools," KUTV Local 12, January 8, 2020, https://katv.com/news/nation-world/dream-come-true-for-students-homework-banned-at-some-utah-schools.
12. Barbara S. Okun and Guy Stecklov, "The Impact of Grandparental Death on the Fertility of Adult Children," *Demography* 58, no. 3 (2021), https://doi.org/10.1215/00703370-9015536.
13. Lizzie O'Leary on Twitter, May 3, 2023, https://twitter.com/lizzieohreally/status/1653748294013648896.
14. Percentages are from a *New York Times* interactive feature, "How Many Households Are Like Yours," June 17, 2011, https://archive.nytimes.com/www.nytimes.com/interactive/2011/06/19/nyregion/how-many-households-are-like-yours.html.
15. Hayford and Morgan, "Religiosity and Fertility in the United States."
16. Bastian Mönkediek, "Patterns of Spatial Proximity and the Timing and Spacing of Bearing Children," *Demographic Research* 42 (January–June 2020), https://www.jstor.org/stable/26936796?seq=4#metadata_info_tab_contents.
17. Lyman Stone, "In Georgia, a Religiously-Inspired Baby Boom?" Institute for Family Studies, October 11, 2017, https://ifstudies.org/blog/in-georgia-a-religiously-inspired-baby-boom.

Chapter 9: Posthuman: How Our Tech Has Changed Us

1. Dawn C. Chmielewski, Michelle Quinn, and Alana Semuels, "The Wait Is Over. The Scene from 2007 When the iPhone First Went on Sale," *Los Angeles Times*, June 30, 2007, https://www.latimes.com/business/technology/la-fi-iphone-debut-20070630-story.html.

2.   Jiyoung Chae, "'Am I a Better Mother Than You?': Media and 21st-Century Motherhood in the Context of the Social Comparison Theory," *Communication Research* 42, no. 4 (2015), https://doi.org/10.1177/0093650214534969.

3.   Naomi Kaye, "Quitting Social Media Made Me a Better Parent," Motherly, July 1, 2021, https://www.mother.ly/health-wellness/mental-health/internet-safety-social-media/.

4.   Sang Yup Lee, "How Do People Compare Themselves with Others on Social Network Sites? The Case of Facebook," *Computers in Human Behavior* 32 (March 2014), https://doi.org/10.1016/j.chb.2013.12.009.

5.   Marie Morganelli, "When People Compare Themselves to Their Social Media Friends, It Can Help or Hurt Their Feelings," University of Florida College of Journalism and Communications, May 13, 2021, https://www.jou.ufl.edu/insights/when-people-compare-themselves-to-their-social-media-friends-it-can-help-or-hurt-their-feelings/.

6.   Sarah Fielding, "The Rise of Social Media Therapy," Verywell Mind, September 29, 2021, https://www.verywellmind.com/the-rise-of-the-mental-health-influencer-5198751.

7.   See: "World's Toughest Job (unofficial) MMBC Mother's Day Commercial," YouTube video, 7:37, May 7, 2016, https://www.youtube.com/watch?v=VVhP4ORAMV8, and "Is this the worlds toughest job? | Happy Mothers Day," YouTube video, 6:00, March 28, 2019, https://www.youtube.com/watch?v=Wc7DZlM9Tr0.

8.   Amy Orben et al., "Windows of Developmental Sensitivity to Social Media," *Nature Communications*, March 28, 2022, https://www.nature.com/articles/s41467-022-29296-3.

9.   Manju George et al., "Psychosocial Aspects of Pornography," *Journal of Psychosexual Health* 1, no. 1 (January 2019), https://journals.sagepub.com/doi/10.1177/2631831818821535.

10. Mateusz Gola et al., "Can Pornography Be Addictive? An fMRI Study of Men Seeking Treatment for Problematic Pornography Use," *Neuropsychopharmacology* 42 (2017), https://www.nature.com/articles/npp201778.

11. Darcel Rockett, "'I Was Absorbed in Pornography for Hours and Hours': How Porn Is Affecting Kids," *Chicago Tribune*, April 3, 2018, https://www.chicagotribune.com/lifestyles/parenting/sc-fam-porn-addiction-in-youth-0417-story.html.

12. Shankar Vedantam, "Researchers Explore Pornography's Effect on Long-Term Relationships," NPR, October 9, 2017, https://www.npr.org/2017/10/09/556606108/research-explores-the-effect-pornography-has-on-long-term-relationships.

13. Nick Bilton, "Tinder, the Fast-Growing Dating App, Taps an Age-Old Truth," *New York Times*, October 29, 2014, https://www.nytimes.com/2014/10/30/fashion/tinder-the-fast-growing-dating-app-taps-an-age-old-truth.html.

14. Mary Harrington, "Love in the Marketplace," *Plough*, May 17, 2021, https://www.plough.com/en/topics/life/relationships/love-in-the-marketplace.

15. Mary Killen, "Dear Mary, How Do I Find a Girlfriend Who Loves Grouse Shooting?" *Spectator*, April 8, 2023.

16. Arianna Brandolini (@answeranxiety), "Here is how you break up with a friend," TikTok, https://www.tiktok.com/@answeranxiety/video/7186671544469343534?lang=en.

17. Kat George and Jay Polish, "7 Ways to Cut a Toxic Friend Out of Your Life," Bustle, July 9, 2015, https://www.bustle.com/wellness/how-to-cut-toxic-friend-out-experts.

18. Zoe Weiner, "7 Tips for Eliminating Toxic People from Your Life," Mental Floss, March 22, 2017, https://www.mentalfloss.com/article/93521/7-tips-eliminating -toxic-people-your-life.

19. "Signs of a Toxic Person," WebMD, December 18, 2022, https://www.webmd .com/mental-health/signs-toxic-person.

20. Lara Bazelon, "Divorce Can Be an Act of Radical Self-Love," *New York Times*, September 2021, https://www.nytimes.com/2021/09/30/opinion/divorce-children .html.

21. Sarah Lopez, testimony at hearing on "The Impact of the Supreme Court's Dobbs Decision on Abortion Rights and Access Across the United States," House Oversight and Reform Committee, July 13, 2022.

22. Michael J. Sandel, "The Procedural Republic and the Unencumbered Self," *Political Theory* 12, no. 1 (February 1984), https://www.jstor.org/stable/191382.

Chapter 10: The Mystery of the Sex Recession

1. Kate Julian, "Why Are Young People Having So Little Sex?" *Atlantic*, December 2018, https://www.theatlantic.com/magazine/archive/2018/12/the-sex -recession/573949/.

2. Julian, "Why Are Young People Having So Little Sex?"

3. "Harry Enten, "Americans Less Likely to Have Sex, Partner Up and Get Married Than Ever," CNN, February 14, 2022, https://www.cnn.com/2022/02/14 /health/valentines-day-love-marriage-relationships-wellness/index.html.

4. Julian, "Why Are Young People Having So Little Sex?"

5. Jean M. Twenge, "Have Smartphones Destroyed a Generation?" *Atlantic*, September 2017, https://www.theatlantic.com/magazine/archive/2017/09/has-the -smartphone-destroyed-a-generation/534198/.

6. "What Predicts Masturbation Practices," Relationships in America. This article was no longer available online as of early 2023.

7. See, for instance, Nick Bilton, "Is *The Handmaid's Tale* the Allegory of the Trump Era?," *Vanity Fair*, June 23, 2017, https://www.vanityfair.com/news /2017/06/handmaids-tale-trump-era-inside-the-hive-podcast; Emily Nussbaum, "A Cunning Adaptation of 'The Handmaid's Tale,'" *New Yorker*, May 15, 2017, https://www.newyorker.com/magazine/2017/05/22/a-cunning-adaptation-of-the -handmaids-tale; Moira Weigel, "We Live in the Reproductive Dystopia of 'The Handmaid's Tale,'" *New Yorker*, April 26, 2017, https://www.newyorker.com /books/page-turner/we-live-in-the-reproductive-dystopia-of-the-handmaids-tale.

8. "How U.S. Religious Composition Has Changed in Recent Decades," Pew Research Center, September 13, 2022, https://www.pewresearch.org/religion/2022/09/13 /how-u-s-religious-composition-has-changed-in-recent-decades/.

9. Amanda Barroso, "Key Takeaways on Americans' Views of and Experiences with Dating and Relationships," Pew Research Center, August 20, 2020, https:// www.pewresearch.org/fact-tank/2020/08/20/key-takeaways-on-americans -views-of-and-experiences-with-dating-and-relationships/.

10. Maria Konnikova, "Casual Sex: Everyone Is Doing It," *New Yorker*, June 25, 2016, https://www.newyorker.com/science/maria-konnikova/casual-sex-everyone -is-doing-it.

11. Christine Emba, *Rethinking Sex: A Provocation* (New York: Sentinel, 2022), 12.

12. Ashley Boucher and Carli Velocci, "Hugh Hefner and Feminism: *Playboy* Brought Progress, But Mostly Destruction," The Wrap, September 29, 2017, https://www.thewrap.com/hugh-hefner-feminist-legacy/.

13. See (or better yet, don't) the lyrics of "WAP" or Beyoncé's "Heated."

14.   Philip Galanes, "Do We Need to Thank the Wedding Guests Who Didn't Give Gifts?," *New York Times*, March 31, 2022, https://www.nytimes.com /2022/03/31/style/wedding-thank-you-social-qs.html.

15.   Emba, *Rethinking Sex*, 37.

16.   Nicholas H. Wolfinger, "Want to Avoid Divorce? Wait to Get Married, but Not Too Long," Institute for Family Studies, July 16, 2015, https://ifstudies.org /blog/want-to-avoid-divorce-wait-to-get-married-but-not-too-long/.

17.   Jay Teachman, "Premarital Sex, Premarital Cohabitation, and the Risk of Subsequent Marital Dissolution Among Women," *Journal of Marriage and Family* 65, no. 2 (May 2003), https://doi.org/10.1111/j.1741-3737.2003.00444.x.

18.   Galena K. Rhoades and Scott M. Stanley, "What Do Premarital Experiences Have to Do with Marital Quality Among Today's Young Adults?," National Marriage Project, http://before-i-do.org/.

19.   Dara Katz, "The Millennial Marriage Trend That Actually Increases Your Chances of Divorce, According to a Relationship Coach," PureWow, May 30, 2021, https://www.purewow.com/family/millennials-marriage-trend-divorce.

20.   Christine Emba, "Consent Is Not Enough. We Need a New Sexual Ethic," *Washington Post*, March 17, 2022, https://www.washingtonpost.com/opinions /2022/03/17/sex-ethics-rethinking-consent-culture/.

21.   Emba, *Rethinking Sex*, 37.

22.   Dustin Guastella, "Anti-Social Socialism Club," Damage, March 22, 2023. https:// damagemag.com/2023/03/22/anti-social-socialism-club/.

23.   Richard Fry, Ruth Igielnik, and Eileen Patten, "How Millennials Today Compare with the Grandparents 50 Years Ago," Pew Research Center, March 16, 2018, https://www.pewresearch.org/fact-tank/2018/03/16/how-millennials-compare -with-their-grandparents/.

24.   Julissa Cruz, "Marriage: More Than a Century of Change," *Family Profiles*, National Center for Family & Marriage Research, Bowing Green State University, https://www.bgsu.edu/content/dam/BGSU/college-of-arts-and-sciences /NCFMR/documents/FP/FP-13-13.pdf.

25.   Janet Adamy, "U.S. Marriage Rate Plunges to Lowest Level on Record," *Wall Street Journal*, April 29, 2020, https://www.wsj.com/articles/u-s-marriage -rate-plunges-to-lowest-level-on-record-11588132860.

26.   Kaitlyn Greenidge, "What Does Marriage Ask Us to Give Up?," *New York Times*, January 4, 2022, https://www.nytimes.com/2022/01/04/opinion /marriage-divorce.html.

27.   Daniel A. Cox, "From Swiping to Sexting: The Enduring Gender Divide in American Dating and Relationships," Survey Center on American Life, February 9, 2023, https://www.americansurveycenter.org/research/from -swiping-to-sexting-the-enduring-gender-divide-in-american-dating-and -relationships/.

28.   Ethan Czuy Levine et al., "Open Relationships, Nonconsensual Nonmonogamy, and Monogamy Among U.S. Adults: Findings from the 2012 National Survey of Sexual Health and Behavior," *Archives of Sexual Behavior* 47, no. 3 (July 2018), https://www.ncbi.nlm.nih.gov/pmc/articles/PMC5958351/.

29.   Candice Williams, "Will Smith Discusses His Marriage with Jada Pinkett Smith, Says It 'Can't Be a Prison,'" *Good Morning America*, ABC News, September 28, 2021, https://www.goodmorningamerica.com/culture/story/smith -discusses-marriage-jada-pinkett-smith-prison-80277192.

30.   Matt Flegenheimer, "Bill de Blasio and Chirlane McCray Are Separating," *New York Times*, July 5, 2023. In the article, the reporter stated that the couple was

not divorcing, and would continue to live together, but that they wanted to date other people, which is basically an open marriage.

31. Jeffrey M. Jones, "Is Marriage Becoming Irrelevant?" Gallup, December 28, 2020, https://news.gallup.com/poll/316223/fewer-say-important-parents-married.aspx.

32. Daniel A. Cox, "A Moral Double Standard on Marital Infidelity," Survey Center on American Life, October 12, 2022, https://www.americansurveycenter.org/a-moral-double-standard-on-marital-infidelity/.

33. Sophie Lewis, "Covid-19 Is Straining the Concept of the Family. Let's Break It," *Nation*, June 3, 2020, https://www.thenation.com/article/society/family-covid-care-marriage/.

34. Maureen Shaw, "The Sexist and Racist History of Marriage That No One Talks About," *Teen Vogue*, November 28, 2017, https://www.teenvogue.com/story/marriage-racist-sexist-history.

35. Clare Chambers, "Feminism, Liberalism and Marriage," American Political Science Association Annual Meeting, 2013, https://www.studocu.com/en-us/document/brown-university/feminist-theoryfeminist-activism-gnss-1960d/feminism-liberalism-and-marriage/30354900.

36. Nathan Yau, "Married People Have More Sex," FlowingData, https://flowingdata.com/2017/07/03/married-people-sex/.

37. Tara Parker-Pope, "Should We All Take the Slow Road to Love?" *New York Times*, July 2, 2019, https://www.nytimes.com/2019/07/02/well/family/millennials-love-relationships-marriage-dating.html.

38. Amanda Barroso, "Key Takeaways on Americans' Views of and Experiences with Dating and Relationships," Pew Research Center, August 20, 2020, https://www.pewresearch.org/fact-tank/2020/08/20/key-takeaways-on-americans-views-of-and-experiences-with-dating-and-relationships/.

39. Parker-Pope, "Should We All Take the Slow Road to Love?"

40. Emba, *Rethinking Sex*, 30.

41. U.S. Census Bureau, "Median Age at First Marriage: 1890 to Present," https://www.census.gov/content/dam/Census/library/visualizations/time-series/demo/families-and-households/ms-2.pdf.

42. Lyman Stone and Spencer James, "Marriage Still Matters: Demonstrating the Link Between Marriage and Fertility in the 21st Century," Institute for Family Studies, October 2022, https://ifstudies.org/ifs-admin/resources/reports/marriagestillmatters-final.pdf.

43. Claire Cain Miller, "Americans Are Having Fewer Babies. They Told Us Why," *New York Times*, July 5, 2018, https://www.nytimes.com/2018/07/05/upshot/americans-are-having-fewer-babies-they-told-us-why.html.

44. Ethan Czuy Levine et al., "Open Relationships, Nonconsensual Nonmonogamy, and Monogamy Among U.S. Adults."

45. W. Bradford Wilcox, "The Group That's Happiest in the Pandemic May Surprise You," Institute for Family Studies, September 29, 2021, https://ifstudies.org/blog/the-group-thats-happiest-in-the-pandemic-may-surprise-you.

46. Raj Chetty et al., "Social Capital I: Measurement and Associations with Economic Mobility," *Nature*, no. 608 (August 2022), https://www.nature.com/articles/s41586-022-04996-4.

47. Melissa Schettini Kearney, "The 'College Gap' in Marriage and Children's Family Structure," NBER Working Paper Series, May 2022, https://www.nber.org/papers/w30078.

48. "The Future of Children: How Cultural Factors Shape Economic Outcomes," *Princeton-Brookings* 30, no.1 (Spring 2020), https://futureofchildren

.princeton.edu/sites/g/files/toruqf2411/files/foc_vol_30_no_1_combined
_v6.pdf.

49.   Emba, *Rethinking Sex*, 23.

Chapter 11: We Need a Family-Friendly Feminism

1.   Candace Owens, "U.S. Birth Rates Decline as the Rotten Fruits of Feminism Increase," Daily Wire, https://www.dailywire.com/news/the-u-s-birth-rates-decline-as-the-rotten-fruits-of-feminism-increase.

2.   Jill Filipovic, "Women Are Having Fewer Babies Because They Have More Choices," *New York Times*, June 27, 2021, https://www.nytimes.com/2021/06/27/opinion/falling-birthrate-women-babies.html.

3.   Claire Cain Miller, "Americans Are Having Fewer Babies. They Told Us Why, *New York Times*, July 5, 2018, https://www.nytimes.com/2018/07/05/upshot/americans-are-having-fewer-babies-they-told-us-why.html.

4.   Michelle Goldberg, "Want More Babies? You Need Less Patriarchy," *New York Times*, May 25, 2018, https://www.nytimes.com/2018/05/25/opinion/american-birthrate-patriarchy.html.

5.   Claire Cain Miller, "Would Americans Have More Babies if the Government Paid Them?," *New York Times*, February 17, 2021, https://www.nytimes.com/2021/02/17/upshot/americans-fertility-babies.html.

6.   Polly Toynbee, "Making It Easier to Be a Mother," *Guardian*, September 24, 2003, https://www.theguardian.com/society/2003/sep/24/childrensservices.comment.

7.   Michelle Goldberg, quoted in Matthew Yglesias, "Feminism as Natalism," ThinkProgress, April 8, 2009, https://archive.thinkprogress.org/feminism-as-natalism-8bed0d247639/.

8.   Henrik Kleven, "The Geography of Child Penalties and Gender Norms: Evidence from the United States," NBER Working Paper Series, January 2023, https://www.nber.org/system/files/working_papers/w30176/w30176.pdf.

9.   Peter McDonald, "Societal Foundations for Explaining Low Fertility: Gender Equity," *Demographic Research* 28, no. 24 (May 2013), https://www.demographic-research.org/volumes/vol28/34/28-34.pdf.

10. Claire Cain Miller, "The 24/7 Work Culture's Toll on Families and Gender Equality," *New York Times*, May 28, 2015, https://www.nytimes.com/2015/05/31/upshot/the-24-7-work-cultures-toll-on-families-and-gender-equality.html.

11. Claudia Goldin, "Hours Flexibility and the Gender Gap in Pay," Center for American Progress, April 2015.

12. Susan Madsen, "Shrinking Families and the State of Motherhood—What Do Moms Need?," *Deseret News*, May 24, 2022, https://www.deseret.com/opinion/2022/5/24/23137994/opinion-working-moms-want-smaller-families-affordable-childcare-household-labor-emotional-burden.

13. Stefan Bauernschuster, Timo Hener, and Helmut Rainer, "Does the Expansion of Public Child Care Increase Birth Rates? Evidence from a Low-Fertility Country," Ifo Institut, Working Paper No. 158 (April 2013), https://www.ifo.de/DocDL/IfoWorkingPaper-158.pdf.

14. Anne Chemin, "France's Baby Boom Secret: Get Women into Work and Ditch Rigid Family Norms," *Guardian*, March 21, 2015, https://www.theguardian.com/world/2015/mar/21/france-population-europe-fertility-rate.

15. "The Influence of Family Policies on Fertility in France," United Nations Expert Group Meeting on Policy Responses to Low Fertility, November 2015,

https://www.un.org/en/development/desa/population/events/pdf/expert/24/Policy_Briefs/PB_France.pdf.

16. Miller, "Would Americans Have More Babies if the Government Paid Them?"

17. National TFR numbers are from World Bank data via Data Commons, https://datacommons.org/tools/timeline#place=country%2FSWE%2Ccountry%2FUSA%2Ccountry%2FDNK%2Ccountry%2FNOR%2Ccountry%2FPOL&statsVar=FertilityRate_Person_Female.

18. Angela Luci-Greulich and Olivier Thévenon, "The Impact of Family Policies on Fertility Trends in Developed Countries," *European Journal of Population* 29, no. 4 (November 2013), https://www.jstor.org/stable/24571482.

19. Lyman Stone provided the analysis on Twitter, February 17, 2021, https://twitter.com/lymanstoneky/status/1362092635956129793.

20. "The Influence of Family Policies on Fertility in France," United Nations Expert Group Meeting on Policy Responses to Low Fertility.

21. Wendy Wang and Jenet Erickson, "Homeward Bound: The Work-Family Reset in Post-COVID America," Institute for Family Studies, August 2021, https://ifstudies.org/ifs-admin/resources/final-ifsparentsreport.pdf.

22. Claire Cain Miller, "The Costs of Motherhood Are Rising, and Catching Women Off Guard," *New York Times*, August 17, 2018.

23. U.S. Bureau of Labor Statistics, "Women Employees-to-All Employees Ratio: Total Nonfarm," retrieved from Federal Reserve Bank of St. Louis, August 5, 2023, https://fred.stlouisfed.org/series/CES0000000039.

24. U.S. Bureau of Labor Statistics, "Labor Force Participation Rate—Women," retrieved from Federal Reserve Bank of St. Louis, August 5, 2023, https://fred.stlouisfed.org/series/LNS11300002.

25. Ilyana Kuziemko et al., "The Mommy Effect: Do Women Anticipate the Employment Effects of Motherhood?" NBER Working Paper Series, December 2020, https://www.nber.org/papers/w24740.

26. Ekaterina Netchaeva et al., "A Meta-Analytic Review of the Gender Difference in Leadership Aspirations," *Journal of Vocational Behavior* 137 (2022), https://doi.org/10.1016/j.jvb.2022.103744.

27. Carly R. Knight and Mary C. Brinton, "One Egalitarianism or Several? Two Decades of Gender-Role Attitude Change in Europe," *American Journal of Sociology* 122, no. 5 (March 2017), https://scholar.harvard.edu/files/brinton/files/knight.brinton.ajs_.pdf.

28. Jordan Weissmann, "America's Insanely Expensive Child Care Is a Serious Economic Problem," Slate, February 11, 2019, https://slate.com/business/2019/02/child-care-day-care-policies-paid-family-maternity-leave-gdp.html.

29. "Despite U.S. Population of Only 330 Million, Biden Says Child Tax Credit Would Put 720 Million Women Back Into the Workforce," Grabien, September 17, 2019, https://news.grabien.com/story-despite-us-population-only-330-million-biden-says-child-tax.

30. David Willetts, "Old Europe? Demographic Change and Pension Reform," Centre for European Reform, September 2003, https://www.cer.org.uk/sites/default/files/publications/attachments/pdf/2011/p475_old_demo_pension-1652.pdf.

31. Lyman Stone, "Why a Child Allowance Is Preferable to Subsidized Child Care," Institute for Family Studies, August 12, 2020, https://ifstudies.org/blog/why-a-child-allowance-is-preferable-to-subsidized-child-care.

32. Wolfgang Lutz, "Fertility Will Be Determined by the Changing Ideal Family Size and the Empowerment to Reach These Targets," *Vienna Yearbook of Population Research* 18 (2020), https://www.jstor.org/stable/27041930.

33. Peter McDonald, "Societal Foundations for Explaining Low Fertility: Gender Equity," *Demographic Research* 28, no. 24 (May 2013), https://www.demographic -research.org/volumes/vol28/34/28-34.pdf.

34. Laurie DeRose and Lyman Stone, "More Work, Fewer Babies: What Does Workism Have to Do with Falling Fertility?" Institute for Family Studies, 2021, https://ifstudies.org/ifs-admin/resources/reports/ifs-workismreport-final -031721.pdf.

35. Lyman Stone and Laurie DeRose, "What Workism Is Doing to Parents," *Atlantic*, May 5, 2021, https://www.theatlantic.com/ideas/archive/2021/05/what- workism-doing-would-be-parents/618789/.

36. Derek Thompson, "Workism Is Making Americans Miserable," *Atlantic*, February 24, 2019, https://www.theatlantic.com/ideas/archive/2019/02/religion- workism-making-americans-miserable/583441/.

37. Juliana Menasce Horowitz and Nikki Graf, "Most U.S. Teens See Anxiety and Depression as a Major Problem Among Their Peers," Pew Research Center, February 20, 2019, https://www.pewresearch.org/social-trends/2019/02/20/most -u-s-teens-see-anxiety-and-depression-as-a-major-problem-among-their-peers/.

38. Anne Helen Petersen, "How Millennials Became the Burnout Generation," BuzzFeed News, January 5, 2019, https://www.buzzfeednews.com/article /annehelenpetersen/millennials-burnout-generation-debt-work.

39. Erin Griffith, "Why Are Young People Pretending to Love Work?" *New York Times*, January 26, 2019, https://www.nytimes.com/2019/01/26/business/against -hustle-culture-rise-and-grind-tgim.html.

40. "Failing on Purpose Survey," American Compass, December 2021, https:// americancompass.org/essays/failing-on-purpose-survey-part-1/.

41. Claire Cain Miller, "The 24/7 Work Culture's Toll on Families and Gender Equality," *New York Times*, May 28, 2015, https://www.nytimes.com/2015/05/31/upshot /the-24-7-work-cultures-toll-on-families-and-gender-equality.html.

42. Ruth Whippman, "Enough Leaning In. Let's Tell Men to Lean Out," *New York Times*, October 10, 2019, https://www.nytimes.com/2019/10/10/opinion/sunday /feminism-lean-in.html.

43. Francesca Fiori, "Do Childcare Arrangements Make the Difference? A Multi- level Approach to the Intention of Having a Second Child in Italy," *Population, Space and Place* 15, no. 5 (September/October 2011), https://onlinelibrary.wiley .com/doi/epdf/10.1002/psp.567.

Chapter 12: You Should Quit Your Job

1. "Home Building Survey Part II: Supporting Families," American Compass, February 2021, https://americancompass.org/essays/home-building-survey -part-2/.

2. Nikki Graff, "Most Americans Say Children Are Better Off with a Parent at Home," Pew Research Center, October 10, 2016, https://www.pewresearch .org/fact-tank/2016/10/10/most-americans-say-children-are-better-off-with-a -parent-at-home/.

3. Wendy Wang and Jenet Erickson, "Homeward Bound: The Work-Family Reset in Post-COVID America," Institute for Family Studies, August 2021, https:// ifstudies.org/ifs-admin/resources/final-ifsparentsreport.pdf.

4. Brad Wilcox, "Why Parents Need the Flexibility of Cash Payments More Than Universal Child Care," *Deseret News*, March 4, 2021, https://www.deseret .com/indepth/2021/3/4/22313418/why-parents-need-the-flexibility-of-cash -payments-more-than-universal-child-care-congress-family.

5. Juliana Menasce Horowitz, "Despite Challenges at Home and Work, Most Working Moms and Dads Say Being Employed Is What's Best for Them," Pew Research Center, September 12, 2019, https://www.pewresearch.org/fact-tank/2019/09/12/despite-challenges-at-home-and-work-most-working-moms-and-dads-say-being-employed-is-whats-best-for-them/.

6. Rasheed Malik, Katie Hamm, and Leila Schochet, "America's Child Care Deserts in 2018," Center for American Progress, December 2018, https://www.americanprogress.org/article/americas-child-care-deserts-2018/.

7. Ann Crittenden, *The Price of Motherhood: Why the Most Important Job in the World Is Still the Least Valued*, 10th anniv. ed. (London: Picador, 2010), 4.

8. "Rosen: Ann Romney 'Never Worked a Day in Her Life,'" *Politico*, video, 0:28, April 12, 2012, https://www.politico.com/video/2012/04/rosen-ann-romney-never-worked-a-day-in-her-life-012678.

9. Ramesh Ponnuru, "Obama's War on Homemakers," Bloomberg View, January 22, 2015, https://www.aei.org/articles/obamas-war-homemakers/.

10. Jahdziah St. Julien, "Work-Family and Gender Justice in the Democratic Presidential Primary Debates," New America, March 2020, https://www.newamerica.org/better-life-lab/reports/work-family-and-gender-justice-democratic-presidential-primary-debates/discussion-how-candidates-framed-work-family-and-gender-workplace-policies/.

11. Matt Bruenig, "The Case for Paying Parents Who Care for Their Own Kids," *New York Times*, April 9, 2022, https://www.nytimes.com/2022/04/09/opinion/paying-parents-for-child-care.html.

12. Jill Filipovic, "It's a Bad Idea to Pay Women to Stay Home," Substack, April 12, 2022, https://jill.substack.com/p/its-a-bad-idea-to-pay-women-to-stay.

13. Tweet from Pima County Democratic Party, July 12, 2021, https://twitter.com/PimaDems/status/1414632823932194828.

14. Helaine Olen, "A Lousy Myth About Moms, Kids and Work Makes a Comeback. Republicans Are Running with It," *Washington Post*, May 9, 2021, https://www.washingtonpost.com/opinions/2021/05/09/just-time-mothers-day-lousy-myth-about-moms-kids-work-makes-comeback-republicans-are-running-with-it/.

15. Gretchen Livingston and Kim Parker, "8 Facts About American Dads," Pew Research Center, July 12, 2019, https://www.pewresearch.org/short-reads/2019/06/12/fathers-day-facts/.

16. Steven Pinker, "Sex Ed," *New Republic*, February 14, 2005, https://newrepublic.com/article/68044/sex-ed.

17. Stephanie Watson, "Oxytocin: The Love Hormone," *Harvard Women's Health Watch*, July 20, 2021, https://www.health.harvard.edu/mind-and-mood/oxytocin-the-love-hormone.

18. Chelsea Conaboy, "Motherhood Brings the Most Dramatic Brain Changes of a Woman's Life," *Boston Globe*, July 17, 2018, https://www.bostonglobe.com/magazine/2018/07/17/pregnant-women-care-ignores-one-most-profound-changes-new-mom-faces/CF5wyP0b5EGCcZ8fzLUWbP/story.html.

19. Stephen Cranney and Andrew Miles, "Desperate Housewives? Differences in Work Satisfaction Between Stay-at-Home and Employed Mothers, 1972–2012," *Journal of Family Issues* 38, no. 11 (August 2016), https://doi.org/10.1177/0192513X16663253.

20. Lyman Stone, "Are Stay-at-Home Mothers Really Miserable?," Institute for Family Studies, April 21, 2022, https://ifstudies.org/blog/are-stay-at-home-mothers-really-miserable.

21.   Stone, "Are Stay-at-Home Mothers Really Miserable?"

22.   Elsevier, "Frequent Consumption of Meals Prepared Away from Home Linked to Increased Risk of Early Death," *ScienceDaily*, March 25, 2021, www.science daily.com/releases/2021/03/210325084824.htm.

23.   Mai Matsumoto et al., "Consumption of meals prepared away from home is associated with inadequacy of dietary fiber, vitamin C and mineral intake among Japanese adults: Analysis from the 2015 National Health and Nutrition Survey," *Nutrition Journal* 20, no. 40 (2021), https://nutritionj.biomedcentral.com /articles/10.1186/s12937-021-00693-6.

24.   Justin Wolfers, "Yes, Your Time as a Parent Does Make a Difference," *New York Times*, April 1, 2015, https://www.nytimes.com/2015/04/02/upshot/yes -your-time-as-a-parent-does-make-a-difference.html.

25.   Joseph Price and Ariel Kalil, "The Effect of Mother–Child Reading Time on Children's Reading Skills: Evidence from Natural Within-Family Variation," *Child Development* 90, no. 6, (November/December 2019), https://doi.org/10.1111 /cdev.13137.

26.   Amber Lapp, "Should Mothers' Labor Force Participation Be a Policy Goal?" Institute for Family Studies, April 25, 2017, https://ifstudies.org/blog/should -mothers-labor-force-participation-be-a-policy-goal.

27.   Carmen Nobel, "Kids Benefit from Having a Working Mom," *Working Knowledge*, May 15, 2015, https://hbswk.hbs.edu/item/kids-benefit-from-having-a -working-mom.

28.   Rachel G. Lucas-Thompson et al., "Maternal Work Early in the Lives of Children and Its Distal Associations with Achievement and Behavior Problems: A Meta-Analysis," *Psychological Bulletin* 136, no. 6 (2010), https://www.apa.org /pubs/journals/releases/bul-136-6-915.pdf.

29.   Anne Firor Scott, *Natural Allies: Women's Associations in American History* (Urbana: University of Illinois Press, 1992), 12.

30.   Emma Green, "What America Lost as Women Entered the Workforce," *Atlantic*, September 19, 2016, https://www.theatlantic.com/politics/archive/2016/09 /what-women-lost/500537/.

31.   Katy Read, "Regrets of a Stay-at-Home Mom," Salon, January 6, 2011, https:// www.salon.com/2011/01/06/wish_i_hadnt_opted_out/.

32.   Scott Cameron, "'Regrets of a Stay-at-Home Mom,'" NPR, January 19, 2011, https://www.kunc.org/2011-01-19/regrets-of-a-stay-at-home-mom.

33.   Christine Emba, *Rethinking Sex: A Provocation* (New York: Sentinel, 2022), 45.

34.   Lara Bazelon, "Divorce Can Be a Radical Act of Self-Love," *New York Times*, September 30, 2021, https://www.nytimes.com/2021/09/30/opinion/divorce -children.html?action=click&module=RelatedLinks&pgtype=Article.

35.   Amy Shearn, "A 50/50 Custody Arrangement Could Save Your Marriage," *New York Times*, October 8, 2022, https://www.nytimes.com/2022/10/08/opinion /married-divorce-parent.html.

Chapter 13: A Culture of Sterility

1.   Paul R. Ehrlich, *The Population Bomb* (New York: Ballantine Books, 1968), 15.

2.   Leah Libresco Sargeant, "Dependence: Toward an Illiberalism of the Weak," *Plough*, December 7, 2020, https://www.plough.com/en/topics/justice/culture -of-life/dependence.

3.   Kim Brooks, *Small Animals: Parenthood in the Age of Fear* (New York: Flatiron Books, 2018), 48.

4. Jill Filipovic, "Women Are Having Fewer Babies Because They Have More Choices," *New York Times*, June 27, 2021. https://www.nytimes.com/2021/06/27/opinion/falling-birthrate-women-babies.html.

5. Brooks, 54–55.

6. Charles Fain Lehman, "Terminally TwentySomething," NeoNarrative, August 17, 2022, https://sotonye.substack.com/p/terminally-twentysomething.

7. "Transcript: Ezra Klein Interviews Alison Gopnik," *New York Times*, April 16, 2021, https://www.nytimes.com/2021/04/16/podcasts/ezra-klein-podcast-alison-gopnik-transcript.html.

8. Wajahat Ali, Twitter, June 27, 2021, https://twitter.com/WajahatAli/status/1409249330368811009.

9. "Tracking Coronavirus in Washington, D.C.: Latest Map and Case Count," *New York Times*, accessed June 28, 2022, https://www.nytimes.com/interactive/2021/us/washington-district-of-columbia-covid-cases.html.

10. Tim Carney, Twitter, June 27, 2021, https://twitter.com/TPCarney/status/1409331789324226563.

11. Rene de Bos, Twitter, June 27, 2021, https://twitter.com/renedebos/status/1409341265481588737. The tweet has since been deleted.

12. Timothy P. Carney, "Biden Says He's Pro-Science. Why Is His Schools Plan Based on Fear?," *New York Times*, February 19, 2021, https://www.nytimes.com/2021/02/19/opinion/coronavirus-schools-biden.html.

13. See, for instance, this interview: Jennifer Couzin-Frankel, "Does Closing Schools Slow the Spread of Coronavirus? Past Outbreaks Provide Clues," *Science*, March 10, 2020, https://www.science.org/content/article/does-closing-schools-slow-spread-novel-coronavirus.

14. Fatima Tokhmafshan, Twitter, April 27, 2020, https://twitter.com/DeNovo_Fatima/status/1254842164640710660.

15. Danielle Wallace, "Maryland County School CEO Suggests Students Will Be Required to Wear Masks Until 'COVID No Longer Exists,'" Fox News, January 26, 2022, https://www.foxnews.com/us/maryland-county-school-ceo-student-mask-mandate-until-covid-no-longer-exists.

16. Ariel Zilber, "Taylor Lorenz Defends China's 'Zero COVID' Lockdowns, Bashes US," *New York Post*, December 1, 2022, https://nypost.com/2022/12/01/taylor-lorenz-defends-chinas-zero-covid-lockdowns/.

17. Paulette Cooper Noble, "My Extreme Anti-Covid Routines: Sterilizing My Eyelids and Soaping My Nostrils," *Washington Post*, September 9, 2020, https://www.washingtonpost.com/outlook/2020/09/09/sterilize-eyelids-soap-nostrils/.

18. Karen Landman, "There's No Such Thing as a Good Cold," Vox, November 29, 2022, https://www.vox.com/science-and-health/23473231/immunity-debt-respiratory-cold-virus-rsv-flu-influenza.

19. Brad Wilcox et al., "The Divided State of Our Unions," Institute for Family Studies, 2021, https://ifstudies.org/reports/the-divided-state-of-our-unions/2021/executive-summary.

20. Tanya Lewis, "The Pandemic Caused a Baby Boom in Red States and a Bust in Blue States," *Scientific American*, May 26, 2023, https://www.scientificamerican.com/article/the-pandemic-caused-a-baby-boom-in-red-states-and-a-bust-in-blue-states/.

21. Jonathan Eig, *The Birth of the Pill: How Four Crusaders Reinvented Sex and Launched a Revolution* (New York: Norton, 2014), 1.

22. Katherine Dee, "Birth Control Pilled," American Mind, July 12, 2021, https://americanmind.org/features/the-church-of-health/birth-control-pilled/.

23. Emily Wax-Thibodeaux, "Men Across America Are Getting Vasectomies 'as an Act of Love,'" *Washington Post*, December 26, 2021, https://www.washington post.com/nation/2021/12/26/men-across-america-are-getting-vasectomies-an -act-love/.

24. Congressional Record, February 27, 2023, https://www.congress.gov/congressional -record/volume-155/issue-145/senate-section/article/S10262-1.

25. Gretchen Livingston, "The Changing Profile of Unmarried Parents," Pew Research Center, April 25, 2018, https://www.pewresearch.org/social-trends /2018/04/25/the-changing-profile-of-unmarried-parents/.

26. "Births to Unmarried Women, by Age and Race," U.S. Department of Education, Institute of Education Sciences, National Center for Education Statistics, https://nces.ed.gov/pubs98/yi/yi07.pdf.

27. Brady E. Hamilton, Ph.D., Joyce A. Martin, M.P.H., et al., "Births: Provisional Data for 2016," Division of Vital Statistics, National Center for Health Statistics, June 2017, https://www.cdc.gov/nchs/data/vsrr/report002.pdf.

28. George A. Akerlof, Janet L. Yellen, and Michael L. Katz, "An Analysis of Out-of-Wedlock Childbearing in the United States," *Quarterly Journal of Economics* 111, no. 2 (May 1996), https://www.jstor.org/stable/2946680.

29. Leah Rivard, "Sen. Ron Johnson: Society Should Provide Opportunities for People to Get Jobs, but Not Responsible for Child Care," News8000.com, January 25, 2022, https://www.news8000.com/news/politics/elections/sen-ron -johnson-society-should-provide-opportunities-for-people-to-get-jobs-but -not-responsible/article_97ea69d5-59cb-560e-bbc1-857d093101e3.html.

Chapter 14: Civilizational Sadness

1. "Number of Births and Deaths in Germany from 1950 to 2022," Statista Research Department, May 2023, https://www.statista.com/statistics/1128099 /births-and-deaths-number-germany/.

2. "Fertility Rate Timeline," Data Commons, https://datacommons.org/tools /timeline#place=country%2FDEU%2Ccountry%2FUSA%2Ccountry%2F FRA%2Ccountry%2FGBR%2Ccountry%2FJPN%2Ccountry%2FITA&stats Var=FertilityRate_Person_Female.

3. "Fertility Rate Timeline," Data Commons.

4. Stefan Bauernschuster, Timo Hener, and Helmut Rainer, "Does the Expansion of Public Child Care Increase Birth Rates? Evidence from a Low-Fertility Country," Ifo Institut, Working Paper No. 158 (April 2013), https://www.ifo .de/DocDL/IfoWorkingPaper-158.pdf.

5. "Germany Passes Japan to Have World's Lowest Birth Rate—Study," BBC News, May 29, 2015, https://www.bbc.com/news/world-europe-32929962.

6. Alex Williams, "To Breed or Not to Breed," *New York Times*, November 20, 2021, https://www.nytimes.com/2021/11/20/style/breed-children-climate-change .html.

7. Pew Research Center, "American Trends Panel."

8. Ezra Klein, "Your Kids Are Not Doomed," *New York Times*, June 5, 2022, https://www.nytimes.com/2022/06/05/opinion/climate-change-should-you -have-kids.html.

9. William A. Burley, "Is Overpopulation Too Grim a Tale?" *New York Times*, April 29, 1990, https://timesmachine.nytimes.com/timesmachine/1990/04/29/099690 .html?pageNumber=157.

10. Jennifer Ludden, "Should We Be Having Kids in the Age of Climate Change?," NPR, August 18, 2016, https://www.npr.org/2016/08/18/479349760/should-we-be-having-kids-in-the-age-of-climate-change.

11. Williams, "To Breed or Not to Breed?"

12. Suzy Weiss, "First Comes Love. Then Comes Sterilization," Free Press, October 25, 2021, https://www.thefp.com/p/first-comes-love-then-comes-sterilization.

13. Todd May, "Would Human Extinction Be a Tragedy?" *New York Times*, December 17, 2018, https://www.nytimes.com/2018/12/17/opinion/human-extinction-climate-change.html.

14. Weiss, "First Comes Love. Then Comes Sterilization."

15. Mike Stobbe, "US Overdose Deaths Hit Record 93,000 in Pandemic Last Year," Associated Press, July 14, 2021, https://apnews.com/article/overdose-deaths-record-covid-pandemic-fd43b5d91a81179def5ac596253b0304?utm_medium=AP&utm_source=Twitter&utm_campaign=SocialFlow.

16. American Foundation for Suicide Prevention, "Suicide Statistics," https://afsp.org/suicide-statistics/.

17. Ryan Burge, Twitter, July 8, 2021, https://twitter.com/ryanburge/status/1413127530396241922.

18. Catherine Pearson, "Why Is It So Hard for Men to Make Close Friends?," *New York Times*, November 28, 2022, https://www.nytimes.com/2022/11/28/well/family/male-friendship-loneliness.html.

19. American Psychological Association, "COVID-19 Pandemic Led to Increase in Loneliness Around the World," May 9, 2021, https://www.apa.org/news/press/releases/2022/05/covid-19-increase-loneliness.

20. Bryce Ward, "Americans Are Choosing to Be Alone. Here's Why We Should Reverse That," *Washington Post*, November 23, 2022, https://www.washingtonpost.com/opinions/2022/11/23/americans-alone-thanksgiving-friends/.

21. Cathy Reisenwitz, "Loneliness Is Self-Reinforcing," Substack, October 24, 2022, https://cathyreisenwitz.substack.com/p/loneliness-is-self-reinforcing?r=5q7u&utm_campaign=post&utm_medium=email.

22. Jennifer Watling Neal and Zachary P. Neal, "Prevalence and Characteristics of Childfree Adults in Michigan (USA)," *PLoS ONE* 16, no. 6 (June 16, 2021), https://www.ncbi.nlm.nih.gov/pmc/articles/PMC8208578/.

23. Lisa Martine Jenkins, "1 in 4 Childless Adults Say Climate Change Has Factored into Their Reproductive Decisions," Morning Consult, September 28, 2020, https://morningconsult.com/2020/09/28/adults-children-climate-change-polling/.

24. Williams, "To Breed or Not to Breed?"

25. Nicholas C. Petris Center on Health Care Markets and Consumer Welfare, "Anxiety Disorder in Millenials: Causes and Consequences," https://petris.org/projects-2/completed-projects-2/anxiety/#:~:text=Anxiety%20is%20a%20growing%20problem,than%20it%20was%20in%202008.

26. Chris Melore, "Nearly Half of Americans Think They're a Better Person Than EVERYONE They Know!" StudyFinds, May 6, 2021, https://studyfinds.org/half-americans-think-better-person-than-everyone/.

27. W. Bradford Wilcox, "Why Are Liberals Less Happy Than Conservatives?," UnHerd, October 10, 2022, https://unherd.com/thepost/why-are-liberals-less-happy-than-conservatives/?=frpo.

28. John Anderer, "Inferiority Complex: 8 in 10 Millennials Believe They Aren't 'Good Enough,'" StudyFinds, November 4, 2019, https://studyfinds.org/inferiority-complex-8-in-10-millennials-believe-they-arent-good-enough/.

29. Lyman Stone, "The Conservative Fertility Advantage," Institute for Family Studies, November 18, 2020, https://ifstudies.org/blog/the-conservative-fertility-advantage.

30. Joey Marshall, "Are Religious People Happier, Healthier? Our New Global Study Explores This Question," Pew Research Center, January 31, 2019, https://www.pewresearch.org/fact-tank/2019/01/31/are-religious-people-happier-healthier-our-new-global-study-explores-this-question/.

31. Gregory A. Smith, "About Three-in-Ten U.S. Adults Are Now Religiously Unaffiliated," Pew Research Center, December 14, 2021, https://www.pewresearch.org/religion/2021/12/14/about-three-in-ten-u-s-adults-are-now-religiously-unaffiliated/.

32. "In U.S., Decline of Christianity Continues at Rapid Pace," Pew Research Center, October 17, 2019, https://www.pewresearch.org/religion/2019/10/17/in-u-s-decline-of-christianity-continues-at-rapid-pace/.

Index

About the Author

TIMOTHY P. CARNEY is a father of six children, a senior fellow at the American Enterprise Institute, and a columnist at the *Washington Examiner*. Tim and his wife, Katie, have raised their family in suburban Maryland and Northern Virginia. Tim grew up with three older brothers in Greenwich Village and later in Pelham, New York. He is the author of *Alienated America*, *The Big Ripoff*, and *Obamanomics*.